JOHN COWPER POWYS:
NOVELIST

John Cowper Powys: *Novelist*

BY

GLEN CAVALIERO

CLARENDON PRESS
OXFORD
1973

Oxford University Press, Ely House, London W.1

GLASGOW   NEW YORK   TORONTO   MELBOURNE   WELLINGTON
CAPE TOWN   IBADAN   NAIROBI   DAR ES SALAAM   LUSAKA   ADDIS ABABA
DELHI   BOMBAY   CALCUTTA   MADRAS   KARACHI   LAHORE   DACCA
KUALA LUMPUR   SINGAPORE   HONG KONG   TOKYO

ISBN 0 19 812049 4
© *Oxford University Press 1973*

*Printed in Great Britain by
Richard Clay (The Chaucer Press), Ltd.,
Bungay, Suffolk*

FOR
John Toft

FOREWORD

THE novels of John Cowper Powys have not yet received the critical attention which is their due. The following book is an attempt to remedy this omission. In it I have sought to analyse the nature of Powys's imagination; to examine all the novels in detail and to evaluate them; to define Powys's art as a novelist; and finally to indicate his significance for English fiction.

Confusion sometimes arises, even at this late date, as to the several identities of the Powys brothers. John Cowper was the eldest of the three famous writers in the family. He was born at Shirley in Derbyshire in 1872, and died at Blaenau Ffestiniog in North Wales in 1963, surviving T. F. Powys, the author of *Mr. Weston's Good Wine*, by ten years, and Llewelyn Powys by twenty-four. He was as unlike his brothers as a writer as they were unlike each other; and he was never taken up by a group of sympathetic and influential admirers as was T. F. Powys. Indeed, the very quality of the latter's achievement stood in the way of John Cowper's recognition, for admirers of *Mr. Weston* and the *Fables* have usually been unresponsive to such books as *Wolf Solent* and *A Glastonbury Romance*.

John Cowper Powys, however, was as great an original as his brother, writing out of a deeply felt world of inner experience; but while his fictional world is his own, it belongs to a genuine tradition. His novels explore the psychology of romanticism, and form a powerful body of work within the English romantic tradition. Writers as diverse as Wordsworth and Pater, Scott and Hardy were influences upon his fiction. But Rabelais and Dostoevsky were his real masters (he wrote studies of them both). To cite these names is to indicate the breadth and variety of his achievement as a novelist.

I have confined myself in this book entirely to his novels, except where reference to his other work illuminates them, or where it seemed relevant to the matter in hand. That work includes eight books of literary criticism and numerous books and pamphlets of popular philosophy, as well as a considerable body of verse and an autobiography. None of these books is without interest, and all of them bear the mark of a highly individual and interesting mind. But, the *Autobiography* apart, they can be regarded as peripheral to his work. The novels are his real achievement.

They are for the most part long, crowded with characters, leisurely in development, heavily descriptive—everything that has been least popular with critics for the past thirty years. And although written out of a twentieth-century consciousness, they belong stylistically to the nineteenth century, so that when set against much contemporary fiction they have a deceptively old-fashioned air. Expressive of a powerful and devious, but genial, personality, their atmosphere is unique in its blending of extravagance and self-mockery, intensity and comprehensive sensuousness. Underlying them all is a prevailing scepticism that never degenerates into bitterness or gloom. Powys, an anachronism in his own time, is prophetic of our own. His extraordinarily subtle attitude to sex and the supernatural makes his work timely as well as permanently valuable. His novels are informed by a serious attempt to come to terms with both the inner and outer aspects of experience: central to them all is an assertion of the power of the imagination to strengthen the individual consciousness, and even to transform the relation of that consciousness to its environment. Powys's central concern might be summed up as the truth of fiction.

He was a late starter. His first major novel, *Wolf Solent* (1929), was not published until he was fifty-seven; and the next thirty years were to be a period of ceaseless literary activity. Previously he had spent over twenty years in the United States as an itinerant lecturer on literature and philosophy; but America nowhere figures in the novels. For these novels, perhaps because they are the work of an elderly man, are retrospective of his youth: Powys's imagination moved in the timeless world of boyhood, making out of it, however, a place in which to explore the abiding nature of the child within the adult. Most of these books were written in the seclusion of up-state New York and the Welsh mountains. This meant that his work, besides being out of step in the time scale with that of his contemporaries, was that of a man who never became known personally in literary circles that might otherwise have given him more consideration. And as a result, it is highly individualistic work, based on a personal rather than a social world. In this respect it relates most forcefully to our increasingly fragmented society. Powys is a novelist whose relevance is likely to increase.

The novels fall naturally into two groups, those written before his move to Wales and those written after it, seven in each group. And each group is itself divided. The first three novels, *Wood and Stone* (1915), *Rodmoor* (1916), and *Ducdame* (1925), were written while their author was still engaged in lecturing, and are in the tradition of late nineteenth-century romanticism, while prophetic of the finer books to come. *Wolf Solent* ushers in Powys's most famous achievement, the great quartet of Wessex novels completed by *A Glastonbury*

Romance (1932), *Weymouth Sands* (1934), and *Maiden Castle* (1936), in which he uses the scenes and world of his boyhood to make a series of explorations of the nature and limitation of romantic experience. *Owen Glendower* (1940) and *Porius* (1951) are the master works of the second part of his career as a novelist, vast historical novels that are epic in their scope and the ultimate expressions of their author's genius. Finally there are the group of fantasies written in extreme old age, of which *Atlantis* (1954) at any rate merits consideration alongside the earlier works. Each group of novels has its own characteristics and qualities, and each develops logically from the one preceding it. It is on these books, together with the *Autobiography* (1934), that Powys's reputation rests.

ACKNOWLEDGEMENTS

I wish to thank Mr. Derek Langridge and Mr. E. E. Bissell for the generous loan of manuscripts, and the Librarian and his staff at Churchill College, Cambridge, who put at my disposal numerous books in the Powys collection there; also Dr. T. R. Henn, Mr. Kenneth Hopkins, Dr. Paris Leary, and Dr. George Steiner for various forms of help and kindness; and most especially Mr. Frederick Davies, Dr. Richard Luckett, and Mr. Angus Wilson, all of whom read the book in manuscript at various stages and made many comments and suggestions.

Of the various critical writings on John Cowper Powys I am especially indebted to Professor Wilson Knight's *The Saturnian Quest*. It is an indispensable basis for all studies of Powys's work.

I gratefully acknowledge permission from the following to reproduce copyright material: Laurence Pollinger Ltd. on behalf of the Estate of the late John Cowper Powys for *Atlantis*, *The Brazen Head*, *A Glastonbury Romance*, *Maiden Castle*, *Porius*, *Rodmoor*, *Weymouth Sands*, *Wolf Solent*, and *Wood and Stone*, Gainstone Press for *Ducdame*; and the University of Wales Press for my own contribution to *Essays on John Cowper Powys*, ed. B. Humfrey.

CONTENTS

CHAPTER ONE

The Novelist and his World

1

No study of John Cowper, Theodore, or Llewelyn Powys can afford to disregard the family to which they belonged. The three brothers stand in varying degrees apart from the literary world of their time; and this detachment can to some extent be accounted for by the intense family, almost tribal, feeling which linked them to each other and gave them the sense of belonging to a self-sufficient world. The patriarchal character of their father, the Revd. Charles Francis Powys (1843–1923), an Evangelical clergyman of the old school, a believer in Biblical inerrancy, who was conservative, disciplined, but spontaneous in emotion and responses, is a formative element in the imaginative development of the brothers. All three rejected the Christianity in which they had been brought up, in ways expressive of their highly individual personalities; but none of them rejected the father who had instilled it, for although austere, disciplined, and formidable, he had a gentleness which could disarm, and an intuitive if uncomprehending knowledge of his children's needs. John Cowper and Llewelyn in particular were repeatedly to recur to their childhood days under the formidable benevolence of a simplicity that was 'majestic ... he used to derive a proud, emotional glory from the simple fact of being able to walk at all, with long steady strides, over the face of the round earth'.[1] This physical self-awareness and sense of kinship with the elements was common to all his children, and it was this, rather than his religious beliefs, which was the foundation of their world.

One speaks of a 'world' advisedly, since the young Powyses grew up in a secluded community, and it was this privacy which was to determine the character of the novels of both Theodore and John Cowper. In them a strong sense of geographical community is balanced by an intense feeling for the sacredness of the individual: both John Cowper's Glastonbury and Theodore's Folly Down are conceived as units within which, and yet against which, the individual must seek to make his way. The Powys literary world arose naturally out of the Powys family world, and this is especially true of John Cowper who,

1. *Autobiography* (Macdonald, 1967), pp. 14–15

in his first seven novels, returned to the days and atmosphere of his childhood in order to further his own self-understanding, the boy in him remaining to the end of his life an active element in his creative work.

Weymouth, Dorchester, and Montacute are the places which saw the upbringing of this numerous and highly talented family of children. Llewelyn in particular has left vivid pictures of life in Montacute vicarage, a life that clearly lacked for little in the way of family affection and imaginative quality; and the self-sufficiency of the group may be gauged by the variety of their endowments and achievements—those of Gertrude Powys as an artist, of ·Littleton Powys as an athlete, schoolmaster, and naturalist, of Philippa Powys as a novelist and poet, of A. R. Powys as an architect, of Marian Powys as an authority on lace: these in addition to the three writing brothers. The young Powyses had a vitality which their parents made no attempt to curb; and while they revered their father they went their several ways in body and mind, unconventional, adventurous, indissolubly attached to one another. There was a strong family likeness between the eleven brothers and sisters, with a wide variety of temperament; a shared intensity with differing expression. They carried their own world within them wherever they went.

This world, in addition to its intense feeling for the natural order inherited from their father, included a love of literature and a delight in the power of the spoken and written word. This was their mother's legacy. Llewelyn has left, in *Skin for Skin*, a memorable portrait of a gentle, self-effacing, almost morbidly romantic woman who contrasted strangely with the reserved and rock-like character of her husband. She had an acute consciousness of the existence and possibilities of cruelty, an awareness that informs the novels of both Theodore and John Cowper; and while both brothers drew on a close-knit family background, a world of private games, nursery tales, long country walks, and unlimited reading, a highly complex feeling for human fears and aberrations complicated the childlike unworldliness of their characters and upbringing.

These fears, and the private worlds which are at once their source and refuge, are the subject of all John Cowper Powys's novels between *Wood and Stone* and *Maiden Castle*. 'My whole life,' he writes in the *Autobiography*, 'has been one long struggle with Fear.'[2] 'We are all in secret fighting for our sanity.'[3] These are two of the main impulses that went to the making of his fictional world, the negative beginning of his romantic quest. His novels are no less a record of

2. *Autobiography*, p. 12.
3. ibid., p. 249.

them than are the *Autobiography* and philosophical books; and his literary output, like that of D. H. Lawrence, is the varied expression of a single point of view. That point of view is urgently related to the pressures endured by the individual in modern society. Again and again Powys emphasizes the essential loneliness of human beings, and many of his finest scenes portray the juxtaposition and occasional collisions of those who are inevitably doomed to live in the creative and destructive universe of their own consciousness. He portrays happiness as consisting in an act of deliberate forgetfulness or escape, in this voicing an apparent irresponsibility to which many incline and to which few admit. He is not only the champion of the solitary man in an age in which gregariousness has become a moral, not to say commercial, virtue, but also the compassionate analyst of the immature.

Powys's reaction to the stresses and strains of his own highly complex personality, a personality from which, he averred, his novels were written to enable him to escape, had both a positive and negative aspect. In *The Complex Vision* (1920) his central contention is that men and women half-create and half-discover the world they inhabit. Mental states are a conditioning aspect of reality. Thirty-five years later, in *The Brazen Head*, he maintains that each human being is opposed not only to itself but to the world outside it.[4] Thus the world and the self can become a refuge from the self and the world respectively; fact and fantasy are protections from each other—the various movements of the soul between the two is the theme of the Wessex novels, and indeed is to be found throughout Powys's work. We find this double movement of attraction and recoil recorded in the books of criticism: in *Suspended Judgments*, an early book of essays published in America in 1916, he writes of Conrad's attitude to his characters that he 'seems to indicate to us ... that since there is no help in heaven or earth for the persecuted child of man, it is the more necessary that in defiance of chance, yea! in defiance of fate itself, man should sink into his own soul and find in the strength of his own isolated and exiled spirit a courage equal to all that can be laid upon it'.[5] Here detachment is seen as heroic endurance (Powys's own characters are more inclined to an unheroic endurance). But a more positive attitude may lie in escape, in a contemplative merging of the self with the exterior world, the elemental world which the mind shapes and seeks to control. So fifteen years later, in his book on Dorothy Richardson, we find him asserting that 'there is something waiting for every lonely spirit, in the quietness

4. *The Brazen Head* (Macdonald, 1956), pp. 19–20.
5. *Suspended Judgments* (Arnold Shaw, 1916), p. 363.

of the non-human, of the inanimate, waiting always there and ready to do much more than soothe and reassure; ready in fact to summon you forth ... into that ... reality within reality which is better than any future heaven'.[6] The rather limp rhetoric of this is tempered to something more positive in the novels he wrote himself.

But the most thorough record of this double reaction to experience, of the self-reliant stoicism and this super-sensuous contemplation of nature, is to be found in his incomparable autobiography. In some ways this is the most remarkable book he ever wrote. He was over sixty when it was published, but it is very far from being a complacent survey of a career nearing its conclusion. Rather it is a self-portrait of astonishing, at times almost oppressive, candour, a chronicle of his consciousness, a sharing and exploration of all his fears and nervous aberrations, his sexual obsessions and sadistic impulses, his physical mannerisms and mystical intuitions. It is a tremendous feat of self-analysis, almost masochistic in its self-exposure, disarming in its frankness, and even something of a smoke-screen thrown up by one who freely acknowledged that he was in many things an actor. It tells little of his work except his lecturing, and nothing of the various women in his life—this by a self-denying voluntary act of chivalry. But for all its chronological vagueness and incompleteness, it remains an enthralling and immensely readable account of what it felt like to be John Cowper Powys, written in a prose at once elaborate and conversational, the prose of his finest work in fiction.

In this book Powys describes what is in effect one source of his own particular art as a novelist, describing how his father would

> tell my two brothers and me, as we sat beside him after tea on the dining-room sofa, an interminable story about two mythic personages called Giant Grumble and Fairy Sprightly. All I can remember now of this never-completed tale was that its villain, the devil of the piece, was always a scientific pedant, called by the narrator 'the Professor', whose sinister activities required all the arts of both Giant and Fairy to circumvent and neutralise.[7]

Powys may not have remembered much of the detail of this saga, but its elements were to colour his own fiction. The alliance of giant and fairy against professor occurs repeatedly there as the forces of sexuality and romantic yearning are pitted against dehumanized curiosity and detachment from life. Giants or men with kindred qualities, often physically repellent, are in several of the novels

6. *Dorothy M. Richardson* (Joiner & Steele, 1931), pp. 43–44.
7. *Autobiography*, p. 4.

associated with wisdom and health; while the sylphlike boy–girl figures of a number of Powysian heroines enact the role of the fairy. One might not inaccurately identify them with the known goodness of natural objects and the creative power of the imagination, the two positives in Powys's world of dualities, of man's activity of discovery and of his activity of creation. The Professor represents more than the false scientific spirit; he stands for the heresy which underlies modern attitudes to science, the heresy that denies a man's derivation from, and participation in, a physical universe as alive as himself. Powys was a convinced animist; and as early as *The Complex Vision* he was able to assert that ' "the illusion of dead matter" is the most formidable expression of evil which we know; and it can only be destroyed by the magic of that creative spirit whose true "opposite" is not hatred or cruelty or violence or destruction, but the motiveless power of a deadly obscurantism'.[8] All his work is by implication a protest against man's exploitation of the natural order; and his 'magician figures' like John Geard, Sylvanus Cobbold, and Myrrdin Wyllt can be seen not so much as eccentrics as witnesses to man's passive, and not merely detached and active, role in the universe.

2

If the family, with its parental figures, its self-contained world, its tensions and boyhood memories, was one great formative influence in Powys's novel writing, his career as a lecturer was the other. Its restricting effect has already been noted, its isolating him from the world of bookmen which, whatever its limitations, would have helped him to receive more critical attention than he did. It had a further drawback, one which, however, was to encourage his virtues as much as his vices. Powys was a fine orator, and thus in great demand; and the exhausting, ramshackle, itinerant existence which took him all over America, denied him any form of settled disciplined routine, and also denied him the chastening influence of a critical audience who knew him at close quarters. A natural spellbinder who half-believed that he had thaumaturgic powers, he made of his lectures great dramatic performances in which he regarded himself as being a kind of medium for the authors of whom he spoke. This identifying of himself with his subject was to be a feature of his fiction: novels, criticism, philosophy were all projections of his inner vision and need for self-expression. And all alike are couched in a style that is at once repetitive and oratorical, a style that at its best can be

8. *The Complex Vision* (Dodd, Mead & Co., 1920), p. 269.

gracious and supple to the calls made upon it, but at its worst extravagant and bombastic. It is his style, perhaps, more than anything else, which makes Powys seem a mere late nineteenth-century leftover—that and his identifying of himself with his audiences. Powys's literary criticism is a totally subjective affair—he commends his authors not by analysis of their qualities so much as of their effect upon himself; literature to him was secondary to living. All his written work was really the work of a preacher, practical in its aims and ends.

An element of preaching characterizes the work of all three Powys brothers. In T. F. Powys, however, this didacticism is matched by a delicately balanced point of view, a rare blend of sardonic pessimism and kindly tenderness: his writing, mannered and archaic though it frequently is, has a conscious art, an ultimate sophistication that keeps it free from mawkishness and cant. Llewelyn's oratory has worn less well: his style seems frequently affected, and not being by instinct a novelist he is the one of the three who falls into the way of bludgeoning his opponents. This is something that John Cowper never does. Stylistically he appears clumsy when compared with his brothers; but his long, endlessly qualifying, endlessly clarifying sentences are the product of a mind more concerned to persuade than to assert. Powys was always conscious of the common reader, the average man, and all those other abstracts whom he so little resembled himself. He wrote both a pamphlet and a book with the title of *The Art of Happiness*; and it is the quest for personal happiness which is the driving power behind his work. His propagation of a way of aesthetic contemplation, his turning to the material world as escape from the self, is the concern of one more anxious to help people than to reform them. Powys was as alive as was D. H. Lawrence to the deadening effects of modern industrial capitalist society and repressive religious beliefs; but he was more prepared to take people as he found them (probably the ability to lecture people in reality was a help to him in this). He was more interested in offsetting the effects of a civilization he had no hope of changing than in establishing separated communities or in identifying a system with its victims. His propagation of popular do-it-yourself culture (he wrote a book commending his own *One Hundred Best Books*—thus anticipating Mr. Cyril Connolly), his romanticism, his animist philosophy and searching out of the springs of happiness, together with his hatred of cruelty (which went to extravagant and inconsistent lengths in his writings on vivisection—there, for once, he refused to give his fellow humans the benefit of the doubt), are alike aspects of his concern with what is fundamental in human nature and thus fundamental to a just society.

3

Powys was not greatly interested in the novel form as such. In his various published essays upon novelists he points to qualities in them that are qualities in his own books—an intensity of visual imagination, a responsiveness to life's physical and psychological undercurrents, and a romantic awareness of beauty and a feeling for its significance. It is as recorders that he values them, just as he regarded himself in his lecturing as a medium for imaginative experiences which he sought to convey to his audience dramatically. His criterion is not any defined standard of literary excellence, or any agreed notion as to what constitutes a proper form, but always the kind of impact made by the writer on the reader's consciousness. His writings on literature are as confessional as his philosophical books or his novels : often he seems to be describing not so much the writer he is concerned with, as himself. Thus, commenting on Dostoevsky, he remarks that

his special greatness as a writer of fiction is to be found in the fact that he is *not* just a mouthpiece, still less a calm and critical interpreter, but a true medium; that is to say, we have the curious feeling, as we listen to what his most disturbing characters are uttering, that he himself is as startled, shocked, awed and impressed by what they reveal as are their hearers.[9]

Again, in a much earlier essay, printed in *Visions and Revisions* in 1915, he points out that Dostoevsky 'has the power of making all other novelists seem dull in comparison; dull—or artistic and rhetorical'.[10] The combination of those two adjectives is significant : Powys's whole conception of novel writing is one of spontaneous *activity*, an urgent communication between writer and reader. Thus he can write :

Though not a single one of his books ends 'happily', the final impression is the reverse of hopeless. His very mania for tragedy, his Dionysic embracing of it, precludes any premature despair. Perhaps a profound deepening of one's sense of the mysterious *perversity* of all human fate is the thing that lingers, a perversity which is itself a kind of redemption, for it implies arbitrariness and waywardness, and these things mean power and pleasure, even in the midst of suffering.[11]

John Cowper Powys's own novels likewise embody an imaginative world in which one can find reflected one's own inner desires and

9. *Dostoievsky* (John Lane, 1946), p. 8.
10. *Visions and Revisions* (Macdonald, 1955), p. 190.
11. ibid.

processes, and from which one draws a heightened awareness of the universal aspects of the human condition. They are not transcripts of life but explorations of it, and were written instinctively rather than from calculation. Their greatness, however, includes a marrying of such instinctive creation with a sure and consistent inner logic; their apparently unwieldy bulk is sustained by imaginative coherence. Acts of self-discovery, they induce self-discovery. 'The books that are the most valuable in this world are not the books that pretend to solve life's mystery with a system. They are the books which create a certain mood, a certain temper—the mood, in fact, which is prepared for incredible surprises—the temper which no surprise can overpower.'[12]

The passage reveals his dislike of dogmatism. Powys was not a 'literary' novelist in the sense that Henry James was: he was not consciously experimenting with or contributing to an art form. He had none the less a respect for the kind of skill James exemplified. James indeed was to become one of his favourite novelists, and he refers in a letter to Louis Wilkinson, dated 3 November 1940, to 'this Colossus of Subtlety & Pure Brain & Flawless Values'[13]—praise however, which is not much in keeping with his own usual scale of values. Where technique of a more experimental kind is concerned, his essay on *Finnegan's Wake*, reprinted in *Obstinate Cymric*, is instructive.

No doubt Frank Budgen's memory of every word exchanged between them about dreams and the dream-basis of *Finnegan's Wake* is clear, true, and absolutely to be trusted. Moreover, I suspect that Joyce himself, could he return to earth, would refuse to contradict these interpretations of his devoted champions. But I remain unconvinced. I hold the view that the really great thing in writers of genius and the things that will influence posterity are *not* the things which are premeditated and intended, but the things that rise up from the depths of the writer's unique soul, and are diffused through his work. He naturally talks a lot about these precious 'patterns' to sympathetic and admiring friends. What the devil else should he talk about? No doubt the friends of the author of the *Faerie Queene* knew every detail about that damned allegory.[14]

These remarks are certainly relevant for any critic of Powys's work, whatever they may be for that of Joyce. And they show in a particular instance where his own priorities lie: with the fundamental and instinctive rather than with the cerebral or ratiocinative. He would have agreed with Lawrence's dictum that 'the business of art

---

12. *Visions and Revisions*, pp. 193–4.
13. *Letters to Louis Wilkinson* (Macdonald, 1958), p. 81.
14. *Obstinate Cymric:* Essays 1935–1947 (The Druid Press, 1947), pp. 35–6.

is to reveal the relation between man and his circumambient universe, at the living moment'.[15] All his novels constitute an attempt to capture that moment in all its various manifestations.

Powys's interpretation of 'the living moment' is related to his conception of dualities. For him, evil lay in what he called 'malice'—a preference of death to life, the refusal of the imagination's function of shaping and transforming the material world apprehended by the senses. His denunciation of cruelty as the one unpardonable sin arises from his belief that cruelty is the fruit of unimaginativeness. His reverence for life led him to postulate consciousness for all forms of matter; and certainly his own life, as recorded in the *Autobiography*, was governed by a profound sense of kinship with the material world. In the early novels he is most concerned with the duality within the self, with the conflict between the demands of love and the need for solitude; in the later ones, as he grew older and more purely contemplative, the emphasis is more on man's relation with the inanimate. But both relationships, with the passions as realized in relations with other people, and with the external order, constitute living moments, moments, that is, when the self is called upon to realize its identity.

Central to both relationships is his belief in the importance of memory, of sensations begotten of memory and apprehended in moments in and out of time—moments such as are analysed in their different ways by Wordsworth and Proust, Traherne and Vaughan, Blake and C. S. Lewis. This particular romantic vision transfiguring what normally passes for reality is not by Powys given the metaphysical development pursued by the others: rather he sees in it, its cultivation and cherishing, the key to happiness. It is a mark of that inner integrity which is necessary to all fruitful relationships. As he wrote in *The Complex Vision*, 'And this is not so much an escape from life as a transfiguring of the nature of life by means of a newly born attitude toward it. This attitude toward life ... is the attitude which the soul struggles to maintain by gathering together all its different memories of those rare moments when it entered into the eternal vision.'[16] And again.

This 'idea of communism', in which the human implications of the eternal vision become realized, is simply the conception of a system of human society founded upon the creative instinct, instead of upon the possessive instinct in humanity ... It only implies a liberation of a force

15. 'Morality and the Novel' from *Selected Literary Criticism* (Heinemann, 1955), p. 108.
16. *The Complex Vision*, p. xviii.

that already exists, of the force in the human soul that is centrifugal, or outflowing, as opposed to the force that is centripetal, or indrawing.[17]

All Powys's magician figures are studies in men who are attuned to the external world in this way; and his novels are, every one of them, concerned with the apprehension of life as it is in itself. Consciousness was to him the supreme mystery, the supreme point of interest, and the clue to all personal relationships; and he refers with distaste to 'that deplorable modern heresy which finds in bric-à-brac and what are called "objets d'art" a disproportionate monopoly of the beauty and wonder of the world'. [18]

Powys does not provide us with any aesthetic or critique of the novel, because he simply was not interested in a critical approach which lends itself to making that kind of distinction. But it is perhaps worth noting that he always referred to his own novels as 'romances'. The term might be used as one of denigration, as when we refer contemptuously to 'the purveyors of popular romance', meaning the kind of sentimental love-story once supposed to be read by servant girls but in fact universally enjoyed as embodiments of day-dream and as wish-fulfilment. Powys's work hardly falls into this category. More strictly the term might be said to refer to that kind of novel which draws its inspiration from ballad motifs, traditional legends, saga, heroic or epic poetry. This heroic or bardic quality is also lacking in John Cowper Powys's work: *Owen Glendower* comes nearest to it, but is clearly something very much more. The term 'romance' might also be applied with justice to tales involving the use of the supernatural—perhaps with the derisive note of 'romancing' attached; but again, whereas Powys's novels involve a certain element of the supernatural this is only one strand in them, and it is in any case treated within the novel as being a para-normal part of actuality. But if the normal definitions of romance hardly serve to define these books, so do they call in question our normal usage of the word 'novel'.

That usage is conditioned by the large amount that has been written on the novel since the turn of the century. In considering it two methods of critical approach stand out, each with a variety of modifications, methods associated most readily with the names of Percy Lubbock and of Dr. F. R. Leavis. Lubbock's highly influential book *The Craft of Fiction* was first published in 1921, and was to be followed by many others dealing with novel writing from a primarily aesthetic viewpoint. 'Form' became a key word. Lubbock's own writ-

17. *The Complex Vision*, p. xix.
18. *Suspended Judgments*, p. 407.

ing was clearly influenced by his editing of the novels of Henry James: the fact that Dr. Leavis's own very different approach to the novel also owes much to James is indicative of the dangers attendant on any quest for critical objectivity. The position held by Lubbock is the result of an examination of the means employed by various writers to achieve verisimilitude: the over-all impression left by his book is of a concern with method rather than with content, and this in spite of his declaration that the two are in fact inseparable. 'The best form is that which makes the most of its subject—there is no other definition of the meaning of form in fiction. The well-made book is the book in which the subject and the form coincide and are indistinguishable—the book in which the matter is all used up in the form, in which the form expresses all the matter.'[19]

The logical outcome of this is Lubbock's praise of *The Ambassadors* as the ultimate in 'the art of dramatizing the picture of somebody's experience'—for such a dramatization is in fact what Lubbock's definition of the relation of form to content implies.

Dr. Leavis, in his immensely influential *The Great Tradition* which was published twenty-seven years after Lubbock's book, shifts the balance of criticism from a preoccupation with form to the evaluation of content. But to say this is not to imply that he, any more than Lubbock, recognizes any distinction between the two:

As a matter of fact, when we examine the formal perfection of *Emma*, we find that it can be appreciated only in terms of the moral preoccupations that characterize the novelist's peculiar interest in life. Those who suppose it to be an 'aesthetic matter', a beauty of 'composition' that is combined, miraculously, with 'truth to life', can give no adequate reason for the view that *Emma* is a great novel, and no intelligent account of its perfection of form.[20]

For Dr. Leavis *The Ambassadors* is very far from being the crown of James's achievement; but then his interests and concerns are different from Lubbock's. Both critics would presumably agree with James's own comment that 'A novel is a living thing, all one and continuous, like any other organism, and in proportion as it lives will it be found ... that in each of the parts there is something of each of the other parts'.[21] The operative words here are 'as it lives': its life is the guarantee both of its 'form' and of its 'content'. The evaluation of that life comes through the subjective apprehension of the critic reinforced by examination of the text. The fallibility of the

19. *The Craft of Fiction* (Cape, 1921), p. 40.
20. *The Great Tradition* (Chatto & Windus, 1948; Peregrine Books, 1962), p. 17.
21. *The House of Fiction* (Hart-Davis, 1957), p. 34.

critic lies in the necessary subjectivity—a failure of imaginative sympathy, a doctrinaire position, may cost him his insight into truth; but the evaluation must be submitted not only at the bar of individual aesthetic sensibility but at that of commonly received tradition as well. Criticism is not an absolute science, but a mediating activity in which the moral faculties are engaged as fully as the intellectual or aesthetic ones—if the three can be ultimately separated, which they cannot; and it is the mark of the truly engaged critic that, like Eliot and like Leavis, he can on occasion admit to a modification of his views.

This diversionary note on the problems of criticism has been necessary on account of the eccentricity of Powys's own position, and because of his apparent failure to measure up to the exacting standards of the two critics singled out. But this is only true if their standards are seen as the expression of a dogma, rather than as standards for a methodology. That is to say, if we adopt the first interpretation, that of dogma, then by the measurement of the flawless construction and singleness of viewpoint of *The Ambassadors* Powys's novels must be accounted as sprawling, shapeless monsters (a judgement that Louis Wilkinson made popular), while compared with *Middlemarch* they seem to reveal a childish immaturity of outlook which dismisses them from the need for any careful or considered judgement.

4

One embarrassment that faces any sympathetic critic of Powys's work is his own lack of pretension. The self-deprecating comments on his work in the *Letters to Louis Wilkinson*, letters written to an admirer of the terse and economic style and art of a de Maupassant, and to one who avowedly preferred his brother Theodore's novels to his own, should be treated with some reserve, for there can be no doubt that Powys took his own novels very seriously; but what they do indicate is that he did not take himself too seriously when writing them. The very casualness of his approach, his omission to make any elaborate plan, and his reliance on the inspiration of the story and characters themselves as they formed in his mind, make him a throwback to the improviser of tales and narrator of marvels: he is concerned not with his own art but with the urgency of what he felt it in him to say. Emphasis has already been laid on his gifts as a lecturer, gifts as much dramatic and hortatory as expository; and he is an actor and preacher in his novels as much as a literary artist. The peculiar spell which they cast is in part the fruit of this eloquence, this romantic self-projection; and yet its magic is something more subtle than that of a preacher, however eloquent. It lies in its own attitude towards itself. Powys liked to describe himself as a charlatan; and yet the ascription is only in part sincere. He was possessed of that particular kind of gift known by the Welsh as the *hwyl*, a sense of intoxicated possession that still leaves room for scepticism because it is not to be identified with the character of the recipient.[22] Powys believed passionately in what he was trying to say; but he never confused his message with himself, he never made a personal issue out of it. This detachment, very different from the enthusiasm of a Lawrence, has led to his being written off as flippant or at best only half-serious; but in fact it springs from an awareness of the multiplicity of human experience and the impossibility of any one single human consciousness being able to apprehend it all. This awareness enables him to believe and disbelieve at one and the same time; or, to put it more precisely, to hold the possibility of disbelief in the back of his mind in the very act of passionate assertion—and vice versa.

It is this ambiguity of approach which governs his attitude to novel writing. His emphasis on the fact that he is telling a story puts his medium in perspective: what he is saying is in terms of a particular convention. He makes no attempt to persuade the reader that he is transcribing actual events as they occur or have just occurred—he is telling a story, is writing *fiction*, the truth of which resides not simply in any verisimilitude it may have but in its representational quality, in its capacity to carry the burden of the author's vision of what constitutes reality. In the finest of the novels, where his imagination is working at full stretch, we willingly assent to the reality of the portraiture; the tale itself is self-authenticating, the magician has proved his credentials. At his worst Powys fails to convince, and his magic collapses into masquerading; but his innate humility saves him from being discredited by this. This is especially true of *A Glastonbury Romance* where the absence of pomposity in the novel as a whole allows not only for assent to its more extravagant moments but even carries the failure of its more outrageous taxes on assent—such as the description of Tom Barter's soul leaving his body after his murder. The fact that the author is himself ready to question the truth of what he asserts frees one from resentment at such a description being essayed in the first place—frees those, however, who are in basic sympathy with his method and approach: there remain many people who cannot endorse his vision of life and who find his method

22. I am indebted to Miss Carol Hughes for drawing my attention to this point.

of presentation, which is inseparable from it, equally unacceptable.

For the enjoyment, perhaps even the appreciation, of Powys's novels depends upon a readiness to share his point of view. In terms of 'the great tradition' of Jane Austen, George Eliot, and Henry James, he will always be an alien: the kind of sensitivity to moral issues, to social pressures, and the balanced portrayal of dramatic conflict which is most peculiarly theirs is a kind of sensitivity he did not possess—or, more strictly, his own awareness of these things is mediated through a different choice of material; he simply is not concerned with the portrayal of society as they record it. He has more in common with Conrad and Lawrence: the particular awareness of man as himself a part of the elemental creation, which is one aspect of Conrad's work, is central to John Cowper Powys's vision, while in his contemptuous rejection of artificial 'society' and its corrupting conventions he is as absolute, though not so continuously insistent, as is Lawrence. But he makes his points out of a fictional world peculiarly his own.

A quotation from *The Craft of Fiction* is relevant here. Commenting on Henry James's use of the terms 'picture' and 'drama' in reference to the final novels, Lubbock extends the term 'picture' from James's definition to include what he calls the 'panoramic' method of Thackeray, a term which can also be applied to Powys's art as a novelist. 'It is a question ... of the reader's relation to the writer; in one case the reader faces towards the story-teller and listens to him, in the other he turns towards the story and watches it.'[23] Powys's work in particular depends upon the part played by the narrator, who is never a character in the story although his presence is always felt. In this respect there is a marked difference between the early novels and those from *Wolf Solent* onwards. In the former Powys keeps himself firmly in the background, and *Rodmoor* and *Ducdame* particularly are written in a style that is comparatively detached and cool. But with *Wolf Solent* there comes a remarkable change. Gone is any attempt at formal grace of presentation or construction, gone any attempt at being 'literary', a quality which is more marked in *Ducdame* than in any other of the novels—*Ducdame*, the book that was revised by the very 'literary' Llewelyn Powys. In *Wolf Solent* Powys discards his earlier restraint; he is concerned to record everything that he can about his hero—not only his innermost thoughts, his religious and sex sensations, but his outward habits, his taste in clothes and food, all his phobias and nervous obsessions. And to do this he elaborated a method of narrative that was based on the leisurely chronicles that he himself liked reading and which is very

23. *The Craft of Fiction*, p. 111.

patently a *tale*, a story, even though the tale is not as eventful outwardly as the build-up might lead one to expect.

What John Cowper Powys does is to use the apparatus of narrative to distance and objectify what is in fact a highly subjective picture of the human scene. His particular kind of romance, or novel, includes all three senses of the term romance that have been outlined above. In the first place it has for its subject-matter the nature and significance of that kind of day-dreaming, that longing for fulfilment, of love and power, which the popular romancers exploit. All Powys's novels, from *Wood and Stone* to *All or Nothing*, touch on this theme. In *Wood and Stone* the day-dreaming element is less pronounced than in the subsequent books; but even in this, the most conventional of the novels, the social cross-currents and treatment of action are secondary to the part played by mental states.

The second kind of romance, that implicit in the ballad or the epic, has as its popular characteristic a feeling for the representational significance of man's activity. Here human relationships are not self-contained within a social fabric, do not draw their significance solely from themselves. They are seen as expressions of man's oneness with the natural order, a oneness known in imaginative contemplation as much as in physical being. This kind of romance (*The House of the Seven Gables* is a good example), with its strong feeling for landscape, whether sparsely indicated as in the traditional ballads or elaborately invoked as in the novels of Scott or Hardy, carries with it a diffused feeling of significance which, while less precise in its application than the kind of moral significance evoked by a novel by George Eliot or James, nevertheless is a basic feeling which can be applied from the centre of one's conscious being to all the circumstantial activities of life. It is a kind of seminal awareness of meaning, a feeling that is at its root religious. Powys's novels, while informed by an undercurrent of scepticism, induce such a feeling of generalized or epic significance by using the narrative method, the kind of dramatic presentation peculiar to this kind of symbolic story.

As for the 'supernatural' romance, it is included in Powys's work as an element in any human experience that is not closed or doctrinaire. In confronting what is perhaps the central difficulty for a contemporary reader of that work—I mean the ostensibly magical or supernatural elements that occur specifically in *A Glastonbury Romance* and the later novels, but implicitly in all—it is necessary to divest oneself of current dogmatic presuppositions. Powys's world is a world in which *anything* may be possible; his novels take that view seriously, and the individual has to interpret these supernatural phenomena as best he may for himself. The author's own lack of dogmatism allows for a kindred reasonableness in his readers. The most immediately obvious fact about this element in his work is that it places it alongside a well-worn and popular tradition: what Powys does is to subsume that tradition, and the half-belief which underlies it, into his total vision of what is possible and of what a novel should contain.

For it is in his content, in his subject-matter, and in the method he uses to deploy it, that Powys's originality as a novelist resides. For sheer *breadth* of subject-matter few can equal him. His total vision is all-embracing, and he refuses to fine down and select. This is perhaps the chief reason why he is rejected by many academic critics. His simultaneous descriptions of the smallest physical phenomena and the wildest metaphysical speculation, his fascination with trivial habits and private day-dreams as well as with the movements of thought and religious beliefs, his encompassing of the sublime and the bathetic within a single scene, do not lend themselves to the kind of sifting and appraisal which is the keynote of much contemporary criticism. He provides a field-day for the source hunters, and another, more frustrating one, for the system makers; but he defeats the moral evaluator, simply because his material extends far beyond the field where moral discriminations can take effect. This is not to say that his work is morally insignificant—a reading of *Wolf Solent* alone should discount that accusation—but it includes morality in its total vision of what it is to be a man, rather than defines that vision by it.

Such width of scope, such ambition, is not, of course, of itself enough to make a good novel: large claims for Powys's genius require critical substantiation. The succeeding analysis of the novels will, it is hoped, indicate something of the nature of their achievement as well as their faults and limitations. The latter are, at first glance, more obvious than the former: the cumbersome frame, the verbosity, the apparent unsophistication, and, more damning, the apparent immaturity—all these together with their detachment from the contemporary scene are enough to discourage serious appraisal. But many of Powys's faults are only faults if we insist on asking from him what he is not concerned to give: there is *Ducdame* to show that he could write a neatly turned novel if he wanted to. The great sprawling books that he did write were necessary for the embodiment of his particular vision. Lawrence when he wrote *The Rainbow* consciously sought out a new form to carry what he had to say; Powys in his Wessex novels preferred to adapt the kind of long romance he had enjoyed in childhood to seek out the roots of the buried childhood life in which he saw the key to the kingdom of heaven. The apparent *naïveté* of his literary approach is part of his method: clumsy compared with the obvious artistry of Conrad or Jane Austen, it is in fact the ideal vehicle for his message. For Powys is a novelist with an urgent message, however leisurely and unexcited his voicing of it may seem to be.

As much as Lawrence he believed in the necessity for getting back to the instinctual roots in man, if civilization was to be saved. But whereas Lawrence lived out his vision in the very facts of his existence, in his marriage and journeyings, his rejection both of the narrow religious life of his childhood and the shallow literary society of Cambridge and London—whereas Lawrence wrote about contemporary society out of his own experience and in the hope of changing it, Powys, for all his insistence on the necessity for individual wholeness and integrity, fought a solitary battle against depression and frustration, fears and illogical aversions. That his writing partook of the nature of a personal exorcism does not, however, invalidate its more general significance. His championship of the individual amid all the pressures of modernized and mechanized society, and his peculiarly mental apprehension of physical phenomena through his cult of sensationalism, were as heartfelt and are as relevant as Lawrence's appeal for tenderness and sensitivity and hatred of demagogic forces. Powys lacks Lawrence's brilliant concurrence of intellectual and emotional sincerity; but, although less obviously 'engaged', his own wisdom was as hard-won and is particularly well attuned to the 'ordeal of consciousness'. Concerning himself primarily with the individual self-awareness of his characters, he none the less manages to evoke an imaginative world that could be seminal for society's growth.

But Lawrence is not a great novelist simply because he has an urgent prophetic message; and Powys's insight and relevance for the predicament of men and women in an industrialized society are not of themselves sufficient to justify the claim that at its best Powys's work as a novelist deserves a critical attention as serious as that accorded to writers such as Lawrence and even Graham Greene or Aldous Huxley. Only the adequate and transforming embodiment of that message in a number of actual novels can do that.

And in the Wessex novels and the two Welsh histories it happens: it is on these six works, with the *Autobiography*, that Powys's reputation should ultimately rest. What then is their importance? It is, I would suggest, because in them Powys has contrived to present dramatic fables or portraits of an attitude to life which is rooted in our earliest consciousness and to relate it dramatically to a wide variety of representative experiences. In *Wolf Solent* and to a lesser extent in *Maiden Castle* it is to love and personal responsibility; in *Weymouth Sands* to anxiety and failure; in *Glastonbury* and the Welsh novels to religion, memory, and politics. These are of course broad generalizations, but they spring from an analysis of the novels and are, I hope, sufficiently supported by them. In all six novels the external world is like and yet unlike the world we know—it is coloured by the controlling imagination of the author, and is at one and the same time presented and interpreted. What gives this world its particular persuasiveness is the power and consistency with which it is imagined—witness Powys's command of the prolonged scene, scenes, or episodes like the Midsummer Day walk to Maiden Castle, the christening of Nell Zoyland's baby in *A Glastonbury Romance*, or the Horse Fair in *Wolf Solent*: for sheer command of detail, for density of pictorial imagination Powys has no equals among his contemporaries, unless it be James Joyce. The profound sensual apprehension of his world permits its enlargement into the realm of perception, and prevents the accounts of mental states from becoming rarefied. The settings of Powys's novels are realized with total actuality; but because of the style of his narrative and his deliberately old-fashioned approach they are sufficiently distanced for us to accept imaginatively the spiritual extensions. He evades the built-in disbelief of his time by a stylistic side-step backwards.

Within this stylistically abstracted world, however, the issues and struggles of the protagonists are of a familiar and intimately personal character. An intense inwardness balances the external vividness. Portraiture in Powys's art is not simply a question of characteristics or caricature (though he can create a Dickensian grotesque when he wants to—witness Finn Toller in *A Glastonbury Romance*, and a host of others in the same book), but is rather used as a medium for and transmitter of psychic experience. His men and women, obsessively real though they are, are centres of a number of intangible worlds of experience; hence the use of emblematic notation in *Wolf Solent*, the various reveries and dream states recorded in *A Glastonbury Romance* and *Weymouth Sands*, the magical processes in the later works. In every case it is a four-dimensional world which his characters inhabit, and, by inhabiting, condition. Powys takes his acute sensory and psychological perceptions and makes of them a portrait of reality which contains the elements of the world we know, and yet which invests it with a significance extending beyond itself— but not in spite of itself. Meaning is extended, not imported from elsewhere. They are poetic rather than religious novels.

Powys himself, in the best of his philosophical books, *The Meaning of Culture*, provides a definition of poetry which underlines this point. Distinguishing between what is meant by beauty and what is meant by poetry, he describes the former as a 'revelation of a non-human absolute', whereas poetry is for him a 'revelation of an accumulated human tradition of certain primitive reactions to life',[24] 'something profoundly and emotionally humanized'.[25] 'Poetry hovers over everything that has been ... a permanent accessory, a daily tool, long enough for a certain organic identification to have grown up between the diurnal usages of our race and this or that fragment of material substance'.[26] It is this kind of poetry which informs all of Powys's novels; and the awareness of it which is the salvation of his characters. Such a living sense of continuity with the past, matched by an acute sensory response to the present, is the foundation of his particular way of life, the *tao* expounded in all his writings, whether criticism, philosophy, or fiction.

The succeeding analysis of the novels will, it is hoped, consolidate the critical position posited above. The particular kind of novel which John Cowper Powys produced demands a considerable suspension of disbelief, but it demands also a seriousness of attention if its full complexity and richness are to be realized. As a craftsman he has had nowhere near his due, and the picture of a great chaotic and muddle-headed sprawler made current in popular journalistic criticism needs the refutation which a close study of the major novels will provide. But craftsmanship as such will never make the significant novelist that John Cowper Powys so richly is when writing at his full stretch. His peculiar gift of evoking the private mythology by which a person lives, and to do so not only discursively, by definition and description, but by his use of what may be called a common literary and cultural subconscious, is the measure of the deep cultural roots from which his fiction springs. His own world is mediated through a world of books. This is not achieved by any erudite system of references, but is more a matter of style and approach. Just as his father told stories to him in his boyhood, so his own narrative method has all the careful particularity and the incantatory repetition beloved by children: he thus appeals to the deepest and oldest conscious memories of his reader. And this way of looking and feeling becomes in his hands something formative and comprehensive, so that if his novels of contemporary life seem semi-mythological, his historical romances and his fantasies are oddly realistic, despite their remoteness of setting or eccentricity of subject. The same attitude informs them all and is flexible to every

24. *The Meaning of Culture* (Jonathan Cape, 1930), p. 71.
25. ibid., p. 62.
26. ibid., p. 64.

call upon it. His novels are written out of that single-minded passion which makes for poetry, springing from a delight in the tale as such and from a profound concern for human beings. His very faults as a writer are instructive and his virtues, far out-topping them, are virtues which call for critical adaptation if they are to be truly apprehended. It is the artist who is the measure of the critic.

CHAPTER TWO

The Early Novels

1

In the preface to *Wood and Stone*, written in, for him, an unusually formal style, Powys sets forth his intentions in writing the novel and his ideas as to what the function of a novel is. The central theme of this particular book is one from which his later fictional world was to spring—the nature of power. The contrasting characters of his father and mother may have dictated the preoccupation, but it is couched here in more philosophical terms, and seen as one of the basic human issues. Is aggression or passivity to be regarded as the ultimate human wisdom? The question so put relates at once to the personal life-illusion, dreams, and ambitions of the individual; however much Powys tries to do so, he cannot evade the personal nature of his inspiration. The great abstractions of Love and Power and Pride and Sacrifice used and capitalized in this preface only make sense in personal terms. His formal intention may be philosophical, to seek out the mainspring of the law of life; but his actual achievement was to be more practical, to portray the various shifts which the human psyche is put to in order to maintain its sanity in a constantly changing world of values. Already Powys is sceptical of any ultimate philosophical answer to his problem; but he believed that truth of a more immediate kind is attainable through art. Indeed, for him, fiction was a more satisfactory method than was formal philosophy for getting at the truth, since the 'whole question is indeed so intimately associated with the actual panorama of life and the evasive caprices of flesh and blood, that every kind of drastic and clinching formula breaks down under its pressure'.[1] The sentence is indicative of the approach that Powys was to follow in his fiction, a curious combination of broad sweep and detailed analysis, a simultaneous panoramic awareness of the phenomenon of life in general and a fascinated interest in the most obscure and miniscule workings of the inner mind. Of the general world of social contacts and organization that lies in between he shows little awareness.

The preface also contains his own credo as a literary artist. The purpose of art, as against the spirit of 'the Professor', is to 'keep the

1. *Wood and Stone* (Arnold Shaw, 1915), p. viii.

horizons open ... She must hold fast to poetry and humour, and about her creations there must be a certain spirit of *liberation*, and the presence of large tolerant after-thoughts.' This is a good description of his own work at its best. He goes on to comment on the popular fiction of the time.

The curious thing about so many modern writers is, that in their earnest preoccupation with philosophical and social problems, they grow strained and thin and sententious, losing the mass and volume, as well as the elusive-blown airs, of the flowing tide. On the other hand there is an irritating tendency, among some of the cleverest, to recover their lost balance after these dogmatic speculations, by foolish indulgence in sheer burlesque—burlesque which is the antithesis of all true humour.[2]

There is an element of prophecy in the words; and Powys's own novels were to be a lifelong protest against both a falsely limiting 'realism' and an irresponsible use of satire. His approach to novel writing in his later works may not have been so solemn or deliberate as here, but his underlying seriousness of purpose was never to be abandoned. Fiction was concerned with truth.

Wood and Stone suffers, unlike John Cowper Powys's later novels, from this deliberation of approach: the contrast between the forces of power and self-sacrifice is too laboured, being asserted rather than worked out at the dramatic level. The plot is slight, and suffers from a proliferation of characters and incident; the two main themes of the novel, the tyranny of the Romers, father and daughter, over their financial dependants, and the mental breakdown and collapse of the stonemason James Andersen, bear little relation to each other. The Romers themselves are cleverly analysed, but hardly brought to life; they are fore-runners of characters to be more fully developed in later books. There is no question that Powys's sympathies lie with their victims, so much so that the nature of aggression is one-sidedly presented, and the relations between Mortimer Romer and the eccentric recluse Maurice Quincunx (in whom it is easy to detect elements of the characters of both John Cowper and Theodore Powys) and between Gladys Romer and her companion, the symbolically named Italian girl, Lacrima, are inadequately developed. Gladys is Powys's first portrait of a sadist and her scenes with Lacrima are a disturbing evocation of that particular torture known as teasing. Lacrima herself is less interesting; but as a type she interests Powys very much indeed.

The Pariah is one who is born with an innate inability to deal vigorously and effectively with his fellow animals. One sees these unfortunates every

2. *Wood and Stone*, p. x.

day—on the street, in the office, at the domestic hearth. One knows them by the queer look in their eyes; the look of animals who have been crushed rather than tamed ... the Pariah does not venerate the Power that oppresses him. He despises it and hates it ... And it is this difference, separating him from the rest, that excites such fury in those who oppress him ... The pure-minded capable man, perceiving the rancorous misanthropy of this sick spirit, longs to trample him into the mud, to obliterate him, to forget him. But the man whose strength and cunning is associated with lascivious perversity, wishes to have him by his side, to humiliate, to degrade, to outrage.[3]

Such perverse relationships are recurrent in Powys's fiction.

In this novel the Romers are defeated, not only by a final upsurge of spirit in the pariahs themselves, but also by the energy and single-minded action of two other Powysian types. Luke Andersen, the cynical young stonemason, is clearly a portrait of Llewelyn Powys, just as James Andersen is a portrait of John Cowper himself in his more disturbed moods. Luke with his animal magnetism and flagrant amorality is worlds away from the sado-masochistic relations between Lacrima and Gladys; and he is balanced in the book's structure by Vennie Seldom, first of another long line, that of the old maids, those wise women who have a detachment from life that puts them above the struggle between the rival strengths of force and weakness. Both Luke and Vennie are in their different ways 'beyond maturity'; and in both of them we see longings for a state of existence transcending both space and time, beyond both good and evil. And the detachment of Luke and Vennie is contrasted with the fate of James Andersen and the parish priest Hugh Clavering, both of whom are the victims of their passions—and, in the case of the latter, of his own moral sense and infatuation with Gladys Romer. Clavering is contrasted half-humorously with the ironically drawn Papist theologian Francis Taxater, a portrait of Powys's friend, the church historian J. W. Williams. The *deus ex machina* who rescues the pariahs is an American painter, a most implausible character who is the only American in Powys's fiction.

The use of landscape is twofold. In the first place it underlines the themes of the novel and serves a symbolic function; it is here that the book is most indebted to the influence of Hardy. Powys was to use all the principal scenes of his boyhood in turn, and in this book Montacute is described under the thin disguise of 'Nevilton'. The images of wood and stone which control the presentation of the opposing forces of love and the will to power are related to the two hills which dominate the Montacute scene—Montacute Tor itself and

3. ibid., pp. 84–5.

Ham Hill. The latter is here called Leo's Hill, and its quarries, owned by Romer, are symbolic of capitalist power—though it must be admitted that Powys's attempt to import a political aspect to his study is a failure: neither here nor in *A Glastonbury Romance*, the one of the later novels most clearly foreshadowed in *Wood and Stone*, is he able to make his political agitators convincing. They are beyond his range of imaginative, though not of his intellectual, sympathy. The quarries are where the unhinged James Andersen meets his death; already we can see Powys's characteristic use of landscape to point his themes. But the use to which he puts Leo's Hill is rather laboured; more effective is his account, under the name 'Nevilton Hill', of Montacute Tor, the traditional burial place of a fragment of the True Cross. There is a fine and very characteristic passage in which Hugh Clavering climbs the hill, tormented by his infatuation with Gladys. From it he observes on one side the nun-like Vennie Seldom pacing to and fro in a white dress in a field far below; on the other he watches two young lovers closer at hand, embracing. The nature of voyeurism was of great interest to Powys; but in this scene, with its intensely realized physical actuality and masterly juxtaposition of images he fuses psychological insight with physical intimations of an unusual kind. The hill and what happens on the hill reflect and control each other; man is seen as being at once a part of nature and transcending it. What Powys is moving towards is a portrayal of man as himself a part of nature not only in his physical sense but also in his imaginative intuition.

Although Powys has frequently been described as a great master of scene painting it is only in the early novels that we find passages which might be called objectively descriptive, though detailed pictures of weather and cloud effects persist until the end. At his best he could write with graphic particularity, as in the following passage:

The afternoon was very hot, though there was no sun. The wind blew in threatening gusts, and the quarry-owner noticed that the distant Quantock Moors were overhung with a dark bank of lowering clouds. It was one of those sinister days that have the power of taking all colour and all interest out of the earth's surface. The time of the year lent itself gloomily to this sombre unmasking. The furze bushes looked like dead things. Many of them had actually been burnt in some wanton conflagration; and their prickly branches carried warped and blighted seeds. The bracken, near the path, had been dragged and trodden. Here and there its stalks protruded like thin amputated arms. The elder-bushes, caught in the wind, showed white and metallic, as if all their leaves had been dipped in some brackish water. All the trees seemed to have something of this dull, whitish glare, which did not prevent them from remaining, in the recesses of their foliage, as drearily dark as the dark dull soil beneath them. The grass of the fields had a look congruous with the rest of the scene; a look as if it had been one large velvety pall, drawn over the whole valley.[4]

This sombre note sounds throughout the book, and the heavy soil of Somerset is repeatedly pictured in a sinister light; images of death and decay recur. In one passage the very landscape becomes an expression of Lacrima's plight, caught between the tormenting attentions of Gladys and the more brutal advances of the farmer, Goring.

As she ascended the shadowy lane with its crumbling banks of sandy soil and its over-hanging trees, she felt once again how persistently this heavy luxuriant landscape dragged her earthwards and clogged the wings of her spirit. The tall grasses growing thick by the way-side enlaced themselves with the elder-bushes and dog-wood, which in their turn blended indissolubly with the lower branches of the elms. The lane itself was but a deep shadowy path dividing a flowing sea of foliage, which seemed to pour, in a tidal wave of suffocating fertility, over the whole valley ... In a curious way it seemed as if this Nevilton scenery offered her no escape from the insidious sensuality she fled.[5]

Indeed at times in *Wood and Stone* it seems as though the author was positing some collusion between nature and the forces of evil; but in the last resort he remains sceptical if a shade ambiguous as to the reality of spiritual forces. There is a certain play upon supernatural dread—or rather dread of the praeternatural—in the chapter called Auber Lake, a chapter which reflects not altogether happily Powys's admiration of Poe; but in Lacrima's compassion for the mad girl, in spite of her own fear of her, we have the kind of confrontation which is handled with far greater sensitiveness and subtlety in the Lenty Pond episodes of *Wolf Solent* and the visit of John Geard to Mark's Court in *A Glastonbury Romance*. In each case the final affirmation is of human values, of the power of love and sanity over fear and superstition. Powys recognizes the awareness of the supernatural as being an aspect of man's awareness of nature; but he never isolates it from its context. His taste for Gothic romances leads him up to the brink of attempting something in the same kind himself; but his common sense always gets the better of him. This conflict in him can lead to bathos, though a bathos that he learned to deploy deliberately. In *Wood and Stone* the prevailing mood is questioning, speculative, and, where human motives are

4. *Wood and Stone*, pp. 370–1.
5. ibid., pp. 294–5.

concerned, disenchanted. All the characters have to settle for the second best.

None of them is idealized, with the exception of the Hardyesque country girl Dinsie Lintot, who seems to have strayed into the novel out of some old Victorian romance. The Romers have their good qualities, while Mr. Quincunx, described with such discerning humour for much of the novel's length, is revealed as chillingly selfish in the final count—revealed, but not denounced. This novel is the work of a man in early middle age: there are no moral histrionics.

There is plenty of dramatic atmosphere, however, if little dramatic action; and the story moves at, for Powys, a remarkably swift pace. The sentences and paragraphs are short, but the book itself is very long. Its principal weakness is a failure of dramatic engagement: the author perpetually obtrudes himself between the reader and his characters. In time he was to learn the art of letting himself act as a filter rather than simply as a commentator. The novel being a first novel is inevitably experimental, and reflects the author's tastes and admirations rather than his actual capacities. And the style reflects this. In the same year that Lawrence was at work upon *The Rainbow* Powys was writing in a stale, ponderous, bookish manner, full of slack adjectives such as 'incredible', 'whimsical', 'indescribable', and of arch euphemisms such as 'daughter of Eve', which were to remain a permanent, though diminishing, blot upon his work.

Nevertheless the book still stands in its own right as a part of a total corpus and not simply as a prentice work. It is developed with an unerring interior logic: if the ultimate conclusions are negative, despite the escape of the pariahs, it is because there is a basic contradiction in human experience that makes a mock of all attempts at rationalization. *Wood and Stone* may not be Powys's most tragic book; but it is arguably his most bitter one.

2

Powys's first seven novels fall into two groups, which might be loosely described as panoramic and dramatic: these labels, however, should be taken as being descriptive of tendencies or of over-all character rather than of actual content. To the first group belong *Wood and Stone, A Glastonbury Romance,* and *Weymouth Sands.* In these books, against a carefully realized geographical background, Powys presents a series of parallel dramas exploring various aspects of power and weakness as they manifest themselves in politics, in religion, in sexual love, in solitary lust, in mysticism, in commercial enterprise, in scientific experiment. Not that these themes are given abstract treatment; rather, they are explored through their relation to the individuals who are their exemplars. In *Wood and Stone* and *A Glastonbury Romance* there is some attempt at a master plot, and the second book has a bizarre metaphysical framework of the author's own invention; but in *Weymouth Sands* Powys abandons any attempt at a containing structure, and contents himself with a series of only accidentally related studies in failure and frustration. But *Rodmoor*, *Ducdame*, and *Wolf Solent*, and to a lesser extent *Maiden Castle* are centred round a single individual. They develop a particular theme, the relation of a man's private world to his environment and personal relationships; and in them Powys establishes the point of view central to all his major novels. And if that point of view is a balanced and sceptical one it none the less derives from a very thorough exploration of the impulses behind romanticism.

Rodmoor is a far more intense, dramatic, and deeply felt novel than *Wood and Stone*, and is written with greater spontaneity and force. Alone among Powys's novels, except for part of *A Glastonbury Romance*, it is set in East Anglia; and in it he distances his theme by putting to a tragic purpose a landscape with happy associations for himself. For the book is a tragedy, though it includes elements which the author was to push on to other, more affirmative conclusions. The landscape perfectly harmonizes with the bleakness of the tale. Rodmoor itself is a decaying port backed by immense salt-marshes and eroded by the sea, and the novel is haunted by a feeling of isolation and of menace. The geographical notation of *Wood and Stone* is here reversed. Now it is the woods and orchards and gardens of the inland country which are friendly and the sea which is the enemy and destroyer: agoraphobia replaces claustrophobia. The huge marsh skies, the swirling turbulent river, the dikes and withy beds and sand dunes are evoked with great power, and the novel suggests a landscape by Ruysdael. It is notable that when as here and in *Ducdame* Powys is describing a region not so much specific as distilled from a general impression he is far more vivid than when depicting a place whose appearance he is familiar with and thus takes for granted.

The plot of *Rodmoor* relates to those of *Ducdame* and *Wolf Solent*, and is in the nature of a preliminary sounding. It concerns the breakdown of the hyper-sensitive Adrian Sorio through his inability to come to terms with his own life, and through his love for two different women. Here in embryo we have the dominant Powysian motives —the relation of man to his own self-consciousness, and the relation of his necessarily self-protective private world to that of others. Adrian finds sanity and deliverance from fear with the faithful and simple Nance Herrick, but his spiritual affinities with Philippa Renshaw. Philippa is native to Rodmoor and to the wild and dangerous elements that surround it; and she and her gigantic brother Brand are presented as members of a doomed race. The Herricks (Nance and her sister Linda) come from the outer world, just as in *A Glastonbury Romance* the Crows are aliens in Somerset and themselves a Norfolk family descended from the Danish raiders —race plays an important part on Powys's fictional world. *Rodmoor* is dedicated to 'The spirit of Emily Brontë', and a kindred contrast to that between the Earnshaws and the Lintons is clearly contemplated. But *Rodmoor* is far more ambiguous than its great original. Adrian's dilemma is unresolved, and the book ends on a note of complete agnosticism.

Adrian is an ex-mental patient in terror of being taken back to the asylum. He suffers from an agonizing physical self-consciousness.

I'm porous to things ... It's just as if I hadn't any skin, as if my soul hadn't any skin. Everything that I see, or hear ... passes straight through me, straight through the very nerves of my inmost being. I feel sometimes as though my mind were like a piece of parchment, stretched out taut and tight and every single thing that comes near me taps against it, tip-tap, tip-tap, tip-tap, as if it were a drum! That wouldn't be so bad if it wasn't that I know so horribly clearly what people are thinking.[6]

He tries to rationalize his fear by writing a book based on the idea that the impulse to destruction may in fact be the life-force itself. He explains himself to Philippa.

The secret of things being found, not in the instinct of creation but in the instinct of destruction, is only the beginning of it. I go further— much further than that ... this 'nothingness', this 'death' ... to which everything struggles is only a name for *what lies beyond life*—for what lies ... beyond the extreme limit of the life of every individual thing. We shrink back from it, everything shrinks back from it, because it is the annihilation of all one's familiar associations, the destruction of the impulse to go on being oneself! But though we shrink back from it, something in us, something that is deeper than ourselves pushes us on to this destruction. This is why, when people have been outraged in the very roots of their being, when they have been lacerated and flayed more than they can bear, when they have been, so to speak, raked through and combed out, they often fall back upon a soft delicious tide of deep large happiness, indescribable, beyond words.[7]

6. *Rodmoor* (Arnold Shaw, 1916), p. 288.
7. ibid., pp. 324–5.

This theme is to be more critically examined in the two novels that succeeded *Rodmoor*: here Adrian dies in illustration of this quest, not in exploration of it.

He is the centre of a number of human contrasts and conflicts. There is the tension between Nance and the perverse intellectual Philippa; there is the contrast between the life-affirming Doctor Fingle Raughty and the life-denying cynical aesthete Baltazar Stork (Powys's choice of names is as eccentric as Hardy's); between Brand and Linda—a vivid portrayal of a sado/masochistic attraction; between the life-affirming priest and his life-denying supporter Helen Renshaw, mother of Brand and Philippa, a character drawn with considerable complexity of shading, at times sinister and at others sympathetic.

Adrian's quest for some mental or spiritual haven beyond this present life is symbolized in a strange bisexual figure seen by him in vision after reading a passage from de Gourmont's *Litany of the Rose*. This figure has two embodiments, with differing notations. The 'good' angel is Adrian's son Baptiste, left behind in America, and out of sight throughout the action of the novel; and the 'bad' one is Philippa. The two are irreconcilable: just when Nance telegraphs to Baptiste to come and save his father from breakdown Adrian dies, and Philippa drowns herself by dragging his body out to sea. The action is unmotivated, but appropriate to a novel which is concerned more with states of feeling than with moral choice.

This is not to say that there isn't a fine controlling intellect at work. Philippa herself is sympathetically drawn, understanding Adrian's feelings better than the simple Nance does. But, as in all Powys's novels, no one is seen from one point of view alone. The lofty Philippa can be humorously treated, as in the scene when Adrian tries to persuade her to let him haul her up into the loft of a windmill.

Philippa looked at him with angry dismay. All this agitating fuss over so childish an adventure irritated her beyond endurance. His proposal had, as a matter of fact, a most subtle and curious effect upon her. It changed the relations between them. It reduced her to the position of a girl playing with an elder brother. It outraged, with an element of the comic, her sense of dramatic fastidiousness. It humiliated her pride and broke the twisted threads of all kinds of delicate spiritual nets she had in her mind to cast over him. It placed her by his side as a weak and timid woman by the side of a willful and strong-limbed man. Her ascendancy over him, as she well knew, depended upon the retaining, on her part, of a certain psychic evasiveness—a certain mysterious and tantalizing reserve. It depended—at any rate that is what she imagined—upon the inscrutable look she could throw into her eyes and upon the tragic glamour of her ambiguous red lips and white cheeks. How could she possibly retain all these characteristics when swinging to and fro at the end of a rope?[8]

When this passage is coupled with the more dramatic scenes it can be perceived how Powys is never enveloped by his use of melodrama, his evocative and highly coloured moments being pigmentation in a fully realized design.

Adrian is destroyed by the confluence of three weaknesses—his excessive responsiveness to the inanimate (he as much as Rodmoor itself is being eroded); the romantic yearning which is at war with his actual circumstances; and his resultant difficulty in achieving a satisfactory relationship with women. These three areas of experience are recurring features in the succeeding novels.

In *Rodmoor* we find the oblique Powysian method of presentation. While being a master-hand at the evocation of the atmosphere and undertones of drama, Powys is no master of plot. But his novels are not so much stories as portraits of a view of life: the various dramatic scenes have their symbolism stressed less within the scene itself (as it is, for example, in Gerald's struggle with the mare in *Women in Love*) than in their relationship with each other. Powys's novels are pictorial rather than dramatic in conception, and need to be interpreted in this way if their force is to be understood.

This is exemplified in his use of landscape for the furthering of his themes. Adrian is telling Baltazar of his physical sensitivity, his imaginative horror of the bodies of men and women when these are divorced from their personalities:

There began to fall upon the place where they sat, upon the cobble-stones of the little quay, upon the wharf steps, slimy with green sea-weed, upon the harbour mud and the tarred gunwales of the gently rocking barges, upon the pallid tide flowing inland with gurglings and suckings and lappings and long-drawn sighs, that indescribable sense of the coming on of night at a river's mouth, which is like nothing else in the world. It is, as it were, the meeting of two infinite vistas of imaginative suggestion —the sense of the mystery of the boundless horizons seaward, and the more human mystery of the unknown distance inland, its vague fields and marshes and woods and silent gardens—blending there together in a suspended breath of ineffable possibility, sad and tender, and touching the margin of what cannot be uttered.[9]

This passage is very characteristic of its author in the way in which it moves from the close particularity of the opening with its clearly felt physical objects (the cobble-stones, the slimy steps) to things clearly seen (the rocking barges, the pallid tide), and then through

8. *Rodmoor*, p. 319.
9. ibid., p. 203.

an increasing fluidity and subjectivity into an invocation of another dimension of reality altogether. Again and again Powys counterpoints his characters' more troubled sensations with such reminders of their natural environment, a blend of outward and inward vision. What he is moving towards in a passage such as this, as he is in *Rodmoor* as a whole, is what had been more tentatively advanced in *Wood and Stone*—the portrayal of man as himself being a part of nature not only in his physical senses but in his imaginative intuition.

Like all Powys's novels *Rodmoor* has atmospheric vividness, an urgency of communication underlying the leisurely technique. Its finest moments are those in which the characters encounter natural forces and are brought face to face with their own part in them, as in the chapter called 'Sun and Sea' or the episode where Philippa discovers the dead woman in the lonely house upon the marsh. There is a good example of Powys's technique in the chapter called 'Broken Voices', in which Adrian and Baltazar row out to sea against the incoming current in quest of a half-killed sea-gull:

A buoy, with a bell attached to it, sent at intervals, over the water, a profoundly melancholy cry—a cry subdued and yet tragic, not absolutely devoid of hope and yet full of heart-breaking wistfulness. The air was hot and windless; the sky heavy with clouds; the horizon concealed by the rapidly falling night. Sorio seized the stake with his hand to keep the boat steady. There were already lights in the town, and some of these twinkled out towards them, in long, radiating, quivering lines . . .

Sorio sighed heavily. 'I vowed to myself,' he muttered, 'I would never talk to anyone again about him; but the sound of that bell—isn't it weird, Tassar? Isn't it ghostly?—makes me long to talk about him.'

'Ah! I understand,' and Baltazar Stork drew in his breath with a low whistle, 'I understand! You're talking about your boy over there. Well, my dear, I don't blame you if you're homesick for him. I have a feeling that he's an extraordinarily beautiful youth. I always picture him to myself like my Venetian. Is he like Flambard, Adrian?'

Sorio sighed again, the sigh of one who sins against his secret soul and misses the reward of his sacrilege. 'No—no,' he muttered, 'it isn't that! It isn't anything to do with his being beautiful. God knows if Baptiste *is* beautiful! It's that I want him. It's that he understands what I'm trying to do in the darkness. It's simply that I want him, Tassar.'

'What do you mean by that "trying to do in the darkness", Adriano? What "darkness" are you talking about?'

Sorio made no immediate answer. His hand, as he clung to the stake amid the rocking of the boat, encountered a piece of seaweed of that kind which possesses slippery, bubble-like excrescences, and he dug his nails into one of these leathery globes, with a vague dreamy idea that if he could burst it he would burst some swollen trouble in his brain.

'Do you remember,' he said at last, 'what I showed you the other night, or have you forgotten?'

Baltazar looked at his mistily outlined features and experienced, what was extremely unusual with him, a faint sense of apprehensive remorse. 'Of course I remember,' he replied. 'You mean those notes of yours— that book you're writing?'

But Sorio did not hear him. All his attention was concentrated just then upon the attempt to burst another seaweed bubble. The bell from the unseen buoy rang out brokenly over the water; and between the side of their boat and the stake to which the man was clinging there came gurglings and lappings and whispers, as if below them, far down under the humming tide, some sad sea-creature, without hope or memory or rest, were tossing and moaning, turning a drowned inhuman face to- wards the darkened sky.[10]

This passage is the end of a chapter: no event develops from it. It works through its images and their relationship to fill out the mood and matter of the book as a whole. The voyage against the tide after the half-dead bird which is never found is emblematic of Adrian's desperate striving after his own self-destructive impulse and his failure to help the broken and maimed who have suffered as he has suffered. The buoy, so poignantly related to Baptiste, is a danger sig- nal and at the same time a lure. Only the seaweed is tangible, that and the post of which Baltazar has already remarked, 'Nothing could possibly cling to it, unless it had hands to cling with.' And the seaweed bursts into nothing. The natural world mirrors and controls the world of the imagination, dictating and responding to Adrian's moods. The scene is poetically apprehended, embodies a weariness, a nostalgia, a longing that leads logically to a desire for death. But this mood is mediated through language that is both precise in visual and tactile content and perfectly controlled in rhythmic movement. The 'leathery' seaweed, the bell crying 'brokenly' are as carefully placed as are the rocking movement of the final phrases which in- deed convey the sense of an unknown creature in the depths.

The novel is not, however, always as successful as here. The style, though less stiff and contorted than in *Wood and Stone*, is frequently cumbersome and arch; the conversations are often curiously unreal —dialogue was a weak point in Powys's work; and the plot always seems about to develop dramatically and never does until the end, when the violence seems as a result a shade contrived.[11] But the central weakness is the character of Adrian, who remains shadowy

10. *Rodmoor*, pp. 209–11.

11. For an amusing and perceptive parody of *Rodmoor* the reader is referred to Louis Wilkinson's *Bumbore: a Romance* (Warren House Press, Southrepps, Norfolk 1969).

and imperfectly observed compared with the vivid characters who surround him. As a result his dilemma and breakdown enlist one's sympathies less for him than for the more convincing Nance, from whose viewpoint the final tragedy is not ennobling but preposterous. Powys was at the stage of contemplating a problem, without as yet analysing it. Although Adrian is a stage nearer a full depiction of neurosis than is James Andersen, *Rodmoor* still suffers from a failure of literary nerve on the author's part.

3

There is no such conflict of viewpoint in *Ducdame*, Powys's most compact and tightly constructed novel. In none of the others is he so responsive to the moods and rhythms of nature, and none of them leaves so vivid a recollection of their setting. That setting is Dorset, and its woods and coverts and hill slopes and water meadows are described with love and sensitivity. Indeed the human drama is so informed by them as to be almost secondary in its effect. Like *Rodmoor*, *Ducdame* recounts the destruction of a man whose inner desires seem to be at war with the forces, or some of the forces, of nature. Rook Ashover, an introspective young squire, is trapped between his love for his forlorn lower-middle class mistress Netta, and the need to propagate a son to carry on the family line. The book's final conclusions are not negative: Rook comes to accept his nature as itself a part of the life force which urges him to continue his family into the future. Once again the setting predominates and sets the tone; but instead of the dreariness and vast agoraphobia of *Rodmoor* the world of *Ducdame* is secluded and enclosed.

Dead leaves that had lain softly one upon another in the mouths of old enmossed fox holes or under clumps of fungi at the edges of woods were now soldered together, as if by tinkling metal, with a thin filigree of crisp white substance. The wet vapour distillations clinging to the yellow reeds down by the ditches began to transform themselves into minute icicles. Birds that had reassumed their natural thinness fluffed out their feathers again as they hopped about searching for sheltered roosting places. In every direction there were tiny rustlings and tightenings and crackings as the crust of the planet yielded to the windless constriction, crisp and crystalline, of a gathering hoar frost.[12]

Along with such meticulous precision is a frequent resort to what Professor Wilson Knight calls 'etherealizing', the suggestion of other dimensions opening out of space and time. A good example of this

12. *Ducdame* (Grant Richards, 1925), p. 136.

is the description of the swan seen by Rook and his brother Lexie.

The bird was so beautiful that the vision of it passed beyond the point where either of them could share the feelings it excited with the other. It seemed to bring with it an overpowering sense of awe; for both the Ashovers regarded its advance in spellbound silence. It was as if it were floating on some mysterious inner lake that was, so to speak, the platonic idea, or the ethereal essence, of the actual lake which they were contemplating. It might have been swimming on an estuary that had suddenly projected itself into our terrestial spaces from a purer level of existence, some tributary of the Eternal and the Undying, that flowed in for one ineffable second of time, converting the watery element it mingled with into its own ethereal substance.

But Powys never loses touch with physical reality: so the account proceeds:

The spell of its approach was broken as soon as the bird itself realized that the Ashover brothers were not two motionless tree-trunks, but alien and disturbing invaders. It swung round with a proud curve of its great neck and an eddy of the blue water about its white feathers, and sheered off toward the centre of the pond.

Rook and Lexie regarded its departure with concentrated interest; but now that the magical moment had passed they were able to note the almost humourous effect of the swan's attempts to retain his impassive dignity, to show appropriate indignation, and at the same time to put a good clear space of deep lake water between himself and the onlookers.[13]

It is a measure of Powys's inclusiveness that the one kind of experience is not cancelled by the other: he can move from intensity to humour in a single scene.

Chapter XIX of *Ducdame* is one of the finest things in all of Powys's fiction; and an analysis of its development brings one very close to the heart not only of this novel but of his work as a whole. It is, quite simply, the description of a walk; but in it Powys achieves a perfect correspondence between outward and inward action.

The time is Midsummer: nature is at her full flowering and Rook's life at its nadir. His mistress, Netta, has left him; his other love, Nell, the local parson's wife, is closely watched by her husband; and he is now unhappily married to his cousin Ann, at the urging of his mother, who wants an heir for the house of Ashover. Only his brother Lexie is left to him; and Lexie is slowly dying. The chapter describes Rook's journey to meet Lexie for a picnic together at an old manor house called Comber's End. The accounts of the foliage and scenery

13. *Ducdame*, pp. 330-2.

are supplemented by Rook's inner thoughts as he gives way to his depression and remorse.

He felt responsible at that moment for the unhappiness of all the lives within his reach ... He saw life at that moment in a different light from any that he had seen it in before. He saw it as a place where not to have become involved in any other existence was the only cause for real thankfulness to the gods; in any other existence than such as was organically linked with his own.[14]

These thoughts lead on to a more generalized conclusion, as he follows the course of a long lane lined with pollarded willows.

The world was full enough of 'honourable men' struggling frantically to get the advantage of one another in this race for success, for fame, for recognition, for achievement. What did it matter? Far, far better, to live harmlessly in some quiet untroubled place, watching season follow season, month follow month, aloof and detached; leaving the breathless procession of outward events to turn and twist upon itself like a wounded snake![15]

But this conclusion, natural to one with an assured income, is not allowed to stay at that. Its logical outcome is despair. 'He began to walk more slowly and driftingly along that interminable lane. He felt as if he had already been following it for half a day; and it still stretched straight in front of him, without any sign of an end or of a turning.'[16] The length and straightness of the lane, the almost hypnotic power of its direction, permeate the whole of this passage. There follows an acute description of the condition of the passive man, of the unassertive character whose dissection Powys excelled in.

He stopped for a while, leaning over a gate and gazing into the green slime of a cattle-trodden ditch, across which three orange-bodied dragonflies were darting with as much arrogance as if it were a Venetian lagoon.

He had a feeling that some deep inarticulate grievance, much less clearly defined than these other causes of misery, was obscurely stirring within him. He tried to plumb the recesses of this emotion and he came to the conclusion that it was a blind repulsion at the idea of being married to Lady Ann. He suddenly found himself actually trembling with a convulsive fit of anger against his wife. It was as if he had never realized before how profoundly his life illusion was outraged by his marriage. The thought that he was irretrievably committed to this brilliant highhanded companion; the thought that his life was no longer to be a series of sweet solitary sensations, but a thing which was only half his own, stripped the magic from earth and air and sky! ... His mind began running up and down the events of his life. He had drifted into this culde-sac in a sort of anaesthetized trance. Something very deep in his nature

14. ibid., p. 300.   15. ibid., p. 301.   16. ibid., p. 302.

had always preserved an absurd faith in his power of extricating himself from any trap. This faith no doubt depended on his emotional detachment; on those remote translunar journeys of his mind that seemed to reduce all human relations into a misty puppet show, seen through the smaller end of a telescope!

He cast about in his brain until his mind trailed its wings and sank huddled and drooping from sheer exhaustion in the attempt to find some outlet from his dilemma.

To and fro those orange-bodied dragon-flies darted. To and fro across the oozing footprints of the cattle, between great heaps of dung, clouds of infinitesimal midges hovered and wavered; while in a corner of clear water a group of tiny black water beetles whirled round and round, as if they were trying to outpace their own small shadows which answered to their movement, down there on the sunlit mud, in queer radiated circles like little dark-rimmed moons.[17]

The relation of reflection to observation is delicately indicated by the use of the phrase 'mind trailed its wings'; and the assimilation of Rook's mind to what he sees has already been prepared for by the 'arrogance' of the dragon-flies and the likening of human affairs to a puppet-show—something watched as Rook is watching the midges and beetles. But a development of his feeling comes with the further assimilation of his mind with what he is half-consciously observing. His detachment recoils upon itself; he becomes what he is looking at.

That the universe could be envisaged as a place where human characters were hammered and chiselled into some premeditated mould of valour or resignation never so much as crossed the threshold of his consciousness. His vision of things would go on to the very end drawing its quality from just such vignettes of the ways of nature as he was staring at at that moment—those casual heaps of cattle dung, those dancing midges, that green pond slime, those revolving jet-bright beetles!

He was sick and weary of thinking; of thinking round and round in the same circle. He was like a hunted gladiator who, in his blind race for life, keeps seeing the same impassive faces looking down upon the same heart-breaking circuit of the arena.[18]

Self-pity is here placed in perspective by a kind of imaginative sleight of hand: the image of the gladiator is an image of how Rook feels to himself; but since it arises from the circular movement of the insects in relation to Rook's fixed gaze we are aware of its fundamental falsehood. Powys is able in this way to dissect Rook's feelings without sitting in judgement upon them: he simply indicates by his use of imagery their place in the over-all reality.

17. *Ducdame*, pp. 303-4.
18. ibid., p. 304.

Rook's thoughts of his wife lead him to a dread of the feminine principle, to feelings of drowning and of suffocation. These emotions are furthered by his almost hypnotized staring at the muddy stagnant pool; and this in turn affects his exterior vision:

... the hedges ceased to be green under that halcyon sky. They became gray like the colour of wood-ashes. The trunks of the willows, too, became gray; and the lane itself under his feet, its deep clay-stiffened cart ruts and its margins of silverweed and feverfew, became gray as the face of some enormous dead creature upon which he was treading.

A paralysis of dizziness seized him, mingled with an abysmal loathing for he knew not what. He staggered as he walked and he found himself feebly shaking his head as if to make some overt protestation against a vision of things that his reason still assured him was unreal.

And then it was that a rider, mounted upon a tall gray horse, came cantering toward him and, pulling up when he reached him, turned his horse round and proceeded to ride by his side along the lane, talking to him as he rode ...

[Rook] was not in the least surprised to detect in his companion's face a certain unmistakable resemblance to his own, nor was he startled or in any way shocked when the youth addressed him as 'Father'.

'It is just dizziness,' Rook found himself saying. 'It has nothing to do with what I have been suffering.'

'You must not suffer, Father,' the youth said gently, stroking his horse's neck with a light hand.

'I thought just now,' Rook retorted, 'that there was no human being in the world unhappier than I am.' ...

He placed his hand on the edge of the rider's saddle and the boy laid his own upon it and began caressing it.

'There's no need for you to tell me, Daddy,' he murmured. His voice became so low and faint just then that Rook glanced at him anxiously. And it was not only that his voice seemed to sink away like a wind that sighed itself into silence among feebly stirred grasses. His very form and face grew shadowy and indistinct.[19]

The whole encounter with his unborn son is described with great tenderness; but what clinches its effect is the way in which interior vision is fused with the external setting of the vision to produce an experience which is in the strictest sense supernatural. And in his dialogue with the boy, or rather revelation of himself to the boy, for the boy himself says little, Rook comes to a self-acceptance which is at the same time a vindication of his desire for freedom as well as a defeat of his self-pity:

'It was the green slime,' the man began again, in a hurried husky voice, his brain full of the one obstinate desire to make a very difficult point

19. ibid., pp. 307–8.

clear. 'And the cattle dung,' he added, pressing the horseman's hand against his saddle.

'What they made me think was that no one who makes any effort to change his nature or to change any one else's nature has any right to be alive upon the earth.' His voice subsided but he was still driven on by that desperate impatient sense that he *must* make everything plain before the lad cantered off.

'Slime—dung—not one gray feather——' he gasped wildly; and then, in a sudden burst of exultant freedom: 'No one is worthy to live,' he cried with a loud voice, 'who doesn't know—who doesn't know——'

'What, Daddy?' whispered the voice at his side.

He flung the words into the air now with a ringing triumphant voice.

'Who doesn't know that all Life asks of us is to be recognized and loved!'

The young rider suddenly snatched up the hand with which Rook had been so desperately retaining him and raised it to his lips. Then he gave him a smile the penetrating sweetness of which diffused itself through every fibre of the man's body.

'Goodbye, Daddy,' he murmured gently; and whispering some quick word to his horse he gave the bridle a shake and cantered away down the lane.[20]

The ghost is a ghost from the future; and in due course, at the time of Rook's own death, the child is born. What Powys is doing in *Ducdame* is to suggest a mystically apprehended unity between man and the natural world of vegetation and seasonal change; and to assess its significance for human relationships. Rook in his inner isolation is both sympathetically presented and yet analysed unsparingly in terms of the havoc that he wreaks on others: and in *Wolf Solent* the process is carried still further. In *Ducdame* the problem remains relatively in the background, and subordinate to the depiction of the natural setting. Nature is therefore not presented as sinister: this only happens as it reflects Rook's own feelings. But *man* in nature is often a disturbing element, as, for instance, in the character of Binnory, the idiot boy; or the twin monsters begotten by Rook's father on a gipsy girl—an example of Powys's use of the grotesque to stress the unity of all forms of life and the need to recognize it. But there are no absolute judgements to be made: Binnory knows the monsters affectionately as 'the half-beasties', and of Binnory himself Powys comments, 'this child, whose half articulate utterances and facial distortions would have been horrible in a city, fell naturally into his place among wilting hemlocks and lightning struck trees and birds eaten by hawks and rabbits eaten by weasles'.[21] In its context the comment is not a bitter one.

20. *Ducdame*, pp. 309–10.   21. ibid., p. 36.

It is the grandmother of the monsters, Betsy Cooper (named after an old gipsy woman known to the Powyses at Montacute), who tells of Cimmery Land, the kind of dream world of escape for which Rook longs, a world of impersonal existence as part of earth and water, 'the land where folks do live like unborn babes'.

As [Rook] listened to the old woman and watched the smoke of her pipe floating up into the illuminated sun-ray where it broke at once into a hundred silver-blue undulations, it came over him that this Cimmery Land of which she spoke was the thing that he had so often vaguely dreamed of; dreamed of on lonely roads at twilight; dreamed of lying on his bed listening to the sounds of the morning; dreamed of under the walls of old buildings in the quiet places of historic cities, when the noons fell hotly and the shadows fell darkly, and from hidden fountains came the splash of water.[22]

In this passage we have the appearance of one of Powys's central concerns, the cult of sensations, sensory and imaginative, as a way of life. In *Ducdame* it is regarded with a certain mistrust. The imagery used in speaking of Cimmery Land relates to the water meadows where Rook meets his unborn son and where he is shown to be in revolt against the natural forces of birth, death, and rebirth, as symbolized in his own marriage to Lady Ann. But in accepting his part in the natural order he has to accept also the peculiarity of his own nature. In *Ducdame*, through his portraits not only of Rook but of Lady Ann and Nell Hastings as well, Powys is portraying another, more personal, life of super-sensory perceptions to which some people are more sensitive than others. It is here that he shares the same territory as Proust, of whom he wrote, '[his] *real theme* ... has to do with the most evasive element in our secret personal life, namely with those obscure feelings of delicious ecstasy which are as hard to arrest or analyse in their swift passage as it is hard to explain why such small, slight, trivial, and casual chances are the cause of their rising up out of the depths'.[23]

Powys analyses these states repeatedly in his work, but nowhere more thoroughly than here. Following his meeting with his son, Rook arrives at Comber's End, and in the beauty of the scene finds the confirmation of his inner life. Powys goes on to remark that 'in addition to the ordinary gregarious human life, led by us in contact with others and in the stress of our normal pursuits, there is another, a more intimate life, solitary and detached, that has its own days and months and years, such as are numbered by no measurings of

22. ibid., p. 265.
23. *The Pleasures of Literature* (Cassell & Co., 1938), pp. 625–6.

common time, by no computation on any terrestrial almanac'.[24] In the *Autobiography* he describes the central part taken by such sensations in his own consciousness, and in his philosophical books recommends their systematic cultivation as a key to happiness. But it is in the novels that they are treated dynamically in relation to their context.

In *Ducdame* Rook is portrayed as the tragic victim of his sensations: he is a born solitary trapped by his very weakness into a situation which destroys him. He finds an interior resignation, but his dilemma remains: the novel does not end on the triumphantly happy note of the visit to Comber's End. His torpor and voluntary inactivity are coolly anatomized; but they spring from an urge to escape from the burdens of living. The parson, Mr. Hastings, is more deeply pessimistic. Like Adrian Sorio he is engaged on a book to prove that all life tends towards self-destruction; and this book and Rook's unborn child are presented as being in a kind of mystical opposition. But Hastings is no more portrayed as being evil than Rook is portrayed as being good. There is compassion and humorous understanding for them both.

Ducdame is as firmly planned as *Rodmoor*, and Rook, as much as Adrian, is the centre of a number of conflicts and is torn between the elements of life and death. But the struggle is complex. Lexie, who means life to Rook, is physically dying while the superbly healthy Ann is a kind of living death to him. Betsy too, from her occult hinterland, speaks for a kind of life. Aligned with Hastings's self-destructiveness is the forlorn and touching figure of Netta, who voluntarily forsakes Rook for the sake of his duty to his family, but who from his point of view is someone he lives by. All these forces are held in a firmly controlled tension; and the novel, for all its tragic qualities, is shot through with a benignly sardonic humour.

In Rook Ashover Powys achieves his fullest portrait yet of the kind of man who is his unique contribution to fiction, the man who fails to achieve his fulfilment in normal human contacts and who seeks oblivion in the impersonal forces of nature. The character is not romanticized. Rook sees his plight and limitations clearly, and is granted the oblivion he craves; but there is a goodness in his death and, before it, a reconciliation with what has oppressed him. This reconciliation, however, remains at a mental level and is not worked out dramatically, so that the novel, despite its pictorial vividness, has a feeling of unreality. Hastings and his book are essentially implausible; while the isolation of the setting, the absence of a community, the shadowy nature of most of the characters (Hastings's

24. *Ducdame*, p. 315.

young wife Nell being a notable exception) rob the novel of some of its force, and give it a curiously entranced effect. The book is oddly lacking in Powys's normal preoccupation with the day-to-day details of ordinary life, and the action goes on more through the minds of the characters than in dramatic conflict. But for all these shortcomings *Ducdame* is a significant and rewarding novel, and a haunting portrayal of the interaction between a man's private fears and self-distrust and the physical world which he inhabits. Appearing as it did in the mid-1920s, it is an undeservedly neglected elegy for the solitary romantic spirit.

CHAPTER THREE

The Wessex Novels

THESE four novels, while distinct in mood and treatment, have a number of features in common. Each of them is set in a specific and vividly evoked geographical location associated intimately with Powys's boyhood. *Wolf Solent*, the most dramatic and carefully wrought of the four, depicts the country where the author spent his unhappy schooldays, and is, appropriately enough, concerned with the individual's struggle to preserve his personal identity and self-respect amid the conflicting claims of family, society, and romantic love. *A Glastonbury Romance* and *Weymouth Sands* are more loosely constructed, more relaxed in mood; but in other respects they differ sharply. *Glastonbury* is, as its title would suggest, about religion in the broadest sense, the religious attitude to life, its nature and implications: the book is the longest and most ambitious of the novels, and the most uneven in quality. In it Powys attempts to provide a metaphysical framework to contain his numerous parallel plots, but his imagination and powers of literary organization were not of the kind to make this a successful attempt. The book survives for its individual characters and their stories rather than as an over-all statement. *Weymouth Sands*, on the other hand, makes no attempt to provide such a frame, and is more of a composite portrait than are the other books. Weymouth being the scene of Powys's happiest boyhood memories, the book is his most serene and naturalistic. Its main concern is the portrayal of the tides of attraction and repulsion that flow between people in their singularity and loneliness. *Maiden Castle*, the shortest of the quartet, is set in Dorchester, another happy boyhood home, and provides Powys's most distilled consideration of the themes of the other novels and relates them to each other. It is a kind of summing up; after it Powys turned to the past and to fantasy to express his interests and speculations. One feels that he did, in the writing of these four novels and the *Autobiography*, succeed in coming to terms with himself and his own life. The later books are far more serene in tone, and in the case of the two historical ones, *Owen Glendower* and *Porius*, profoundly impressive; but they lack the tension and complexity of the Wessex novels. It is on the latter that discussion of Powys's achievement and stature is likely to centre.

1

Wolf Solent is the novel which made its author's name and is among his very finest. Certainly it is the one to commend itself most readily to the modern world, despite the strange anachronisms it contains. Powys in returning in memory to the places of his boyhood returned in time as well; but instead of boldly declaring that his book was set in the late nineteenth century he blent with the manners and customs of that time other attitudes and attributes belonging to the present day—the world of 1929. Thus he was, as H. P. Collins observes, 'capable of filling the heavens with aeroplanes and leaving the roads virgin of motor cars'.[1] But the novel's psychological acuteness is twentieth century; and it has a structural unity and an elaboration and control of imagery that belie the contention that Powys was incapable of systematic organization.

The central theme is the nature of reality and the nature of illusion as mediated through the conflicting claims of the self, with its projections into dream and fantasy, and the claims of other personalities with which that self is surrounded. The story of Wolf Solent's struggles with his inner fears and aberrations, and with the demands upon him of his mother, his wife, and his mistress, becomes also a penetrating study of the difference between men and women, and of the nature of insecurity and jealousy. It is narrated throughout from Wolf's point of view. In this way Powys imposes a structural unity upon his long narrative and complexity of material, though at the cost of a blurring of critical vision. Wolf himself is 'placed', and very clearly placed, by a number of different characters; but since it is through his own eyes and ears that we receive those criticisms, their force is lessened. Rather it is to the plot and to the undercurrent of imagery that we must look for elucidation of the author's viewpoint.

None the less Wolf himself is Powys's mouthpiece for most of the time. With his sardonic humour, his agonizing sensibility, his animistic passion for sticks and stones, he is one of the most clearly realized characters in twentieth-century fiction, and his progress, for all its remoteness of setting and apparent limitation of concern, remains relevant to other times and situations. The book is in one sense a myth of man's self-assertion against the pressures of a collectivist and materialistic civilization, symbolized here in Wolf's rejection of London. But the novel is a critique as well as a defence

1. H. P. Collins. *John Cowper Powys: Old Earth-Man* (Barrie & Rockliff, 1966), p. 73.

of the individualistic life, and makes no glib or confident moral judgements. Thus is may be read also as an examination of the implications of the 'back to nature' movements which were a feature of the literature between the wars, and with which Powys himself is mistakenly identified. A genuine countryman, he knew what he was writing about, and in *Wolf Solent* examines ruthlessly the implications of man's involvement with his physical environment. There is a carefully worked out balance of values.

Wolf Solent is set on the borders of Somerset and Dorset, in the country where Powys spent his unhappy schooldays at Sherborne, disguised here under the name of Ramsgard—Blacksod being Yeovil, and Kings Barton probably the village of Nether Compton, which lies between the two. Powys knew every square mile of the district, and the names of the principal landmarks occur again and again like the chanting of a litany. The various localities have symbolic value. Wolf's return to Dorset is a return to his roots, to the place where his father lies buried. Ramsgard is the place of tradition and ancient pieties. Here is the home of Selena Gault, the eccentric ugly woman who is spiritual mother to Wolf just as she had been the Platonic lover of his father; here is the Abbey Church, embodiment of religion and the burial place of ancient kings; and it is in Ramsgard that Wolf finds his hitherto unknown half-sister Mattie, and with her a sense of responsibility for others. Here is the Past.

Blacksod, on the other hand, represents the Present. It is the place where Wolf finds and marries the beautiful Gerda, the daughter of a local stonemason; where he discovers his soul-mate, Christie Malakite, whose father is a bookseller of unsavoury reputation; and it is the place where his high-spirited mother comes to live and to shame him by her enterprise and independence. It is in Blacksod that he is made aware of his own limitations and of the hard reality of other people and their habits and demands. But Blacksod and Ramsgard are subtly related. It is in Ramsgard, for instance, that Wolf sees the old man with the cat, who becomes for him an image of the death-dealing nature of self-sufficiency; while Blacksod, the place where he feels most harassed and depressed, is also the place where he encounters the schoolboy, Barge, whose goodness saves his sanity.

Besides London, two other places have particular significance—Weymouth and Kings Barton. The former is, as always in Powys's fiction, a symbol of happiness, and, as in *Wood and Stone*, it is a symbol of escape as well. It is the enchanted place to which Christie moves at the end of the novel, taking with her Olwen, the fairy-like offspring of her father and sister. It represents the kind of liberation which for ever eludes Wolf until he has balanced his self-love with his self-distrust. But it is Kings Barton whose atmosphere really pervades the book. Here takes place the great crowd scene of the School Treat, which serves to focus the action, and in which all the principal characters are brought together. For much of the time Kings Barton is the haunt of rumour, of inactivity, and illusion; the inhabitants are neurotic or perverse, and the village seethes with tales of suicides and ghosts. Its centre is Lenty Pond, like Auber Lake in *Wood and Stone* a place of ill-repute, but, unlike its predecessor, described in quiet naturalistic terms. For the pond, when faced, as in the scene where Wolf finds his employer and the poet Jason Otter, both of them hitherto sinister figures in his eyes, watching two boys bathing, it becomes innocent of anything but its own physical nature, a place to be enjoyed. Powys's handling of the image of Lenty Pond is a fine example of his essential wisdom and sanity.

The landscape is evoked less by direct description, as in the earlier novels, than by indirect methods such as the noting of smells and scents, of cloud and wind effects. The leafiness and heavy clay of Dorset are contrasted with the alluvial plains of Somerset, the watery landscape with which Wolf feels most affinity. Dorset, however, is the scene of the struggle for Wolf's soul by his father and mother which is a leading motif in the book. There is here a reversal of the usual parental roles, the father representing the passive feminine principle, the mother the masculine active one. It is to the spirit of his father that Wolf runs for protection from his mother's demands upon him, and significantly the father is represented as having been a man without shame or moral sense. It is by such notation that Powys makes his critical points.

Wolf, like other Powysian heroes, is also torn between two women who love him, and both of whom he loves. Powys is realistic about romantic love, and portrays Wolf as feeling a need for both women. Gerda is given pagan associations, and her gift of imitating the blackbird's song shows her affinities with the natural world. She is a kind of earth-spirit, though at the same time an ordinary country girl, house-proud, greedy, anxious for a settled life and enough money for the housekeeping. Sensuous without being particularly interested in sex, she is the most appealing character in the book.

Christie is of very different mettle. She is given vegetative associations in keeping with the imagery employed for Wolf's private daydreams, is likened to a water nymph and to a changeling. In Wolf's mind she is linked to the mystic hill of Glastonbury and is an almost asexual embodiment of intellectual companionship. But Christie also represents something abnormal. The first sight of her is as of one entranced, and she belongs to the boy–girl type which recurs in Powys's fiction. Her relationship with her father is subtly handled; she may share in Wolf's private world of the imagination but she asserts roundly that she is also of the world of the incestuous old bookseller. When Wolf has his chance to possess her he fails to take it, and this failure is due not only to his own indecision but also to a virginal quality in her akin almost to the magical. But throughout all this Christie remains a convincing study of a withdrawn, sensitive, but toughly realistic girl. The scenes between her and Wolf have great tenderness and delicacy.

Two figures who are also in apposition are Selena Gault and the gardener, Roger Monk. If she is given witch-like notations, he is a kind of giant, a symbol of the brute intransigence of matter and of the sexual instinct. His name, though paradoxical, is expressive: it is he who starts Wolf's mind on its jealous harrying of Gerda, and who terrifies the hyper-sensitive Jason Otter. He dominates Squire Urquhart, Wolf's employer, who is engaged in composing a scabrous book of county annals—sex in the mind as opposed to normal sexuality. And like Miss Gault, Monk is associated with a grave. The scene at the book's commencement where Wolf visits his father's grave in her company is balanced by one at the end in which Monk, tidying the grave of Wolf's predecessor as the squire's secretary (around whose death much speculation has hovered) disabuses Wolf of his misconceptions about the inhabitants of Kings Barton, and puts the supernatural in its place. Both he and Miss Gault are given ugly, almost non-human characteristics, and may be likened to the Grail-bearer figures of Mad Bet in *A Glastonbury Romance* and Broch o' Meifod in *Owen Glendower*.

Another grouping is that of Mattie Smith with Darnley Otter, Jason's brother, the only two of the major characters to be undisturbed by inner conflict. Mattie is at once Wolf's responsibility and a symbol of security for him, not being a threat to his private world in the way that his mother and Gerda and even Christie are. Darnley provides a kind of masculine acceptance that is given a faint sexual overtone towards the end. His eyes are likened to the colour of mackerel (the fish being a symbol of Wolf's inner identity —a good example of Powys's method of implying relationships in terms of naturalistic description). Darnley, like Christie, is a virginal figure, and unattracted to women. His marriage to Mattie corresponds to Wolf's final acceptance of life in his own limitations and thus throws light on Wolf's predicament. When he watches Darnley and Mattie embrace Wolf notices that Darnley's eyes are 'like those of a man who pulls himself together, naked, tense, exultant, on the brink of a rapid torrent'.[2]

There is a further correspondence to be noted: that between Jason Otter and the 'man on the Waterloo steps'. The latter is a man regarded by Wolf as an epitome of that kind of suffering which challenges belief in a benevolent creator. He recurs to Wolf's inward sight repeatedly—in the squire's garden, in Gerda's face, in Christie's bedroom, in dreams, above all in the person of Jason Otter. Jason is Wolf's real adversary, Jason with his pitiless mockery, his endless capacity for suffering, his raw nerves demanding to be hurt. He is helplessness incarnate, Wolf's own inadequacy made palpable. He acts as a kind of malevolent chorus, and his three haunting poems serve as a commentary on Wolf's developing self-awareness. Wolf's interior dialogue with the man on the Waterloo steps is paralleled by his actual dialogue with Jason.

Linked to the character and importance of Jason is the treatment of sexual abnormality. It is here that Powys strikes a note peculiarly his own. The fact that Squire Urquhart, Jason, and the parson T. E. Valley, are homosexuals becomes apparent as the book proceeds; but it is never treated as a 'problem': even the squire's necrophily and Malakite's incest appear quite simply as two manifestations of the way in which human nature can behave. There are few sexual aberrations which are not touched on somewhere in Powys's novels, but the treatment is compassionate and calm. What interests him most is the voyeurism which is necessarily attendant on any sexual taste precluded by society; and he is notably successful in portraying that little-described but common aspect of sex, the arousing of desire without the readiness or capacity to act upon it. Urquhart, Jason, and the parson all feel guilty, and their resultant unhappiness is the poison in the air of Kings Barton. Wolf himself is voyeuristically inclined, and stimulated by the adolescent curiosity of Gerda's brother Lobbie and the young shop assistant Bob Weevil, by whom he is eventually cuckolded. This part of the novel is most skilfully handled. Voyeurism in the sexually normal Wolf leads to abnormality; but in Jason and Urquhart to an almost beatific peace— as in the scene at Lenty Pond. The delicacy with which these ambivalences are treated furthers the theme of the relation of daydreaming to action, of illusion and reality.

The main theme, however, is that of Wolf's growth in the capacity to live with himself and thus with other people—or, rather, his ability to do the first after failing in the second: the novel ends on an ambiguous note. The marriage to Gerda is unsuccessful; and

2. *Wolf Solent* (Macdonald, 1961), p. 545.

Wolf's love for Christie, although returned, only ends in separation. Thus far the outcome of the book is tragic; but the real meaning is to be found in Wolf's soliloquys, where there is a dynamic progress through hope and despair towards a stoical acceptance of his own nature and circumstances. The peculiar, and to some tastes repellent, character of the book lies in its preoccupation with internal states of feeling while providing a lively pattern of external action. There is a certain obviousness about the way in which Powys weds the two elements: after some violent quarrel or disturbance Wolf, like Rook before him, is dispatched on a long solitary walk to provide a background and vehicle for his meditations—a fact which is, however, amusingly adverted upon by Jason: Powys could make fun of his own limitations. The meditations themselves are overwritten and become monotonous, and are only partially successful in their attempt to exteriorize half-conscious sensations. The switch from direct speech to monologue without any corresponding switch of idiom tends to make accounts of obscure thought processes sound like clumsy speeches. Powys suffered here from his addiction to novels of the past. A glance at the technique of his contemporaries would have helped him: as it is, in *Wolf Solent* we have a nineteenth-century medium stretched almost beyond its capacity to contain a twentieth-century subject-matter.

Nevertheless the book is a notable contribution to the literature of introspection. Wolf's inner musings are at once its subject and its vehicle. The account of his mental states, particularized as they are, may be personal to the author; but if they are read as representative of secretive fantasies and half-thoughts the relevance of the novel becomes apparent. Powys analyses Wolf's thought processes through a dramatizing of their interaction with external stimuli. In the first half of the book he gives free play to Wolf's changing moods, using them to establish the feel of the supporting characters and the scenic atmosphere, and to build up the tissue of rumours around the death of Redfern, Wolf's predecessor. This also serves to heighten Wolf's life-illusion, not only in his passive response to nature, but also in his sense of participation in a moral battle between good and evil. Under the sanctions of religion and traditional pieties, as in Ramsgard Abbey, his soul feels to him like a piece of crystal, a resistant entity of fixed shape; in other moods he feels it as something infinitely evasive and adaptable, 'a cunning that could flow like air, sink like rainwater, rise like green sap, root itself like invisible spores of moss, float like filmy pond-scum, yield and retreat, retreat and yield, yet remain unconquered and inviolable!'[3] But with the dawning of a

3. ibid., p. 4.

socially orientated moral sense as a result of taking Mattie under his protection, there is a disturbance of his private world; and his revolt against this takes the form of a quickened sense of, and revulsion from, his own body, not dissimilar to that experienced by Adrian in *Rodmoor*. Wolf's doubt as to the morality of continuing to accept payment for helping Urquhart with his 'evil' book still further disturbs his balance. With his mother and Gerda financially dependent on him he is faced with a moral choice which is neither clear-cut nor concerned solely with himself.

This crisis is prefigured in the above-mentioned scene at Lenty Pond, which is central to the book's moral scheme. There, confronted with the 'purged and almost hieratic' look on the squire's face, and Jason's resemblance to 'an enraptured saint, liberated from earthly persecution and awakening to the pure ecstasies of Paradise', Wolf is forced to wonder whether there really is a deep psychic struggle between himself and Urquhart. The doubt disquiets him.

He knew very well why it had this effect. His whole philosophy had been for years and years a deliberately subjective thing. It was one of the fatalities of his temperament that he completely distrusted what is called 'objective truth'. He had come more and more to regard 'reality' as a mere name given to the most lasting and most vivid among all the various impressions of life which each individual experiences ... one of his own most permanent impressions had always been of the nature of an extreme dualism, a dualism descending to the profoundest gulfs of being, a dualism in which every living thing was compelled to take part ... it was profoundly necessary to his life-illusion to feel the impact of this mysterious struggle and to feel that he was taking part in it.[4]

His life in Blacksod sees the destruction of this belief. His jealousy of Gerda and Bob Weevil arouses a feeling of self-contempt in him that annihilates desire, making his private world seem meaningless. Then he momentarily attains (for Powys's leisurely realism allows for a good deal of ebb and flow) a sense of identity in suffering that eliminates his egoism; but this escape is not at first understood as involving the loss of self in another, at least not in the form of encounter. What Wolf craves is identification, 'to flow like a serpentine mist into the grave of his father, into the mocking heart of his mother, into the ash tree, into the wind, into the sands on Weymouth beach, into the voice of the landlord of the Farmer's Rest'. That this is a subconscious desire for death is made clear in the passage which concludes Chapter 18, 'The School Treat'. Wolf's awareness of the erotic attraction of Gerda for Bob, and the look of sexual rapture on

4. *Wolf Solent*, pp. 285–6.

a girl's face, arouse a nameless desire and unease. He has regarded Urquhart's preoccupation with 'evil' as a form of reversion to primeval matter born of a longing for sterility; but his own reaction to what Proust calls 'Gomorrah' leads him to a very different response to that desire. Walking furiously to overcome his lust, he sees in the twilight the huge watery plain of Somerset with Glastonbury Tor 'like the phallus of an unknown God' rising from the midst of it; and here he finds the embodiment of his own private mythology. In Powys's initial account of the latter he says that Wolf's 'magnetic impulses resembled the expanding of great vegetable leaves over a still pool—leaves nourished by hushed noons, by liquid transparent nights, by all the movements of the elements—but making some inexplicable difference, merely by their spontaneous expansion, to the great hidden struggle always going on in Nature between the good and evil forces'.[5] But now the vision has met its objective correlative.

It was as though he had suddenly emerged, by some hidden doorway, into a world entirely composed of vast, cool, silently-growing vegetation, a world where no men, no beasts, no birds, broke the mossy stillness; a world of sap and moisture and drooping ferns; a world of leaves that fell and fell for ever, leaf upon leaf; a world where that which slowly mounted upwards endured eternally the eternal lapse of that which slowly settled downwards; a world that itself was slowly settling down, leaf upon leaf, grass-blade upon grass-blade, towards some cool, wet, dark, unutterable dimension in the secret heart of silence!
Lying upon that rank, drenched grass, he drew a deep sigh of obliterating release. It was not that his troubles were merely assuaged. They were swallowed up. They were lost in the primal dew of the earth's first twilights. They were absorbed in the chemistry, faint, flowing, and dim, of that strange *vegetable flesh* which is so far older than the flesh of man or beast!
He stretched out one of his hands and touched the cool-scaled stalks of a bed of 'mares tails'. Ah! how his human consciousness sank down *into that* with which all terrestrial consciousness began! ...
He was a leaf among leaves ... among large, cool, untroubled leaves ... He had fallen back into the womb of his real mother ... He was drenched through and through with darkness and with peace.[6]

This passage is a good example of the author's strengths and weaknesses. The overwriting, the poeticizing, the verbal inflation, and the resort to italics and exclamation marks, are vices of Powys's style disfiguring *Wolf Solent* more than the other novels, but present in varying degrees in them all. But with them we find here his mastery

5. ibid., p. 8.
6. ibid., p. 389.

of prose rhythms, his powers of incantation and sensuous perception, the vivid particularity of, for example, the 'cool-scaled' stalks. Above all the passage exemplifies Powys's awareness of man's evolution and of the continuing identity of earlier modes of consciousness: Powys is not so much a nature mystic as a medium for infra-physical awareness. Wolf's mythology is here identified with his non-human origins: the moral sense is lost in them. But the life drawn from the moral sense, the life which has to be lived because he is a human being, still awaits him; and in the succeeding movements of the book the dying which Wolf experiences in his vision is related to the dying of his self-esteem. His return to work for the squire against his own inner convictions, and his failure to consummate his love for Christie, alike prove deleterious. He feels as though he were dying with the autumn vegetation. His fear when he finds that Christie is willing to give herself to him is treated with tender humour; but there is a deeper side to the incident. Wolf is stricken with disgust when he realizes that to be one with Christie means being one with the repellent and unnatural Mr. Malakite; but in the moving scene where he fails her Christie's bedroom is given a descriptive colouring that links it with Wolf's vision of the Glastonbury plain—just as Christie herself has been associated with Glastonbury, home of the mystic grail, through her supposed descent from Merlin.

Following his failure Wolf becomes obsessed with the excremental and disgusting aspects of the body. Faced with Gerda's adultery he half-decides to drown himself in Lenty Pond, to be confronted with the physical at the place of death itself. Dorset has conquered him. His journey to the pond follows his glimpse of the disinterment of Redfern's body, the dead made actual. But he fails to drown himself through simple fear of the coldness of the water, the fear of matter rather than of spirit.

The reuniting of matter with spirit is the penultimate stage in Wolf's progress. His mythology is gone, now that he can no longer stand outside the dualistic struggle and see himself pledged to the side of good; and his cult of sensation is gone because 'it implied a certain kind of Wolf who was enjoying it, and that kind of Wolf was stone dead'. But a new selflessness is being born: he is tender to Gerda and Bob, and sacrifices his private dream of taking Christie to Weymouth by promising to take Gerda there instead; and he finally receives his word of salvation from the abhorred lips of Mr. Malakite, who on his death-bed, after having tried to assault Christie, shrieks the single word 'forget', in contra-distinction to Wolf's suggested 'forgive'. Wolf's dualism is smashed; he realizes that whatever might be the case with good, evil is relative, not absolute, and that he is a single being, body and soul inseparable. His liberation is completed at Redfern's graveside, when Monk reveals to him the conversion of Urquhart and the true, matter-of-fact significance of Redfern's disinterment. The ghosts of Kings Barton are dispersed; and a similar moment occurs at his father's graveside when he defends his mother against Miss Gault and thus finally identifies his interests with the present instead of with the past. The liberators, the grail-bearers, are the three monsters, the ugly ones—Selena Gault, Mr. Malakite, Roger Monk. The underlying point as to the necessity of loving the squalid and the outcast, and of accepting the excremental factor in life, if wholeness is to be attained, is at the heart of Powys's vision.

But Powys was a cynically benevolent realist, and there is a wry postscript in the last chapter, a masterpiece of balanced irony. Wolf is set alongside the worldly, accomplished Lord Carfax, who succeeds in everything where he himself fails.[7] Faced once more with Gerda's infidelity and with the very jealousy which had goaded her into it in the first place, he knows himself to be alone; but in a field, placed with a Powysian appropriateness 'behind the pigsty' he also knows, in a kind of golden heathen theophany, that he is now whole and can face his life. This happiness is the confirmation of an earlier vision.

Powys has affinities with Blake, Wordsworth, and Proust in his concern with the romantic view of reality and its significance. He carries the matter a stage further than Proust does, by dramatizing it and relating it to the world in which it is known. Early in the novel he describes Wolf's sight of a field of kingcups.

It was along the edge of a small tributary full of marsh-marigolds that they approached the river-bank. Gerda was so impatient to hear a water-rat splash that she scarcely glanced at these great yellow orbs rising from thick, moist, mud-stained stalks and burnished leaves; but to Wolf, as he passed them by, there came rushing headlong out of that ditch, like an invisible company of tossing-maned air-horses, a whole wild herd of ancient memories! ... They had to do with wild rain-drenched escapes beneath banks of sombre clouds, of escapes along old backwaters and by forsaken sea-estuaries, of escapes along wet, deserted moor-paths and by sighing pond-reeds; along melancholy quarry-pools and by quagmires of livid moss. Indescribable! Indescribable! But memories of this kind were —and he had long known it!—the very essence of his life. They were more sacred to him than any living person. They were his friends, his gods, his secret religion. Like a mad botanist, like a crazed butterfly-collector, he hunted these filmy growths, these wild wanderers, and stored them up in his mind. For what purpose did he store them? For *no* pur-

7. Wolf's relationship with Lord Carfax may possibly reflect some of Powys's feelings towards Louis Wilkinson.

pose! And yet these things were connected in some mysterious way with that mythopoeic fatality which drove him on and on and on and on.[8]

This almost mystical apprehension is represented in the novels as man's sure defence against the afflictions he endures either from society, his fellows, or his nervous aberrations. It is this stress upon perception as a creative element in personality which distinguishes Powys from other novelists, even from Lawrence, with whom he has at first sight so much in common. He stresses man's loneliness, and the private worlds in which each man and woman must in the last resort live alone. In his next two novels he portrays the complexity of those worlds and their interaction; in *Wolf Solent* he is more concerned to establish the identity of one man's world, and to place it in relation to conscience and the demands of love.

The kingcup passage also provides another link in the web of associations and symbols that bind this at first sight unwieldy narrative together. The magical happiness associated with the golden flowers is in another passage evoked by the sight of the blue sky. For much of the novel's action the skies are clouded, though their ultimate blueness is frequently referred to. Blue is here the colour of natural happiness, just as gold is the colour of magical or supernatural happiness. Wolf's joy at the sight of the kingcups is recalled in the final scene in the buttercup field, where an otherwise purely mental experience is given a more general validity by this use of the imagery of gold. Generally, however, it is the greenness of nature which is stressed, together with its watery elements. Green is a blend of blue and gold: nature is the place of making and meeting. It is the use of tonality such as this which justifies the description of Powys as a poetic writer.

Among several linking images in the novel Jason's statue of Mukalog the rain god is prominent. Rain is given sinister associations here, as distinct from sunlight. At one point Wolf, looking at the sunset, seems to see the idol at its heart menacing him, a sign of that cruelty in nature which it is necessary for humanity to forget if happiness is to be attained. And Powys, a disciple of Rabelais, is a firm believer in the healing power of happiness based on the tolerance of every human aberration except cruelty. It is when Wolf throws the idol over the wall into the buttercup field and then has to search for it there, that he attains his final revelation. There are several such images in the book, recurring like leitmotifs, a kind of internal system of references whereby the events of the plot are subsumed into a larger composite portrait of Wolf's consciousness. It is

8. *Wolf Solent*, p. 95.

only in relation to him that the other characters exist.

This is not to say that they are not extremely vivid, Jason and Urquhart, for example, being felt powerfully as presences. Wolf's mother is portrayed more in the round, her blend of warmth and cruelty most neatly caught. Her relationship with her son is searchingly examined, especially in the great quarrel scene that follows Wolf's sight of the boys bathing in Lenty Pond. The acceptance of one sexual taboo is followed by Powys's resolute facing of a still greater one.

She drew in her arm and buried her face in the sofa, her body heaving with long, dry, husky sobs.

Wolf surveyed her form as she lay there, one strong leg exposed as high as the knee, and one disarranged tress of wavy grey hair hanging across her cheek. And it came over him with a wave of remorseful shame that this formidable being, so grotesquely reduced, was the actual human animal out of whose entrails he had been dragged into light and air.

His remorse, however, was not a pure or simple emotion. It was complicated by a kind of sulky indignation and by a bitter sense of injustice. The physical shamelessness, too, of her abandonment shocked something in him, some vein of fastidious reverence. But his mother's cynicism had always shocked this element in his nature; and what he felt now he had felt a thousand times before—felt in the earliest dawn of consciousness. What he would have liked to do at that moment was just to slip out of the room and out of the house. Her paroxysm roused something in him which, had she known it, she would have recognized as something more dangerous than any responsive anger. But this feeling did not destroy his pity; so that, as he now sombrely contemplated those grey hairs, and that exposed knee, he felt a more poignant consciousness of what she was, than he had ever felt at the times when he admired her most and loved her most.

He let himself sink down in his chair and covered his mouth with his hand as if to hide a yawn. But he was not yawning. This was an old automatic gesture of his: perhaps originally induced by his consciousness that his mouth was his weakest and most sensitive feature and the one by which the sufferings of his mind were most quickly betrayed.

Then he suddenly became aware that the sobs had ceased; and a second later he received a most queer impression, namely that one warm, glowing, ironical brown eye was fixed upon him and was steadily regarding him— regarding him through the disordered tress of ruffled hair that lay across it . . .

He fell on his knees in front of her and she let her touzled forehead sink down till it rested against his; and there they remained for a while, their two skulls in a happy trance of relaxed contact, full of unspoken reciprocities, like the skulls of two animals out at pasture, or the branches of two trees exhausted by a storm.

Wolf was conscious of abandoning himself to a vast undisturbed peace

—a peace without thought, aim, or desire—a peace that flowed over him
from the dim reservoirs of prenatal life, lulling him, soothing him,
hypnotising him—obliterating everything from his consciousness except
a faint delicious feeling that everything *had* been obliterated.

It was his mother herself who broke the spell. She raised her hands to
his head and held it back by his stubbly straw-coloured hair, pressing, as
she did so, her own glowing tear-stained cheeks against his chin, and
finally kissing him with a hot, intense, tyrannous kiss.

He rose to his feet after that and so did she; and, moved by a simultaneous impulse, they both sat down again at the deserted tea-table,
emptied the teapot into their cups, and began spreading for themselves
large mouthfuls of bread-and-butter with overflowing spoonfuls of red-
currant jam.

Wolf felt as if this were in some way a kind of sacramental feast; and
he even received a queer sensation, as though their mutual enjoyment of
the sweet morsels they swallowed so greedily were an obscure reversion to
those forgotten diurnal nourishments which he must have shared with
her long before his flesh was separated from hers.[9]

In its simultaneous realism and extravagance, boldness and delicacy,
this scene is very typical of Powys's work at its best. It also relates to
the description of Wolf's vision of the Somerset plain: in one light
the novel is the story of his real birth.

Wolf Solent is an unnervingly penetrating study of one man's
secret inner consciousness and its relation to the outward realities of
his life; and it is the more effective because of the way in which the
theme of reality and illusion, so critical to his own understanding of
himself, is woven into the novel's plot. There is complete unity between theme and presentation: the novel embodies the predicament,
and in so embodying it resolves it. Wolf's story may seem remote and
fanciful on a first reading; but it is ultimately concerned with problems of personal integrity of a kind so intimate that they lie at the
very basis of human relationships. Wolf's situation between Gerda
and Christie, the two women whom he loves, is common enough;
but what gives the novel its universal quality is not that alone,
vividly though the situation is described, but rather the relating of
it to Wolf's own understanding and feeling for himself. Powys is
honest enough to admit the egoism of man as a necessary com-
ponent in his make-up, and subtle enough to make of a man's secret
day-dreams and innermost illusions a factor in more external, intra-
personal situations. Such a subject in lesser hands might well have
been treated esoterically, have become strained and precious and
unrelated to social life; but Wolf Solent's story takes place within a
group and is mediated through the life of that group. In nothing

9. *Wolf Solent*, pp. 290–1.

else is the sheer comprehensiveness of Powys's imagination so apparent as in this capacity to fuse interior and exterior conditions into a mutually illuminating whole. That he does this by a necessary sacrifice of contemporary similitude, creating a physically plausible world that is yet temporarily abstracted from the one we know, is to point out also that he is not a social novelist, an observer and analyser of society in the manner of George Eliot, Henry James, or, to cite a contemporary practitioner, Anthony Powell. Powys's social world is a psychological one: it is consciousness rather than manners with which he is concerned.

In *Wolf Solent* the consciousness of Wolf himself is the medium of the narrative; but the mental projections, the psychological force, of the other characters are what determine the action. Gerda is not simply a well-observed country girl: she has her own clearly apprehended aura, a mental way of life, a sensibility and way of projecting herself which impinge dramatically on Wolf's own self-enclosure. It is in his exploration of these 'auras' that Powys differs from other novelists. His analysis of character and motive can be acute; but it is never a diagnostic analysis, as in the manner of George Eliot. In this instance it may be instructive to compare a passage from *Middlemarch* with a passage by Powys, which enlarges on the same subject-matter. Here is George Eliot describing Rosamund's attraction for Lydgate:

Lydgate, in fact, was already conscious of being fascinated by a woman strikingly different from Miss Brooke: he did not in the least suppose that he had lost his balance and fallen in love, but he had said of that particular woman, 'She is grace itself; she is perfectly lovely and accomplished. That is what a woman ought to be: she ought to produce the effect of exquisite music.' Plain women he regarded as he did the other severe facts of life, to be faced with philosophy and investigated by science. But Rosamund Vincey seemed to have the true melodic charm; and when a man has seen the woman whom he would have chosen if he had intended to marry speedily, his remaining a bachelor will usually depend on her resolution rather than on his.[10]

The wit, detachment, and balance of this are obvious: and they describe not only Lydgate's particular feelings but, by implication, a whole set of built-in attitudes. The passage, written with care and a controlling sense of irony, is a statement about society as well as one about a particular member of society. This density of presentation is very characteristic of George Eliot: her mind is in full control of her material. Compared with this John Cowper Powys sounds inflated

10. *Middlemarch*, Ch. 11.

and imprecise. Here is the account of Wolf Solent's feelings for Gerda as they walk together through the fields:

Wolf had hitherto, in his attitude to the girls he had approached, been dominated by an impersonal lust; but what he now felt stealing over him like a sweet, insidious essence, was the actual, inmost identity of this young human animal. And the strange thing was that this conscious presence, this deep-breathing Gerda, moving silently beside him under her cloak, under her olive-green frock, under everything she wore, was not just a girl, not just a white, flexible body, with lovely breasts, slender hips, and a gallant swinging stride, but a living conscious soul, different in its entire being from his own identity.[11]

It is of course at once apparent that Powys is attempting something different from George Eliot: he is describing and defining a particular condition of momentary awareness; and so it is throughout his work. There is very little retrospective action, very little analysis of conscious motive, very little dramatic interaction. It is always the present moment which concerns him, the flowering at one and then another particular instant of this or that especial complex of physical–psychic being. It is the visionary intensity which makes his novels so hypnotic in their effect, and which also makes them so demanding to read. In this connection the length and amplitude of the books are a necessary feature. Writing of the crisp and economic kind instanced above in the extract from George Eliot, would have been alien to his purpose, even if it had been congenial to him; and even the passage from *Wolf Solent* is, for all the apparent obviousness of its content (in view of which it might, as it stands, be considered over-diffuse or even banal), even this relatively straightforward passage is developed at length to open out into the imaginative territory which is peculiarly Powys's own:

What he felt at that moment was that, hovering in some way around this tangible form, was another form, impalpable and delicate, thrilling him with a kind of mystical awe. It changed everything around him, this new mysterious being at his side, whose physical loveliness was only its outward sheath! It added something to every tiniest detail of that enchanted walk which they took together now over one green field after another. The little earth-thrown mole-hills were different. The reddish leaves of the newly-sprung sorrel were different. The droppings of the cattle, the clumps of dark-green meadow-rushes, all were different! And something in the cold, low-hung clouds themselves seemed to conspire, like a great stretched-out grey wing, to separate Gerda and himself from the peering instrusion of the outer world.[12]

11. *Wolf Solent*, p. 143.
12. ibid., pp. 143–4.

Here the transforming quality of the imagination is made apparent: the heightened awareness of another personality in turn develops into a heightened perception of the physical environment of that personality. This again is a not unfamiliar state: sufficient at this stage to note the characteristic particularity of Powys's evocation of the scene—a blend of minute observation and of rarefied sensuousness. Both physical reality and psychic response are emphasized. This results in a fusion between the two areas of awareness: 'And if the greyness above and the greenness beneath enhanced his consciousness of the virginal beauty of the girl, her own nature at that hour seemed to gather into itself all that most resembled it in that Spring twilight.' The use of 'seemed' serves, however, to keep the necessary perspective. The two paragraphs that follow bring the experience to its logical extension and conclusion, in a further blending of the two worlds of experience.

Gate after gate leading from one darkening field into another they opened and passed through, walking unconsciously westward, towards the vast yellowish bank of clouds that had swallowed up that sky-road into space. It was so far only the beginning of twilight, but the undried rains that hung still in motionless water-drops upon millions of grass-blades seemed to welcome the coming on of night—seemed to render the whole surface of the earth less opaque.

Over this cold surface they moved hand in hand, between the unfallen mist of rain in the sky and the diffused mist of rain in the grass, until the man began to feel that they two were left alone alive, of all the people of the earth—that they two, careless of past and future, protected from the very ghosts of the dead by these tutelary vapours, were moving forward, themselves like ghosts, to some vague imponderable sanctuary where none could disturb or trouble them![13]

The sequel to this is Wolf's seduction of Gerda, prefaced by his fateful decision to marry her; and the event is seen not simply as something in the forefront of his mind, something that can be logically accounted for merely, but as the inevitable outcome of their two physio-mental states, the conjoining of their individual auras with the overarching physical environment which both affects, and is affected by, those auras. The purely social reference is transcended: action is presented in terms of consciousness. The peculiarly beautiful and uniquely Powysian account of the clouds of withheld rain embodies this area of felt experience, this mental world encompassing the physical one; the connotation is always exact.

In analysing the book's external structure and internal patterning one inevitably neglects its dramatic and pictorial vividness, and its

13. ibid., p. 144.

unflagging narrative power. It creates and sustains an entire world of imaginative experience. Its great variety of mood ranges through the comedy of Wolf's domestic disagreements with Gerda, and the tremulous and finely drawn passages with Christie, to the many complex crowd scenes, and to the unnerving sequences concerning the Squire and Jason, sequences which explore with a kind of delicate familiarity the borderlines of madness. Each scene is presented against a sharply realized background, the atmosphere of the various houses and landscapes being precisely caught. Powys's sense perceptions are keen, his feeling for the erotic extending beyond the specifically sexual realm, so that the novel in its exploration of the darker underside of the human imagination enlarges one's capacity for experience and liberates the mind. Powys is more of a stoic than a pessimist; and for all its remoteness from twentieth-century conditions *Wolf Solent* is a saga, a saga of twentieth-century self-awareness, one of the supreme novels of introspection. In his insistence on introspection as a way of life Wolf belongs to the modern world, however much his fanatical hatred of machines shows him to be reacting against it; but in his relations with Gerda and Christie, Jason and his mother, as in his response to his natural environment, his consciousness is quickened by perennial verities and challenges. His craving for the pre-human inanimate is examined in terms of private vision, of its relation to nature and its origins in physiology; and his 'mythology', his human relationships, and his aesthetic responses are presented as parts of a single reality, and as needing to be reconciled and harmonized. The problems presented in *Rodmoor* and *Ducdame* are to this extent resolved; but the final conclusion is not clear-cut. Wolf has learned to accept himself: whether this will help him with Gerda or Christie we do not know. Life remains mysterious, and it is with its mystery as such in all its multifarious dimensions that Powys was to concern himself from now on.

2

A Glastonbury Romance, for all its many and glaring faults, remains Powys's most enthralling novel and the one in which he expressed himself most fully. Its sheer bulk is overwhelming; but it is big not merely in its length but in the width of its scope and the variety of its themes and plots. It is a pictorial novel rather than a dramatic one: that is to say, its impact is not made primarily through its plot. It is not an epic, though it looks like one at first sight, for most of its dramatic possibilities are thrown away. One might argue that Powys's employment of nineteenth-century narrative methods serves him ill, inasmuch as it conceals the book's true purpose which is, the author declared in the preface written for the 1955 edition, 'to convey a jumbled-up and squeezed-together epitome of life's various dimensions'.[14] To do this he deploys related and contrasting groups of people and describes them in relation to certain central symbols, of which the Grail is the chief. But some kind of progression in time is also part of the scheme, and so a story is needed, and a long story at that. The impression of unwieldiness that the book gives, is largely induced by the sheer slowness of the narrative and the continual proliferation of irrelevancies, which are not, however, irrelevancies from the point of view of the over-all *pictorial* design. 'A Glastonbury Tapestry' might have been a better name for the book.

Nevertheless, the plot does bear a definite relation to the theme. The story of John Geard's attempt to start a new mystical cult at Glastonbury, and the simultaneous establishment of a commune there, serve as machinery by means of which Powys can explore the various attitudes to life which are portrayed in the novel as a whole. The underlying theme of the novel is the nature of the religious sense, and a number of differing responses to the numinous are examined and made palpable through the personal dramas of the characters. Powys, who at this stage of his life seems to have favoured some kind of pantheism, stresses the diversity of people's responses even to symbols accepted in common, so that, for example, John Geard's Christ is not the same Christ as that of the ascetic Sam Dekker. Behind all the beliefs is a mystery, of which the Grail is the somewhat nebulous symbol.

Before going on to examine Powys's treatment of the Grail it is necessary to outline the structure of the book. If from a narrative point of view Powys is a formless writer, this cannot be said of his powers of construction in a more general sense. *A Glastonbury Romance* is built round a series of antitheses. The underlying one is the division of the book into heathen and religious elements, represented geographically by the parts played in the novel by Norfolk and Glastonbury. It is a measure, perhaps, of Powys's wariness in approaching religion, that he should have chosen his beloved boyhood holiday land of East Anglia to be the ancestral home of the Crow family, those descendants of the heathen Danish invaders who are to be the main opponents of John Geard's religious quest and of the magic of the Glastonbury legends. Throughout the book, Norfolk, where the action commences, is continually recalled as a kind of touchstone of sanity and of a recalcitrant resistance to the dominance of the supernatural. The three members of the Crow

14. *A Glastonbury Romance* (Macdonald, 1955), p. xiv.

family who represent the 'opposition' have each of them their corresponding figure in Glastonbury, a figure whose story is a counterpart to their own. John Geard, 'Bloody Johnny', the eccentric half-pagan, unorthodox Christian Mayor of Glastonbury, who attempts in a strange and almost half-hearted way to establish a new religion, is violently opposed by Philip Crow, industrialist, and owner of the Wookey Hole caves. Geard supports the commune, and is exploited by them (but this political element is, as it was in *Wood and Stone*, the least convincing aspect of the book). Philip's raffish and cynical cousin John, while employed by Geard, has the heathen's dislike for the whole Glastonbury cultus, although his cousin Mary, whom he marries, is one of the two people in Glastonbury to see the Grail, the other being John's counterpart, Sam Dekker, the son of the vicar of Glastonbury. The story of Sam's vision of the suffering Christ and his renunciation of his mistress Nell Zoyland in order to live among the poor is told with a most beautiful and honest realism entirely free from sentimentality. The third Crow cousin, Persephone Spear, married to one of the communist leaders, is a more shadowy character, a feminine version of Rook Ashover, full of mystical longings for some state removed from the claims of flesh and blood. Her counterpart in Glastonbury is Owen Evans, an antiquarian bookseller who is one of the most sensitive mediums of the Glastonbury psychic aura, and also the victim of his own suppressed sadism: in both these figures we have people attracted in their different ways to the inhuman. One might call them unbaptized contemplatives.

These six characters are not crudely distinguished from each other: each one has something in common with his counterpart. Thus Bloody Johnny as much as Philip has a desire to control his fellow men, though in a far subtler way; John Crow, although a disbeliever, is sensitive to psychic influences, while Sam, for all his intense religiousness, is a naturalist at heart. Persephone and Evans are both of them romantics and both of them desire oblivion, she from her inability to love, he from his desire to kill. Again, while Persephone, Sam, and Evans are all seeking the Grail, Bloody Johnny, Philip, and John Crow are not. In addition there are two complementary triangle dramas, a Norfolk one between John and Mary Crow and their friend Tom Barter, and a Glastonbury one between Sam, Nell, and Sam's father Mat Dekker, in whom one can detect the lineaments of the Revd. Charles Francis Powys himself. The Crow drama is inarticulate and cerebral, the Dekker one passionate and overt. And all these several dramas are developed alongside each other, and imagined with the utmost vividness and profound understanding from within. Their participants are representative of permanent factors in human awareness, each embodying some religious attitude or attitude to life. Indeed, one might compare the contest between Philip Crow and John Geard to that between the two archetypal animals in Edwin Muir's poem *The Combat*.

These are not the only patterns that can be detected. There are two of those elderly spinsters in whose delineation Powys excelled—the Crows' Aunt Elizabeth from Norfolk, who has for long been in love with Mat Dekker; and, from Glastonbury, Miss Euphemia Drew, in her turn tragically in love with her companion, Mary Crow. The political characters form a quartet, the Christ-like Dave Spear balancing the vindictive Red Robinson, and the anarchist Paul Trent the Marquis of P—— as he is irritatingly called. It is as if Powys is determined to have as fully rounded and balanced a portrayal of a society as possible, and every age group and social element in Glastonbury is depicted. There is a fine cross-section of dwelling places and interiors—the manor house, the church, the low pub, the smart modern villa, the shabby house of Mr. Geard, the brothel, the dairy, the draper's, John's bachelor apartments, the antiquarian bookshop—all are sensuously apprehended and lend colour to the fabric of the novel. However strange the happenings and eccentric the characters we are always in the world of everyday affairs.

Glastonbury is presented as a place rich in both good and evil. Some of the most winning passages in the book concern the group of children known as 'the Robber Band' and their relations with the elderly Abel Twig. They belong spiritually to the world of John Geard, whose two daughters Cordelia and Crummie act as grail-bearers to Evans and Sam respectively. And there is a 'dark' grail-bearer in the person of Mad Bet who lures Evans on to the realizing of his sadistic desires and who is one source of Sam's devotion to the suffering Christ. Indeed the role of the Grail as a central symbol is shot through with ambiguity. In the preface written twenty years after the book first appeared Powys said that 'Its heroine is the Grail. Its hero is the Life poured into the Grail. Its message is that no one Receptacle of Life and no one Fountain of Life poured into that Receptacle can contain or explain what the world offers us.'[15] But the Grail is in the novel a reality that transcends all that seems to embody it; and only the single-minded ones, Sam and Mary, are allowed to see it. The main themes of the novel are, however, all related to the Grail. In the conflict between Bloody Johnny and Philip Crow it is Geard who is on the side of the Grail: his urge to power is not towards political power as is Philip's, but towards the power to influence men through love. He is able to heal the sick and even to

15. *A Glastonbury Romance*, p. xiii.

raise the dead—though the latter incident is treated in a curiously oblique manner, as if Powys were not really sure of his ground here (which is hardly surprising). Geard identifies himself with other people; he is the Merlin figure in the book, the benevolent magician who in the end lays down his life for his enemy. Sam Dekker achieves the Grail both in vision and in interior contentment, but Bloody Johnny lives as if the Grail were his loving cup. The Grail as used by Powys is never a standard of measurement, but represents the fullness of life, and is only seen by those who have somehow attained it. Mary who with Sam is described as one of 'the two noblest hearts in Glastonbury',[16] does so, proudly heathen though she is, since she is generous and great-hearted. To her the Grail, seen as an intense focus of dawn light on the broken arch of the abbey church, is an occasion of simple ecstatic joy. It comes in a different way to Sam, meeting his own nature as the confirmation of his dedication of himself to others.

In view of the frequent charges of formlessness and prolixity made against John Cowper Powys it seems necessary to stress the general purposefulness of *A Glastonbury Romance*. The novel moves forward slowly, but it does move; and although, as has already been stressed, its fundamental nature is pictorial rather than dramatic, its length is not due simply to the author's meandering; the book has a recognizable development. It falls into six parts with a prelude and an interlude. The prelude consists of the first three chapters, those dealing with the Crow family gathering in Norfolk for their grandfather's funeral and John's journey to Glastonbury and his meeting with Owen Evans at Stonehenge—one of Powys's finest scenes when the arch-enemy of the Glastonbury legends meets their most fervent devotee at the mysterious shrine that is older than them all. Stonehenge comes to mean for John a bedrock system of worship by which alone he can live. The prologue also introduces the political element, and the assembling of most of those who are to be a threat to Geard's attempted religious revival. Part I (Chapters 4–12) introduces the Dekker household, and the other principal characters, and brings Bloody Johnny firmly on the scene with his comforting of the cancerous woman: it also contains the idyll of Nell Zoyland's love for Sam. The forces of life are here in the ascendant. This part of the novel concludes with the chapter called 'The Dolorous Blow' in which Philip's quick wits get the better of Geard's inertia. Part II (Chapters 13–16) is heavy with Arthurian overtones and introduces three critical elements in the over-all picture—Geard's identification with Merlin at Mark's Court; the mutual misunderstanding of Sam and

16. *A Glastonbury Romance*, p. 397.

Mary, the two achievers of the Grail (a characteristic piece of Powys-ian irony); and the invocation of the primeval spiritual world of Glastonbury at the Easter Monday party at the house of Mrs. Legge, the town's procuress, when the old pagan religions of fer-tility and death are shown to be lying still only a little way below the surface. The third movement of the novel deals with Bloody Johnny's pageant, which establishes his fame at Glastonbury and brings the 'official' first part to a close. It marks the establishment of Geard's in-fluence against all opposition; but, again characteristically, it is not wholly a success. Part IV (Chapters 20-3), which marks a certain falling off of interest, leads up to Geard's miracle of healing at the chalice well. In the fifth part (Chapters 24-6) the dark forces advance into the foreground, as in Mad Bet's plot to kill John Crow and the disastrous (but brilliantly narrated) christening party at the Zoy-lands. This section is preceded by the remarkable chapter called 'Nature Seems Dead', which forms a kind of interlude, and which relates the action to its physical background. The last four chapters bring the six main stories to an end. There is a balance of powers, Philip's work is destroyed, but his life is saved; while Geard at the triumphant peak of his career goes voluntarily to his death. Evans succumbs only partially to his temptation; while Sam repents of his desertion of Nell too late. The other Crows all run away, John with 'his still-born, never returning opportunity of touching the Eternal' as a lasting loss.

The eternal is suggested in the novel by two main literary expedi-ents. One of these is the use of the Arthurian myth to point, though not to control, the development of the themes. *A Glastonbury Romance* is not a modern reworking of the myth; but the myth is presented as the expression of a number of psychic elements in a place where it is nourished. It is only one of the spiritual forces operating in Glastonbury. At certain moments and occasions the myth is re-enacted: sometimes explicitly as in the rather uncon-vincing comparison of Philip's speech to Geard's supporters with the Dolorous Blow; or with greater powers of suggestion, as when John Crow has his vision of the sword of Arthur at Pomparlés Bridge. John's mood at the time of his vision blends with the spiritual force that motivated Arthur's throwing away of his sword and so he enters into that experience; but in so doing John's mood reinterprets that experience—it is not the one normally associated with the myth. There is even a kind of interplay with the supernatural as in the great scene in the haunted bedchamber at Mark's Court when John Geard reaches out to comfort the disconsolate ghost of Merlin and from then on does in a sense become Merlin himself. And underlying these specific approximations there is a constant undertow of Arthurian and mythological imagery and notations, as when Crummie, hopelessly in love with Sam, plays the role of the Lady of Shalott in Geard's pageant, or when one impish little girl is called Morgan Nelly, relating her only half-ironically to the enchantress Morgan le Fay. Similarly old Abel Twig lives near the site of the primitive lake-dwellers' village, Isaac Weatherwax, the vicarage gardener, is likened to a goblin, or Tom Barter to a sergeant-major. The worlds of imagination and external appearance are indissolubly linked.

Powys's specific metaphysical framework is far less successful. So long as he uses nature as a symbol or agent for human emotions or desires he is a master of his medium; but so soon as he introduces a specific cosmology, he becomes unconvincing, the more so as this cosmological framework of sun and moon and evening star and double-natured First Cause conflicts badly with his simultaneous insistence on the subjectivity of all religious or mystical or imaginative experience. There is a passage at the very beginning of the book which illustrates both his strength and weakness in this respect:

The soundless roaring of the great solar furnace up there in the vast ether became, too, at that moment worse than merely indifferent to the motions of this infinitesimal creature advancing into the bracken-grown expanses of the historic Heath, like a black ant into a flowerpot . . . Humming and roaring and whirling in its huge confluent maelstroms of fiery gas, the body of that tornado of paternity concealed at that moment a soul that associated John Crow not only with such beings as neglected to invoke its godhead but with such beings as in their malicious rational impiety positively denied it any consciousness. Among all the greater gods around him it was the soul of the earth, however, that remained most jealous and hostile. It must have dimly been aware of the narrow and concentrated feeling, exclusive, misanthropic, which John experienced as he approached the home of his dead mother. And thus as it shot quivering vibrations through the greenish-yellow buds upon the hawthorn bushes, through the tender white blossoms upon the blackthorn, through the folded tremulousness of the fern fronds and the metallic sheen of the celandines, to John Crow it refused to give that exquisite feeling of primordial well-being which it gave to the rest. Why, thinking of his mother, he felt so sad, was a strange fact beyond this man's analysis. How could he know that mingled with their awareness of wet, green mosses, of dry, scaly lichens, of the heady-sweet odours of prickly gorse, of the cool-rooted fragility of lilac-coloured cuckoo flowers, of the sturdy swelling of the woolly calices of early cowslips, of the embryo lives within the miraculous blue shells of hedge-sparrows' eggs, the thoughts of the earth-mother throbbed with a dull, indefinable, unappeasable jealousy of a human mother?[17]

17. *A Glastonbury Romance*, p. 23.

And how can the author know?, one wants to ask. The great weakness of *A Glastonbury Romance* lies in the fact that too often what are acceptable as superbly imaginative insights and intuitions of an infinitely suggestive nature are presented as dogmas uttered with a kind of pseudo-gnomic wisdom which lend themselves all too readily to the accusation that John Cowper Powys was a crank. The power of the above passage is undeniable, as is its close attentiveness of external observation and richness of vocabulary; but it is also overloaded and tends, as Virginia Woolf remarked of the Elizabethan dramatists, to 'suffocate our imaginations rather than set them to work'.[18] And in none of the other novels is there quite so much of this overworking of material; the reading of *A Glastonbury Romance* is an exhausting experience as well as an absorbing one.

Nevertheless, the philosophical viewpoint emerging from the metaphysic is clear enough. Powys is a kind of benevolent sceptic in religious and philosophical matters. One aspect of his belief is well expressed in a conversation between Wolf and Christie in *Wolf Solent*.

'I don't understand half of what I read,' Christie began, speaking with extreme precision. 'All I know is that every one of those old books has its own atmosphere for me ...

'I regard each philosophy, not as the "truth", but just as a particular country, in which I can go about—countries with their own peculiar light ...'

... 'I know perfectly well what you mean,' he said eagerly. 'Philosophy to you, and to me, too, isn't science at all! It's life winnowed and heightened. It's the essence of life caught on the wing. It's life framed ...'[19]

Powys is sceptical of absolute truth, and finds belief in it a dangerous thing leading to the desire to impose the acceptance of that absolute on others. His aim in this novel, he declares in the preface, is to advocate 'an acceptance of our human life in the spirit of absolutely undogmatic ignorance'.[20] The key words here are 'acceptance' and 'undogmatic'. Not even ignorance is to be asserted as an absolute, and the mind is to be left open to all impressions; and the uncertainty is to be *accepted*. 'Possess, Enjoy, Defy' is the motto of John and Mary Crow, whose viewpoint approximates most nearly in the novel to the author's own.

The figure of Christ, although a powerful influence in the spiritual

18. 'Notes on an Elizabethan Play', *The Common Reader* (Hogarth Press, London, 1925), p. 74.
19. *Wolf Solent*, pp. 78–9.
20. *A Glastonbury Romance*, p. xvi.

world of Glastonbury, is ambiguous in character and means different things to different people. Thus to John Geard Christ is at once the Master and the power within him, a power with whom he is on homely, not to say familiar, terms; and he makes his own private heretical communion in his front garden on Easter day.

> The East welcomed Mr. Geard with a rush of extremely chilly air; but undeterred by this reception, after listening intently to make sure that Cordelia and Crummie were as fast asleep as their mother, he sank down on his knees in the presence of a little square patch of grass, a few privet bushes, and a tiny round bed with three dead hyacinths in it, and in this position began, with a sort of ravenous greed, tearing open the loaf and gobbling great lumps of crumb from the centre of it. These mouthfuls he washed down with repeated gulps of port wine. As he ate and drank, with the cold wind blowing against his white face, his diabolically dark eyes kept roving about that small garden . . .
>
> 'Christ is risen! Christ is risen!' muttered Bloody Johnny, with his mouth full of the inside of his loaf. 'Christ our Passover,' he went on, 'is sacrificed for us; let us therefore keep the Feast!'
>
> As he uttered these words he tossed off his third tumbler of port wine; and then, emptying the remainder of the decanter upon the gravel outside the threshold where he knelt, he struggled up, heavily and awkwardly, upon his feet and closed the garden door.[21]

The blend here of seriousness, grotesquerie, precise observation, and sheer daring originality is typical of Powys: John Geard, with his strange mixture of gentleness, charlatanism, grossness, and self-sufficiency is one of his supreme creations. He is the least fanatical of prophets; and Sam Dekker, who is single-minded to an extreme, realizes the difference between Bloody Johnny's Jesus and his own.

> 'My Christ's utterly different from Geard's,' Sam said, 'and different from my father's. My Christ's like Lucifer—only he's not evil . . . at least not what I call evil. But He's the enemy of God. That is, He's the enemy of Creation! He's always struggling against Life as we know it . . . this curst, cruel self-assertion . . . this pricking up of fins, this prodding with horns . . . this opening of mouths . . . this clutching, this ravishing, this snatching, this *possessing*.'[22]

But Sam's Christ is not simply an aspect of Sam or a projection of his own awareness. He is an objectified projection, a living image 'created by the unpardonable suffering of all sentient nerves from the zenith to the nadir of the physical universe'.[23] Indeed, it is Powys's contention that men do in part create the gods they worship.

21. *A Glastonbury Romance*, pp. 709–10.
22. ibid., pp. 815–16.
23. ibid., p. 377.

In the fine scene when Bloody Johnny cures the cancerous woman at the Chalice Well an important distinction is drawn between his kind of religious activity and that of Sam. Geard as he wills himself into healing the woman draws on the strength of the Grail.

What Mr. Geard really did—being more practical and less scrupulous than Sam Dekker—was to associate this immemorial *Fetish* with the Absolute, with Its creative as distinct from Its destructive energy. Sam, in his passion for the crucified, opposed himself to the First Cause, as Something so evil in Its cruelty that a man ought to resist It, curse It, defy It, and have no dealings with It. Thus in his loathing of the evil in God, Sam, the Saint, refused to make any use of the beneficence in God; and this refusal was constantly handicapping him in his present 'all-or-nothing' existence. Mr. Geard on the other hand was prepared to make use of this ambiguous Emperor of the Cosmos without the slightest scruple.[24]

Elsewhere Powys remarks that,

Mr. Geard's Christ was a Power to be exploited. In his weird gnostic dialogues with *his* Master, the Mayor of Glastonbury addressed Him like a friend, almost like an equal. He was the Mayor's great magician, his super-Merlin, by whose strength and support he became strong. Never once had it crossed the threshold of Mr. Geard's consciousness that it was his duty to live a life of self-sacrifice.

'I live *as I like to live*,' he would have retorted to any ascetic protest, 'and my Master lives as He likes to live.'[25]

Glastonbury is revealed as being the vortex of a whole crowd of contending spiritual forces, its population divided between those who are enemies of the Grail and those who are its friends. The enemies are the disbelievers, the men of action, the strong, those who seek power and control; the lovers of the Grail are the women of Glastonbury and the weak and receptive and self-giving: we are back in the world of *Wood and Stone*. The novel abounds in warmly sympathetic portraits of the simple and the good, people like Miss Elizabeth Crow or the amiable draper Mr. Wollop, for whom the whole of life is a delightful show both spectacular and sensational. It is the simple of heart who are blessed.

The homosexual theme developed in *Wolf Solent* is carried further here, with a calm delicacy of handling. The curious half-buried love of John Crow for Tom Barter is presented as the survival in him of a boyish sexuality never quite outgrown; that of the boy Elphin for Sam Dekker as the hero worship of a youth. It is the lesbian relationships which are treated with intensity; and Powys wrote few more

24. ibid.. pp. 708–9.
25. ibid., p. 909.

moving scenes than that in which Euphemia Drew begs Mary Crow
not to join her husband on their wedding night:

When Miss Drew came back from crossing the room the two women
confronted each other between the fragile coffee-table and the fireless
grate. The elder wore her usual black silk garment with the heavy brooch
securing the old lace frill on her withered neck. Opposed to her gaunt
figure, Mary's form, in her low-cut white dress and big crimson sash,
looked very young and soft and girlish.

'I'd like you . . . I'd like you not to . . .'

Miss Drew was evidently struggling to say something that tore at her
vitals.

'I'd like——' she gasped again.

'What is it, oh, what *is* it?' stammered Mary, awed, a little scared and
completely bewildered.

'I'd like you not to go to him tonight. I'd like you to stay with me
tonight . . . our last night . . . as you are!'

'Of course, my dear, if you feel it like that——'

'I mean . . . not leave me at all . . . just this once . . . I mean . . . let me
hold you . . . all night . . . close to me——'

Mary's face must have expressed such trouble, such pity, such confused
agitation, that the old woman changed her tone to a quieter one. 'It
would be nothing to you . . . to watch . . . to be there . . . to be near me . . .
just this once . . . and then'—she swallowed a rasping dry sob—'tomorrow
. . . you shall go.'

'Dear! I must think. He'll be at the gate in a few minutes; I must—I
don't know *what* to say. For him to go back alone—through the streets—
to that room—oh, I don't know what to do!'

She flung herself down on a chair, her red sash trailing to the carpet,
lying on the carpet, like a great stream of blood from a stab in her side . . .
Her thoughts kept taking first one road of trouble and then another. 'It
isn't fair!' her heart cried. 'I belong to John. It isn't fair!' And then a
vast pity for this unloved, childless old woman surged up within her.
'After all,' she said to herself, 'it's only for one short night; and how could
I be happy over there, thinking that I'd denied her such a little thing?'

'Let me think,' she whispered, giving Miss Drew a faint smile and a
reassuring nod. 'Sit down, dear—don't stand like that! You make me
nervous. I only want to think . . . just to think . . . a little more.'

But Miss Drew did not show any inclination to sit down. She kept her
eyes fixed upon the girl in the chair, as if that red sash were a death
warrant. And something from her Isle-of-Ely ancestors now rose up in
Mary's nature; something sturdy, earth-rooted and with a smack of indulgent humour in it, like the taste of peat-smoke.

'The poor heart!' she said to herself. 'John and I can surely wait for
twenty-four hours. If *I* can—God knows!—*he* can.'

To her consternation, Miss Drew now rushed forward and with a heart-
rending groan flung herself on her knees at the girl's feet. 'I'm not a bad

woman! I'm not a bad woman!' she sobbed out; and then to Mary's dismay she began pressing the red sash against her lips. 'I'm not ... I'm not a bad woman!' she groaned again, uplifting to the girl a face contorted with shame and passion.

'Miss Drew! *dear* Miss Drew! Get up, for Christ's sake. It's not right for you—it's not right for either of us! Oh, *what* shall I do? What shall I——'

But the other had buried her face in the girl's lap and with her arms outstretched was clutching at the sash where it was wound around the young woman's waist. She was murmuring all sorts of wild things now to which the girl could only helplessly listen, looking distractedly at the clock, which went on with its infernal ticking in exactly the same tone as if its mistress had been pouring out tea for Matthew Dekker.

'Oh, I love you so! Oh, I would give up my life for you! I can't bear it any more—it's lasted too long. But you will? My child, my little one, my only one, you will? You *will* be with me, watch with me, let me hold you, just this one single night? I'm not a bad woman! *Say* I'm not, child! It's ... it's *it's this Love* that's burning my life up!'[26]

It seems worth while to quote from this scene at some length in order to demonstrate Powys's command of the movements of human passion and the tenderness which he has at his command. His writing may be extravagant, rooted in an unfashionable mysticism, filled with intimations of timelessness; but equally it remains in close touch with human sensations and emotions as they are actually felt. In the end Miss Drew lets Mary go—after Mary has agreed to stay; and the whole incident is put in typical Powysian perspective—at once grotesque and tragic—as John waits for Mary to come to him:

... from some remote cowshed somewhere out towards Havyatt Gap, on the road to West Pennard, he could hear the pitiful cry of a beast in pain.

As this cry went on, tossed forth upon the summer night with woeful persistence, John stood and listened nervously, leaning upon his hazel-root stick.

'Damn!' he thought, 'and it must be a pain like that, that this woman's enduring now, only in the heart ... in the heart ... at my carrying off Mary! What a thing—that not one perfect day can be enjoyed by anyone without hearing something groan or moan! What would young Dekker be doing in my case? Well—it's clear what he'd be doing, by what he's done over Mrs. Zoyland! Cleared out of it ... hands off ... and spends his time between Paradise and Bove Town, comforting the sick.'

He resumed his sentry's march, but his mind was beating now against the blood-stained wedge of the world's pain, and he could not give up himself with absolute assent to his good hour.[27]

26. *A Glastonbury Romance*, pp. 636–8.
27. ibid., p. 643.

In the character of Persephone we have another of the boy–girl figures who especially attracted Powys and who are for him projections of the 'anima' pointing to regions of knowledge of which the ordinary world is only a shadow. Persephone arouses passion in both Philip Crow and in Angela Beere, but can find no satisfaction for herself. Powys is remarkably perceptive in his treatment of sexual relations, being always more conscious of people's separateness in the sexual act than in their togetherness: there are several Mrs. Shandys in his work. But not all his love affairs are of the abnormal or frustrated kind, and in the stories of Sam and Nell and in that of the Marquis's daughter Lady Rachel and the poet–farmer Edgar Athling, he portrays love and romance of a straightforward healing kind. The latter couple would seem to represent a kind of healthy norm among the Lovers of the Grail, and the scenes between them have a natural sweetness not quite like anything else in the book. More characteristic of Powys's art is his treatment of the energies of sex, used either for good, as when Cordelia pits her own sexual hold over her husband against his sadistic tendencies; or for evil, as in the terrifying scene at St. Michael's Inn when Red Robinson's sexual frustration sparks off his destructive tendencies, and he becomes horrifyingly aware of a reciprocity between himself and the murderous tramp Finn Toller.

This is further underlined in the stories of Sam Dekker and Owen Evans, which are complementary to each other. In both, a critical point is the necessity of coming to terms with the abhorrent and the ugly. Evans begins to accept his destiny when at Mrs. Legge's party he kisses the bald and repellent head of Mad Bet, herself a sadist, accepting her as his Grail messenger; and it is only when he has confronted his desire in its actual accomplishment that he is freed from it. Mad Bet's plot to kill John Crow is thus Evans's opportunity to rid himself of his obsession. Sam, at the time of his vision of the Grail feels himself pierced through the anus by a spear; and his first act after this is to give an enema to an old man—a scene of quite remarkable tenderness and humour. Again and again the need for accepting every aspect of physical existence is exemplified; and even Philip's conventional, house-proud wife Tillie is a member of 'that secret freemasonry of unfastidious realism that binds all women together'. John Crow, on the other hand, is squeamish; and his vision of Arthur's sword comes to him as he is contemplating with disgust the decomposing body of a cat. The heroic Cordelia is ugly, and like Mad Bet she is a grail-bearer—Powys carries over this kind of notation from novel to novel: the boy Elphin, the idiot boy whom Sam befriends, reminds one of Binnory in *Ducdame*. It is Bloody Johnny's strength that he is at home with the poor and the outcast and the ugly, and does naturally what it costs Sam an effort to do. A good example of his powers, and of Powys's unique quality of imagination, is the first occasion on which he ministers to the cancer-ridden Tittie Petherton.

A gaunt woman, propped upon pillows, who had pulled herself up so desperately to a sitting posture that the bed-clothes were clinging in a disordered mass about her knees, was leaning forward with a terribly fixed stare. She began at once an incoherent and piteous pleading. 'Have you the stuff? Have you brought the stuff? Oh, for Jesus' sake, give me the stuff!' ... The oil lamp reeked vilely, and from the tortured woman's bed there emanated a sweetish-sour and very sickly smell ...
... Mr. Geard came forward. Unobserved by his companions he had removed his coat and waistcoat, and now showed himself in his purple braces and grey shirt. He did not even look at the woman's face. To the astonishment of the others he stretched himself out flat by her side upon the bed, using the little table as a support for one of his great elbows. Mat Dekker could not help noticing that the bulge of his stomach had burst the top button of his trousers. But from this position he rolled his eyes towards the nurse. 'Put summat under me head, will 'ee, kindly,' he muttered, relapsing into the broadest Somerset. The nurse promptly obeyed him, snatching a faded cushion from a chair on the further side of the attic. 'Take thik lamp away, one o'ye, if ye doant mind. No! No! Put the little bugger on floor, Missus, where woant shine in our poor eyes.' Again the astonished nurse obeyed this singular authority, placing the lamp in the centre of the floor, and turning the wick down as low as she dared. 'Now, Tittie, old gurl, thee and me be a'goin' to have some blessed sleep. I be drowsy as a spent bullick, I be. Night to ye both; night to ye all. Tittie and me be all right. Us 'ull be safe and sound till mornin'. And then maybe ye'll bring up a cup o' tea for we to bless the Lord in!'[28]

Whenever he is writing about John Geard Powys is at the height of his powers; nor are the portraits of the Dekkers, of John Crow, and Tom Barter much less vital. The latter in particular is an acute and sympathetic study of a second-rate man obscurely troubled by his limitations, and the more interesting because, unlike most of Powys's major figures, he is not a projection of an aspect of the writer's own personality. With Philip Crow Powys is less at home: men of action were not men whom he really sympathized with or understood; but when he is describing Philip's inner world of fears and dreams he is at once authoritative and convincing. The most disappointing of the character studies in the book is that of Mr. Evans. He is vivid enough certainly, with his tenseness and enthusiasm for the past of Glastonbury, his desperate mysticism and horrible mental temptations; but perhaps because those temptations

28. *A Glastonbury Romance*, pp. 290–2.

were so like those which Powys has recorded as happening to himself, they are not treated with the compassionate detachment normally attendant on his writing. The language becomes slack and over-exclamatory as it touches on Evans's vice, becomes rhetorical and laboured. The whole story, while brilliant in idea, is weak in execution.

There are some fifty characters in this enormous novel, and each one of them is vivid, whether presented in the round or merely from outside. Only one of them is a real failure—Red Robinson who is not only implausibly conceived (which would not necessarily matter, since Powys has a genius for making the implausible imaginatively accept-able) but quite unconvincing in presentation. His cockney speeches and those of his mother are embarrassingly bad. What is notable about the characters most of all is that Powys contrives to make one acquainted not only with their appearance, ways of thought, and characteristic behaviour, but also—and this is perhaps his supreme contribution to fiction—their psychic aura as well, so that they seem to inhabit a dimension deeper than that of which we are normally aware.

In a way it is Glastonbury itself which is the real subject of the book, Glastonbury as a place uniquely constituted for revealing its author's vision of reality. That vision might be described as a naturalizing of the supernatural, the incorporation into a single vision of two normally separate areas of experience. One finds this in his description, quite early in the book, of what he calls 'the immemorial mystery of Glastonbury'.

Everyone who came to this spot seemed to draw something from it, attracted by a magnetism too powerful for anyone to resist, but as dif-ferent people approached it they changed its chemistry, though not its essence, by their own identity, so that upon none of them it had the same psychic effect. This influence was personal and yet impersonal, it was a material centre of force and yet an immaterial fountain of life.[29]

This is but one example upon many in this extraordinary book of the opening out of normal experience into an encompassing order of reality in which relationships are established undreamed of in our usual notions of what constitutes cause and effect. Frequently these examples are preposterous and strained; but throughout the book one is made aware of 'a sensation like that of the presence of a *double world*, every motion and gesture in the first being a symbol of some-thing that was taking place in the second. The sensation was ac-companied by an absolute conviction of the boundless importance

29. *A Glastonbury Romance*, p. 125.

of every thought that a human being had.'[30] The two worlds are
interdependent; and it is the ignoring of the other world which leads
to authoritarianism and self-assertion. The awareness of that world
is the true blessedness, whether it be that of Mr. Wollop who only
'thought of what he saw' or that of Nancy Stickles.

When not in acute physical pain, or in the presence of acute physical
pain, Nancy Stickles enjoyed every moment of life. She liked to touch
life, hear life, smell life, taste life, see life; but she went far beyond Mr.
Wollop and Bert, as she did indeed beyond everybody in Glastonbury,
except its present Mayor, in the enjoyment of religion. To Nancy Stickles,
God was a dignified, well-meaning, but rather helpless Person, like Parson
Dekker; Christ was a lovable, but rather disturbing Person, like Sam
Dekker; the Holy Spirit was, quite simply and quite reverently, a very
large and very voluble Wood Pigeon; but all these entities moved to and
fro in an inner, behind-stage Glastonbury; a Glastonbury with greener
fields, a redder Chalice Well, yellower apples and even bluer mists, than
the one Nancy knew best, but one—all the same—that she felt frequently
conscious of, and towards which her deepest feminine soul expanded in
delicious waves of admiration, hope and love.[31]

The quiet humour of this is entirely devoid of patronage: and its
gaiety is increased when one remembers that Bert is Bert Cole, 'an
infant of five, who in placidity and appearance resembled a giant
mushroom'.

Nancy's kind of mysticism is something more than formal religion,
which for Powys is something exclusive rather than inclusive
and which flourishes when the heat and light of the life-giving sun
are muted in a miasma characteristic of the Glastonbury weather
itself:

On this particular day the weather conditions had assumed a cloud-
pattern, an air-pressure, a perspective of light and shadow, such as
dwellers in Glastonbury recognized as more natural and normal than any
other. Over the surface of the sky extended a feathery white film of
vapour. The effect of this filmy screen upon the sun was to make it seem
as if it shone through a roof of water. As a matter of fact, this vaporous
film reduced the sun-rays to so mild a diffusion that they ceased to be
rays. The sun's orb, thus shorn of its outpouring of radiance, came to
resemble the disk of the moon. The great Luminary was so reduced by
this film of clouds that, like Agamemnon in the toils of Clytemnestra, it
could hardly be said to shine at all. It peered helplessly forth over the
green meadows of Avalon; so that stubborn Christian spirits, such as Mat
Dekker, had the satisfaction of being able to confront the great Light-
Lord, and stare him full in the face without blinking.[32]

30. ibid., p. 913.   31. ibid., p. 658.   32. ibid., p. 254.

The style and content of this passage illuminate another facet of
the novel—its vast range of mythical reference and vocabulary. Powys
writes out of a profound and living relationship with archetypal
myths and their cultural embodiment. Part of his strangeness in the
contemporary literary scene lies in his familiar acquaintance with
what is no longer believed in or taken for granted. He speaks from
an older, more culturally rooted world; and it is perhaps this appeal
to the more primitive and simple instincts in his followers which
secures for him a readership outside the student world among those
whom the psychological sophistication of his work might not otherwise attract.

To say this is not meant to suggest that the book is written only on
one level of intensity: Powys can command a wide range of style.
He can write, with all stops out, a grand pulsating prose, as in the
De Quincey-like invocation to the moon in Chapter Ten, or the
descriptions of the Flood that brings the action to an end;
and he can be simple and concise, as in his last account of Bloody
Johnny.

He had never been an artistic man. He had never been a fastidious man.
He had got pleasure from smelling at dung-hills, from making water in
his wife's garden, from sniffing up the sweet sweat of those he loved. He
had no cruelty, no culture, no ambition, no breeding, no refinement, no
curiosity, no conceit. He believed that there was a borderland of the
miraculous round everything that existed and that 'everything that lived
was holy'.[33]

He can produce a thumb-nail sketch: here is his description of Mrs.
Legge. 'She was a vast, dusky, double-chinned mountain of a woman,
with astute, little grey eyes; eyes that seemed rather to aim at *not*
seeing what she wanted to avoid, than at seeing what she wanted to
see.'[34] He can command a grim humour: here is Finn Toller talking
to himself about Mr. Evans's sadistic voyeurism. 'I'll *have* to let this
gent see it done ... for he's so crazy-bent on't that, if I dunna let 'un
he'll go and give I up to Tarnton Jail. That's where I'll end anyway;
and 'twould be Gibbet Hill, only they hangs 'em behind walls now,
so us pore buggers can't wave to our aunties.'[35] Or the humour can
be more oblique, the style parodying itself so that the jester seems to
be laughing not only at his subject but at himself as well.

[Paul Trent] stopped to take breath and found that he was gesticulating
furiously with his free hand right in front of Miss Crow's face, and that

33. *A Glastonbury Romance*, p. 1117.
34. ibid., p. 488.
35. ibid., p. 1013.

Miss Crow had shut her eyes tight, as if she were in the process of being shampooed, and that in his eagerness he actually *had* emitted a small globule of white sputum which now adhered to the black frill of Miss Crow's maternal but maidenly bosom.

Around this anarchistic spittle, a minute yellowish fly, attracted by the smell of humanity and dreaming perhaps that one of the old-fashioned Glastonbury markets was about to commence, hovered with pulsing and heaving desire.

Paul Trent drew out his elegant pocket-handkerchief from his breast-pocket, and therewith wiped his forehead. Then he hesitated for a minute. He would dearly have liked to have wiped that little bubble from his too voluble mouth which still adhered in annoying prominence to the lady's bosom, but he simply had not the courage to attempt such a deed. It is easier to defy society than to outrage a small propriety; and the man from what Malory calls the country of the Surluse, and what Sir John Rhys calls the Sorlingues, or Les Isles Lointaines, replaced his dainty handkerchief in his breast-pocket and sank back in his place, with an inward sigh and an outward smile. 'No good!' he thought to himself, and a wave of bitter futility swept over him.[36]

This passage is characteristic of much of *A Glastonbury Romance*. In it we find a precise physical realism wedded to a simultaneous feeling for the microscopic insect world and the mental world of literature and legend, of genealogy and satire and farce and pathos, all couched in a style that is both formal and colloquial. Powys has by now come to write with complete confidence and absence of self-consciousness. In his single-minded old-world integrity he is rather like Tom Bombadil in *The Lord of the Rings* over whom the magic of the ring has no power.

He can continue to write badly. The first sentence of the book is notorious, and has been wittily described by Jocelyn Brooke as 'the Becher's Brook of English Fiction'[37] but there are many others as ungainly. More important than these incidental defects, however, is the visionary intensity of the whole. In this novel, more even than in *Wolf Solent*, Powys has created a world. It is neither an abstracted fantasy world, like that, say, of J. R. R. Tolkien or of Mervyn Peake in his Gormenghast trilogy; nor is it a faithful re-creation of a known and recognizable world in the manner of Arnold Bennett or Anthony Powell. It contains elements of both and has something more beside. So vividly has Powys imagined his characters that there seems to be no detail of their thoughts or of their surroundings that he is not prepared to tell us; and this particularly extends far beyond mere

36. ibid., p. 996.
37. Jocelyn Brooke: 'On Re-Reading *A Glastonbury Romance*', *The London Magazine* (Apr. 1956).

outward appearance or conscious awareness. He sees them from the perspective of the whole man, from the knowledge of their total context in time and space, as beings swayed by physical and psychic forces which together constitute the secret of their being. The individual narratives of *A Glastonbury Romance* are subordinate to the overriding creation of a universal portrait. It is this attempt at universality which is central to any appraisal of the book. It is what gives it its especial flavour as distinct from Powys's other novels; it is what makes the writing at times bombastic and inflated; it is what on certain occasions causes the characters to speak inconsistently with their own normal style. It is what weighs the book down with a super-abundance of metaphysical comment; but it is also what in the last resort justifies the super-abundance of physical description.

In many ways it is an anti-dramatic novel, one that is all-inclusive both in tone and content. As a study of the interaction of man and his environment it is unique. The Glastonbury landscape is seldom described directly through the eye; rather it is mediated through our senses of smell and hearing, though a constant, loving ennumeration of place names, street names, and of local landmarks; and through a meticulous and precise evocation of weather conditions, of wind and rain and sunbeams. And the characters live not so much in their mutual interaction but through their sense impressions, their solitary reveries, their own contributions to the encompassing atmospheric world of associations, memories, and half-expressed desires. In this novel, and the one that followed it, Powys realizes his vision of the world as both the product and sustainer of the human imagination. For all its faults of style and implausibility, of occasional childishness and self-indulgent slowness, it remains Powys's masterpiece. It is inferior as a formal work of art to *Wolf Solent* and *Owen Glendower*; but to make such a statement is in itself to comment on the nature of critical theory. None of the other novels has quite the same sustained force of creative energy and in *A Glastonbury Romance* Powys evolved a form for the kind of lengthy novel that he most enjoyed and which here he wrote definitively.

3

Most authors, after completing a work as vast and taxing and comprehensive as *A Glastonbury Romance*, would be content to rest for a time and wait for further inspiration. But John Cowper Powys was a born writer; and thirty years of public speaking had left him only the more eager to project himself in print. The astonishing fertility of his imagination is nowhere more evidenced than in his following

Glastonbury with *Weymouth Sands*, a shorter novel, admittedly, than either the *Romance* or *Wolf Solent*, but fully comparable with them in creative vigour, and even in some respects their superior in visionary power. Moreover it is as different from either as they are from each other, with a distinctive character of its own, a character drawn largely from Powys's feeling for the seaside town which is its setting.

Weymouth Sands was first published in England under the title *Jobber Skald*. Powys had had a libel suit on his hands as a result of the particularity of his Glastonbury descriptions and accordingly was persuaded to play safe by disguising the setting of the new novel with fictitious names. But Sea-Sands is still cleary recognizable as Weymouth, Weymouth the most ubiquitous in the author's fiction of all his boyhood homes. It was here that he was happiest; and now it was to the place which he had treated so lyrically in *Wood and Stone* that he returned for his most searching examination of the meaning of failure and of loss.

More than any other of the novels *Weymouth Sands* advocates or presents a specific way of looking at life and of approaching reality; it is preoccupied with human failure, and with the way in which those who fail in life can come to terms with it and with themselves. The image of the sea is predominant. All the characters of the book are in their several ways lost or astray; bewildered, tormented people, like flotsam thrown up on the shore, where the sea which has nowhere to go pounds endlessly to and fro, and the shrill vicious voice of Mr. Punch, 'like a savage chorus of age-old mockery', screams across the beach. The sea has a twofold meaning in the novel. It resembles destiny or chance to several of the characters; but more significantly it represents the subconscious which alone links them together. For if this is a novel about human separateness and the inability of people to make easy contact with each other, at another level it reveals the underlying unity of human beings with each other and with the elements. Thus the theme of loneliness, developed in a number of the personal histories which make up the body of the novel, is related to the external objects which link the characters through their common imaginative perception. Weymouth, as much as Glastonbury, is here seen as an entity in its own right, an embodiment of the inner cities which all the characters inhabit. Freaks and failures though they are, they are vindicated by their relation to the total order of things. This is at once Powys's most mystical and most compassionate novel; it is also his most humorous and mellow one.

As in *A Glastonbury Romance* the 'plot' is simply a device to keep the book moving; in fact this particular novel has hardly any plot at all. It consists rather of a group of parallel accounts of loss or failure. There is the story of Magnus Muir, the middle-aged bachelor schoolmaster, infatuated with the shop-girl Curly Wix, who in the end loses her to the local magnate Dogberry Cattistock—himself, in his own inner life, a failure; there is Jobber Skald with his self-imposed vendetta against Cattistock, which nearly loses him the love of the heroic Perdita Wane; and most striking of all there is the story of Sylvanus Cobbold, most touching and human of Powys's portrait gallery of religious mystics, who fails to make his message understood and is shut up in a madhouse, partly in order to save the scandal attendant on his passion for young girls. Nearly everyone in this tragi-comic novel is futile or forlorn, like Peg Frampton, drifting from a loveless home into a loveless promiscuity; like Richard Gaul, the neurotic young philosopher who comes to love her, despite his fear of venereal disease; like Rodney Loder, trapped in his own hatred of his father's illness. As the Fool Chorus to it all is Jerry Cobbold, the tragic clown, disillusioned, poised on the abyss, married to a sadistic hypochondriac, and compassionate out of despair. But the final note of the book is not tragic; through it all there flows a current of renewing life and delight in life.

This is made most clear in those passages where the outward appearance of their environment blends with the responses of the characters. At the very beginning of the book Magnus is aware of another Weymouth, almost its Platonic essence:

... as he undressed himself the familiar smell of dead seaweed kept entering his room; and a strange phantasmal Weymouth, a mystical town made of a solemn sadness, gathered itself about him, a town built out of the smell of dead seaweed, a town whose very walls and roofs were composed of flying spindrift and tossing rain. Lying in bed in the faint glimmer from the grate he could hear the waves on the beach, and a great flood of sadness swept over him ... For a while he floated helplessly on the tide of this feeling, watching his big red curtains slowly inflate themselves and bulge forward, only to be sucked back, with the retreat of the wind, into hollow answering concavities. Then something in him gathered itself together, as it always did, to resist this hopelessness ... Then while he settled down under the bedclothes, there came before his eyes once more the spire, the clock, the statue of the king, the outline of the Nothe, as he had felt them when he sat in the cold opposite the deserted donkey stand. And the impression gathered upon him that these simple things had a significance beyond all explanation; that they were in truth the outward 'accidents' of some interior 'substance', that belonged —by a strange law of transubstantiation—to some life of his that was independent of the humiliations of his ordinary experience; independent, for instance, of whether when he went to see Curly tomorrow she made him feel silly and old.[38]

This is Rook Ashover's Cimmery Land brought into the present, known not only as an inspiration or as an escape, but also as a living reality. And this deeper Weymouth, this mystical Weymouth created, as is suggested in another passage, by the communal thoughts of its inhabitants, manifests itself also in the linking imagery of the narrative. Powys is quite specific as to the significance of using such imagery.

There are moments in almost everyone's life when events occur in a special and curious manner that seems to separate that fragment of time from all other fragments.
  One peculiarity of such moments is the vividness with which some particular human gesture limns itself on the sensitive-plate of our inmost consciousness, along with certain inanimate objects ... Another peculiarity of these moments is a sensation as if they were a spiritual screen, made of a material far more impenetrable than adamant, between our existing world of forms and impressions and *some other world*, and as if this screen had suddenly grown extremely thin, thin as a dark, semi-transparent glass, through which certain faintly adumbrated motions, of a pregnantly symbolic character, are dimly visible.
  Such a gesture—to the inner consciousness of this proud girl—was the upraised arm of the man called the Jobber as he flung that seaweed and pebble over the shelving bank into the darkened water; and it was her complete absorbtion in this occurrence that held her feet for a moment, after he had gone, as if rooted to the spot, though she did not turn her head to watch him go ... but kept it hanging down, as if in the humility of a sudden perception of a movement of destiny.[39]

Powys was no believer in destiny in the theological sense; rather he came to pay an ironic homage to what he liked to call 'the great goddess Chance'. But destiny in the Greek sense of *moira* or the Welsh *tynged*, that is to say a kind of personal fatality that was itself in part a product of a person's true nature, and obedience to which was a necessity for proper self-expression and fulfilment, he did believe in. Perdita Wane senses her own personal destiny as being bound up with that of Jobber Skald, and her reaction to his gesture has a quality of recognition. So, a few pages later, her thoughts recur to that world of sense impressions in which her true identity can know itself.

The jobber, when she tried to visualize his identity, seemed to melt away from the clasp of her imagination and to lose himself in the sound of

38. *Weymouth Sands* (Macdonald, 1963), pp. 39–40.
39. ibid., pp. 48–9.

breaking waves, the smell of tossed-up sea-drift, the rocking reflections of ships' lanterns ... she kept seeing the formidable sweep of the tall man's arm as they stopped on the esplanade and he flung that piece of seaweed into the darkness. She kept imagining the way that seaweed was now being washed, to and fro and lifted up and down, as the stone to which it clung rolled over and over on the ribbed sand under the dark tide.

'I am like that seaweed,' she thought, 'only I have no stone to cling to.'[40]

This is the kind of notation employed in *Wolf Solent*, where, for example, trees are used as linking images, such as a lilac branch for Gerda, a laburnum for Christie, or an ash for Wolf. But the stone image is developed far more elaborately in *Weymouth Sands*, where it is related to the stone the Jobber keeps in his pocket as a sign of his determination to kill Cattistock and the great stone by which he and Perdita make love. Both the creative and destructive aspects of his nature are embodied in it, and his initial desperation is underlined by his gesture in throwing it into the sea.

Another element in Powys's vision is strongly present in this novel: his all-embracing reverence for the material world. This extends, as we have seen, to the ugly and the excremental. Jerry Cobbold, world-weary though he is, can yet take delight in one of the back streets of the town.

His face partook of the gusto of his feelings which were those of sweet satisfaction in the dirtiness and littered condition of the piece of road he traversed. The faintest and most pallid tinge of sunlight had just now broken through the clouds and its watery lemon-coloured light fell upon all the horse-droppings and all the broken boxes and all the puddles and all the mud. There were some high hoardings, too, in this ramshackle quarter at the back of the station, upon one of which the clown noted an advertisement of a well-known aperient, held aloft on the pinnacles of a Gothic Cathedral. But the old withered horse-droppings, together with certain wisps of dirty straw, were what seemed to please both this watery sunshine and the senses of Jerry most of all. A bit of blue paper, torn from the hoarding, flapped like a discontented flag in his path; but the comedian's grave eye, as it gloated with a sort of mystical ecstasy on all these manifestations of matter, seemed to rebuke the discontent of this piece of paper. He was soon traversing the yet poorer district of Ranelagh Road, a region that always fascinated him. Ranelagh Road at that time was a sort of poor people's replica of the grand esplanade; and it was above everything a parade ground and rendezvous for the lovers of the children of the poor. Here when the lights were lit at night the natural shyness of the large groups of boys and girls who met there concealed itself under loud guffaws, crude gestures, incredibly gross jests, and hys-

40. *Weymouth Sands*, pp. 58–9.

terical idiotic giggling. All this Jerry Cobbold sucked up with far more relish than he did the plaudits of any audience. Jerry had indeed something in him that went beyond Rabelaisianism, in that he not only could get an ecstasy of curious satisfaction from the most drab, ordinary, homely, realistic aspects of what might be called the excremental under-tides of existence but he could slough off his loathing for humanity in this contemplation and grow gay, child-like, guileless.[41]

The pictorial nature of Powys's art has already been stressed: here we see him resembling not Claude but Lowry. His sensuousness goes far beyond the usual term in its responsiveness and sympathy; and we know from the *Autobiography* that this type of urban landscape made a great appeal to him. Indeed, it is to that book that we must look if we would see in its full roundedness what the life of cities really meant to this particular countryman. Powys was never a mere ruralist: and his elementalism goes far beyond a sensitivity to the more romantic aspects of natural scenery.

Weymouth Sands, like *A Glastonbury Romance*, portrays sensuality as a conscious response to carefully cultivated stimuli. The account of Rodney Loder's secret inner life reminds one of Marcel Proust.

These subtle and insubstantial feelings had gradually become, for this sluggish and unambitious young man, a sort of world within the world, or life within life, and he would rest his chin on his hands as he sat at his desk in the office, or at his table in this pleasant room, and fall into a deep day-dream, or vegetative trance, in which all manner of insignificant little scenes, recalled from his walks into the town ... seemed to grow in importance, until they acquired for him a sort of mystical value, as if they were the casual by-paths or hidden postern-gates, leading into aerial landscapes of other and much happier incarnations.[42]

It is characteristic of Powys's fiction that Rodney, although presented with sympathy and some elaboration in the chapter which bears his name, plays very little part in the subsequent events in the book. But a certain note has been struck in the description of him, and his particular personal dilemma takes its place in the over-all picture.

His sister Ruth likewise has her secret life, 'calm depths and placid gulfs of inhuman detachment',[43] which sustain her as she devotes herself to her sick and exacting father, this response to the inanimate being strong enough to offset the assault on her nerves and patience of a bitter, self-dramatizing invalid. Powys, a lifetime sufferer from gastric ulcers himself, is one of our greatest masters in the depiction of the ravages of pain. Tittie Petherton and James Loder are unforgettable in their suffering.

41. ibid., pp. 221-2.   42. ibid., p. 183.   43. ibid., p. 486.

And yet in the last resort the book is far from being depressing, and this is largely because of the capacity of even the most downtrodden of its characters to hit back at their fate and to accept themselves. This finds its most muted expression early on, when Magnus realizes that 'A coward ... has a right to his own philosophy as well as everybody else; and I must get into the habit of accepting the fact that I am an undistinguished and unworthy person'.[44] But it is Sylvanus Cobbold, Jerry's brother, the pathetically eccentric, childlike, wily, unworldly mystic who knows the greatest heights and depths. Sylvanus is one of Powys's supreme creations, a more human and accessible figure than John Geard, with a curious private cultus and worship of inanimates (in this resembling the John Cowper recorded in the final chapter of the *Autobiography*) and with his innocent mania for young girls (whom he uses in a manner similar to that of certain early Christians castigated by St. Paul in the first epistle to the Corinthians for their dealings with the virgins known as *subintroductae*). Sylvanus sleeps chastely with his girls, but sublimates his sexuality for purposes of interior illumination. But there is nothing esoteric about him in himself; grotesque and extravagant he may be; but like Bloody Johnny he has his underlying element of common sense. Although finally incarcerated in the sinister Hells Museum, his real personal crisis occurs when Gipsy May in a fit of jealousy cuts off his giant moustaches while he is asleep.

'I depended on the idea of myself with those moustaches,' he thought ...'They were Me! ... When boys ran after me in the street and tormented me and when people stared at me on the sands in summer when I paddled with women, that no one else wanted to go into the water with, it was always "Me and my moustaches" ... but what will I do now?'[45]

There is a kind of anti-heroic honesty in this which is extremely touching. Sylvanus is both humble and realistic. 'Yes, I'll take it as fate. I'll shave my lip tomorrow and henceforth I'll shave it till I die. Maybe they'll grow again, in my coffin. Well! They were the longest moustaches ever seen in Weymouth!'[46] The same half-humorous self-assertion supports him when, a prisoner in the asylum and newly separated from the Punch and Judy girl, Marret, whom he loves, he experiences another kind of desolation. The scene is so typical of Sylvanus and of Powys's peculiar mixture of grotesquerie and humour and pathos, that it calls for full quotation.

44. *Weymouth Sands*, p. 26.
45. ibid., p. 413.
46. ibid., p. 414.

Sylvanus stood on the gravel-path that led to the Doctor's private residence and contemplated a garden fork that someone had left stuck deep into a heap of manure. Had this tool been a hoe he would have passed it by ... But he had so often used a fork, just like this, for various purposes at Last House, that the mere sight of it stirred up his old fighting spirit.

'What was it that the poor old Jobber was always muttering?' he thought. ' "A time and times and half a time." Well ... if I *am* destined to die in this place ... and if I'm *not* destined ever to see Marret again ... at least I'll *fight*! That's the whole thing. Suffer ... be miserable ... feel like a worm cut in half ... but one thing a person *can* do, till he's stone-dead, and that's fight ... even though his fighting is all done in the circle of his own mind!'

He felt so grateful to the fork that he actually stepped on the dung heap and bending down, kissed its handle. To kiss the handle of a garden fork would not have arrested any particular attention *where he was*, but it would have fatally lent itself to Perdita's impression of him, as one who, even when alone, was forever acting and showing off. Perdita's view of his character, and indeed the Jobber's view, too, would have been accentuated had they witnessed the sequel.

After walking briskly forward with a happier step, now he had seen the fork in the dung, for both these objects seemed to belong to everything that was outside the Brush Home, it occurred to his superstitious mind that the dung heap might feel neglected. Back therefore he went, and pulling out the fork with a jerk, while with the emergence of the tool came forth a heavy warm scent of long-buried cow droppings, he raised the prongs to his face and kissed *them*. Then he replaced the tool where he had found it and hurried off again.[47]

Here Powys's concern for the inanimate approaches fetishism, an aberration for which he had a particular understanding. Few novelists are his equal when it comes to describing what people do when they are alone. Characters like Sylvanus and Dud No-Man in *Maiden Castle* are really heightened portrayals of the half-buried eccentricities of more ordinary people. In creating his magician figures Powys is suggesting the latent possibilities of a richer mental and physical existence in everybody and putting into a half-humorous embodiment the doctrines advocated more strenuously, though no more persuasively, in his books of popular philosophy.

In Magnus Muir Powys portrays a man as much sunk in his own private world as is Sylvanus, but without the power to make of that isolation a way of life. His infatuation with Curly Wix menaces his own inner world, and there is a grey pathos about his feeble struggle against it. In the end he not surprisingly loses her to Cattistock, re-

47. ibid., p. 520.

turning with a certain gratitude to the ministrations of Miss Le
Fleau, the most motherly of Powys's old-maid figures. It is a mark
of the increased maturity of this novel that she is the only woman in
it to be idealized.

The Jobber is, in some aspects, an enlargement of the figure of Red
Robinson in *A Glastonbury Romance*. His obsessive rage against
Cattistock poisons his love for Perdita and almost causes him to lose
her for ever. It is in keeping with the anti-heroic mood of the novel
that he should neither overcome his hatred nor expel it by action:
chance simply takes matters out of his hands. The story may be read
as an implicit critique of self-dramatization of the wrong kind.
Sylvanus, and to a lesser extent Magnus, know that they are alone
and that their motives are built around their own desire for self-
preservation. Skald makes the mistake of believing that his motives
are rational and therefore justified. He is an appealing figure, with
his great physical strength and mental sensitivity, at once a formidable giant and yet a boy in his emotions. His love for Perdita and
hers for him is powerfully presented, with a simplicity only attained
elsewhere in Powys's work in the story of Sam Dekker and Nell
Zoyland.

The final reconciliation of Perdita with the Jobber conforms to
the novel's final note of resignation to fate. Against the tide of that
fate all the characters are swimming, tossed hither and thither by
contending desires. The book is a network of erotic attraction, and
odd relationships. Sylvanus and his girls are not the only strange
lovers in the book. There is a vivid scene in which Magnus and Curly
are embracing high up on a hillside, and all the while he is thinking
of his father and she is listening fascinated to the sound of her other
lover's motor-horn on the road below: this ability of humans to de-
tach themselves from the closest physical embrace is a frequent motif
in Powys's writings about sex. In *Weymouth Sands* there is a constant
change of sexual or emotional partners. Cattistock is involved in turn
with the dancer Tissty, with Jerry Cobbold's sister-in-law, Mrs. Lily,
and with Curly Wix; Jerry himself is involved with Tissty's sister
Tossty (the eccentric naming of these two is one of Powys's more
irritating gestures) and later on in his turn with Mrs. Lily. Tossty is
obsessed with her sister. Daisy, Mrs. Lily's daughter, is involved with
both Rodney Loder and Peg Frampton; and Peg himself is attracted
both by Richard Gaul and the shady doctor Girodel. Love in a simpler form is shown by the half-witted boy Larry Zed (Powys's finest
achievement in this particular type of character) in his adoration of
both Perdita and Marret; while there are elements of homosexuality
in Sylvanus's attraction for his doctor, Daniel Brush, and of incest

in the hysterical Lucinda Cobbold's relations with her father. But most of these sexual currents are suggested rather than emphasized; the whole tone of the book is tolerant and restrained, and the web of attraction and repulsion is revealed as itself the fabric of life; a desire to meddle and change is here, as in the other novels, the enemy of human happiness and thus of society itself.

As in *A Glastonbury Romance* the central contrast is between the Authorities and Men of Power—Cattistock, his nephew Ballard, Daniel Brush—and the helpless and downtrodden—Peg Frampton, Sylvanus, Larry Zed, and their kind. Between these two extremes are Magnus Muir, Jerry Cobbold, and the Jobber, all of them in their different ways maladjusted—Skald being obsessed with the future (his killing of Cattistock), Magnus with the past (his relations with his father), and Cobbold being disenchanted with life altogether. Their respective lots are Fortune, in the shape of Perdita's love; Resignation; and Compensation of a kind, in the vapid person of Mrs. Lily.

The other contrast in the novel is between love and cruelty. Vivisection, which was for Powys the root evil of modern scientific method, is carried on as a sideline at Daniel Brush's mental home; and a kindred playing with the helpless informs Mrs. Cobbold's character. She is a remarkable portrait, apprehended rather than comprehended, and her speech carries the very tone of suppressed hysteria.

'Out,' she said laconically. 'Always out, when there's trouble brewing! But as a matter of fact Jerry's got his own worries just now. They've sent for him to the Police Station about that brother of his. Jerry is really angry at last ... done with that man for good, I hope! If he hadn't the patience of an angel and if *I* hadn't the patience of—I don't know what—we'd have let them shut him up long ago. Jerry says he's mad; but *I* don't believe it. *I* say he only does it to annoy Jerry and me, and make our life here difficult with everybody. I told Jerry I'd never forgive him if he "went voucher" again or whatever they call it, for him. And I wouldn't either! I've had enough of the man and all this fuss about him. The sooner he's put away the better. How can we be responsible for him I should like to know, when he delights, yes, positively delights, in making us a laughing-stock to the whole town? I told Jerry to tell them plainly—and I think he will—that this is the end. The sooner they arrest him and put him in an institution the better. If Jerry doesn't like the idea of the Country Asylum they could send him to Dr. Brush. The expense will come on us of course. But I'm used to that. If it isn't one thing, it's——'[48]

The gradual quickening of pace from the laconic opening to the

48. *Weymouth Sands*, p. 150.

virulent and interrupted close is masterly; and the passage really
gathers its force with Lucinda's introduction of herself and thus, by
a natural progression, of her own grievances. Powys is a master hand
at portraying angry women, as if he had an intuitive understanding
of how the male looks to the female, a simultaneous awareness of
both points of view. His great quarrel scenes are especially memorable.

As against Lucinda's attitude to Sylvanus we have the views of the
new doctor who in the fine chapter entitled 'Punch and Judy' utters
what is described as an oracle—'I do nothing but listen ... and ...
move ... perhaps ... a few things that have got in the way'—a statement which is as concise an account of the role of the psycho-
analyst as any other. Ironically Powys, who was always suspicious of
anything approaching authority in any scientific attitude makes this
the answer to the question 'how do you go to work with your neurotic
cases, now that you've dropped psychoanalysis?'[49]

In spite of his own clearly defined attitudes Powys portrays both
Lucinda and Dr. Brush with a certain sympathy: their cruelty is
seen as an inability to make proper contact with other people. In
contradistinction the house of Dr. Girodel, which is a kind of un-
official brothel, is a place of refuge for the lonely and frustrated. The
father figures in the book tend to be tyrannical—Peg Frampton's
father, the ulcer-ridden James Loder, even the elder Muir, dead
though he is—but the women are no longer seen, as they were in the.
early novels, as a threat to masculine integrity. Sex indeed is now a
liberating factor, and the role of Perdita with regard to Skald is a
development of that of Cordelia Geard in her attempts to woo Mr.
Evans from his vice. Peg Frampton too is healed through her growing love for Richard Gaul. Even Sylvanus's supernatural intimations
mean less to him than does his love for Marret.

The tall man and the tall girl stared at each other in tense silence. By
some kind-unkind chance a great cloud of smoke rolled between them,
and the girl accepted the sign ... As he watched their retreating figures,
Zed swinging the basket and Marret with her small head, in its boy's
cap, hanging down a little on one side, he was aware of a sensation in the
pit of his stomach as if there were an umbrella inside him that was blow-
ing inside out. But he kept his eyes fixed steadily upon them till their
forms vanished behind a curve of the hill. Then ... his whole figure
dropped and wilted in the grey dawn. It was one of those moments in
a human being's life when the will to live drains away, like water from
a dam that has been lifted.[50]

49. *Weymouth Sands*, pp. 496–7.
50. ibid., pp. 518–19.

Only in *Owen Glendower* does Powys write so movingly of love
as he does in *Weymouth Sands*. One of the finest things in the book
is the figure of the red-haired boy Larry Zed, who lives with Gypsy
May in her hut on Lodmoor; and one of the supreme moments in
all Powys's extraordinary succession of love scenes is that in which
he describes Larry's spiritual ravishing of the passive and at this
moment helpless Perdita. The quietness and tenderness of the prose
is rare in his work; but the insight that went into the writing of the
passage is not.

With the quick spontaneous grace of a wild animal young Zed leapt to
his feet and went over to her side. Very gently, just as if she had been
made of some material more precious than flesh and blood, he stroked
one of her bare hands which lay cold on her lap with the tips of his
fingers. Perdita had closed her eyes; but in a moment she opened them
again, for she felt by his quick breathing that he had fallen on his knees
by her side and had tightened his fingers over the hand he had touched.
For some minutes they stayed together in this position, and then some
thing deep in the girl, which surprised herself by its sudden strength,
stirred within her; and she knew that standing there behind the kneeling
lad, in spite of her reckless mood, in spite of her sense of the futility of
thinking about him, remained, for all she could do, the great lowering
figure of that tall man who threw the seaweed into the sea! But she still
went on gazing softly and tenderly into the face of the kneeling boy; nor
did she stir, nor did she make the least motion to release her fingers,
although, so strong was his feeling, she could feel the burning pulse
throbbing within his wrist. Larry's whole soul gleamed in his green eyes
as he hung over her. His brain felt dizzy; but it seemed to him as
though touching her so, and while she lay there prone and still beneath
him, that a veritable consummation of his desire was taking place. To
his fervid imagination it was enough that their eyes clung together and
that she knew he was ravishing her in his thought. Her bare hand, round
which his fingers burned, was to him then her whole body. For this was
the first time in his life that he had held a girl who knew what he felt
and did not stop him. His green eyes, as they clung to her soft brown ones,
kept saying to her: 'I'm taking you! I'm taking you!' and it seemed to
him that she yielded more and more, as he bent forward, his body pressed
against the side of the couch; and it seemed to him that it pleased her that
he should be seeing her bare figure—as he *was* now seeing it in his intense
imagination—and that it pleased her to lie so hushed and still, so that he
could the more easily enjoy her; and it seemed to him that this strange
passivity, she knowing that he was taking her, was the ultimate essence of
her being offered up to him; and that her lying so still, with her bare hand
in his, while he enjoyed her, was the ultimate sign of what it meant to be
a real, live, mysterious girl; and that this was the secret of all girls, that
they could not know how exciting they were; and that this was their in-

most nature that they stayed so quiet while they were loved.[51]

What is so remarkable about the quality of Powys's imagination is its constant returning upon itself, its awareness of opposing forces, contradictions, ironies—and this without any bitterness or anger. It is because of this that he can both chill and yet not repel by following up his account of Larry's tremulous feelings with the following comment.

How could he know that it was only possible for Perdita to remain so quiet, and to answer his impassioned gaze so calmly because her own thoughts had once more grown pitifully sad. Weary and hopeless was her whole spirit, as she lay on Larry's bed; and all, all seemed futile to her. The fleeting quiver of response that the boy's beauty and passion had roused in her had been stricken cold by that image of the Jobber lowering above him. Perhaps it had been all the while her feeling for the Jobber— for not a night had passed, since she saw him, but she had gone to sleep thinking about him—that rendered her so sensitive to this boy's infatuation.[52]

This novel does not lend itself to structural analysis; but appropriately there is a controlling imagery of the sea. Perdita has dreams of a lover from the sea, whom she finds embodied in the Jobber. She herself comes over the sea to him, and returns across it to her home after his resolution to kill Cattistock has come between them, and returns again across to him when she learns of his remorse. The sea image fills the description of their final reunion. 'He could taste the salt of her tears, pouring, pouring, from what seemed like the whole surface of her face, and she could feel herself rising and falling, up and down, on the crests and troughs of his immense, slow, shaking sobs.'[53] Magnus also loves the sea; and it is a mark of his lack of true affinity with Curly that she should be a girl from an inland village. (Another descriptive pointer is that she should be employed at the Upwey Wishing Well: she is as much of a dream figure to Magnus as Larry's 'Nothing-Girl' is to him.) At the end of the novel we find Magnus wandering by the Fleet, the strange backwater behind Chesil Beach that 'seemed neither to belong to the sea nor to any recognizable portion of the earth' and which is in itself a vivid embodiment of his interior state.

The saltish nature of these *stranded* waters, subject to risings and fallings in regard to their level, but never roused to any tumult comparable to the

51. *Weymouth Sands*, pp. 172–3.
52. ibid., p. 173.
53. ibid., p. 565.

outer sea, gives to their sandy reaches, when they are traversed or even skirted by an observant wayfarer, a quality that is unique. The spot has a strange metallic look, a livid forlornness, as if the brackish element in its mud had not only killed any ordinary plant-growth in its salt-bitten bosom, but had rendered its own amphibious, marine mosses sea-pale, sea-chilly and sea-blighted.[54]

No overt comparison is made between Magnus and the place in which he finds himself: he is simply placed there and outer and inward aspects combine in a single picture.

The sea likewise dominates the lives of the other characters. One critical moment comes during the great storm on the Chesil Bank when Cattistock plunges into the waves to rescue a drowning man, to the delight of the crowds and the chagrin of the Jobber, who finds his purposes mocked by the man's apparent heroism. (But with typical Powysian irony we are to learn that Cattistock performed his deed out of a love of histrionics, and that the victim is non-existent.) The sea likewise dominates Sylvanus's private world. He lives on the far tip of a headland, Portland Bill; and is himself frequently likened to a sea-serpent in appearance. The serpent is a frequent symbol of sex and of magic: significantly the inn on the Isle of Portland where the Jobber and Perdita part and are reunited is called The Sea-Serpent's Head. It is here too that the tragic aspect of the novel is made more evident, when young Sue Gadget, the landlord's daughter feels that 'all the waves of the sea did not contain water enough to wash out the pity and trouble and pain and weariness of being alive in this world'.[55]

The sands from which the book takes its title are, however, the real place of revelation. It is here that Dr. Mabon utters his oracle, attended by the waif-like Caddie Water, the one child in Powys's portrait gallery who resembles the typical little girl of Victorian fiction, both innocent and ailing. A great tenderness lies over this incident. The sands are where the land and sea meet, and Powys contrasts the inhabitants of the dry sands, the mothers and fathers and aunts and uncles, and all the ordinary human bustle of everyday life, with the wet sands 'imprinted by the "printless" feet, light, immortal, bare, of what might easily have been the purer spirits of an eternal class-ical childhood, happy and free, in some divine limbo of unassailable play-time'.[56] In his capacity to blend natural observation with an awareness of the distillation of that observation in art and literature Powys resembles Walter Pater. Again and again he achieves these effects of broadening out from the particular to the universal, to evoke the notion of Platonic archetypes. This is furnished in this

54. ibid., p. 552.   55. ibid., p. 566.   56. ibid., p. 457.

particular novel by the numerous and beautiful descriptions of wind
and sea and sands and marsh, and above all of the light of dawn.
The private dreams and fears of the various characters are taken up
into a freer atmosphere that is partly of their own creating: and
this is conveyed in a style that is notably less exclamatory and inflated than that of the book's two predecessors.

The weak point of *Weymouth Sands* is that of the other Wessex
novels—external plausibility. Cattistock is no more convincing than is
Philip Crow as a man of affairs, though, as with Philip, the inner
man in his private mental world is real enough. More important a
failure is the working out of Jobber Skald's vendetta: it is insuffi-
ciently motivated, the rights and wrongs of the quarrymen which
are its ostensible cause being barely touched upon. Powys was, one
feels, simply not interested. The dialogue too is often awkward, and
there is rather too much 'Mummerset', amusing though Powys's use
of dialect can be. Tissty and Tossty are especially implausible; nor is
it easy to believe that Jerry Cobbold is as famous as he is supposed
to be. Powys's knowledge of Weymouth does in this respect serve
him ill: there is at times a sense of self-indulgence about the descriptions, and the repeated cataloguing of the town's chief landmarks
soon becomes a bore.

And more than any other of the novels *Weymouth Sands* suffers
from the lack of an adequate dramatic framework. There is no real
development; events simply happen one after the other and are
essentially static. As usual, the chapters are far too long. (Indeed
most of Powys's novels could do with a judicious subdividing of the
chapters: they would then seem and feel far less unwieldy than
they do at present.) Powys has little gift (though *Maiden Castle* and
Wolf Solent do to some extent give the lie to this) for describing the
dramatic interaction of his characters; and *Weymouth Sands* in
particular reads at times like a series of monologues. But at its best,
as in the 'Punch and Judy' chapter, the book achieves a narrative
method peculiarly Powys's own. Through it he is able to relate a
group of seemingly disparate events to one another by a linking use of
imagery. In this particular chapter the cry of Punch at the beginning, a cry of cruelty and mockery, is balanced by a cry of exas-
perated anger at the end from the other clown, Jerry Cobbold.
Between these two cries we read of Magnus's disappointment with
Curly, the Jobber's despair at having lost Perdita, the physical agony
of James Loder, and the committal of Sylvanus to the asylum. All
these things are narrated against the background of everyday doings
on the sea-front; and the sadness of them is offset by the vision
of nature and the healing power of the inanimate, as mediated

through the mind of Ruth Loder, and by the oracle spoken by the new doctor who is presented obliquely as something not unlike a Messianic figure: Magnus sees in him 'a specimen of a new type of personality in the world'.[57] But the movement of the chapter remains unobtrusive. Powys does not erect obvious signposts in the manner of some novelists—which may be one reason for his critical neglect. Instead he relies on a unity of tone and colouring to make his points, and in his best writing he works with a fine and furious instinct that produces some of the most brilliantly sustained narrative passages in our literature. *Weymouth Sands* may not be notably rich in these, but it has its own peculiar excellences, and its central message is integral to Powys's work as a whole, the final articulation of something that all the previous novels had been leading up to, namely that, as Dr. Brush discovers in his dealings with Sylvanus, 'not only from the surface of that sea within us *but from all levels and depths of it* we have the power of coming into contact with one another'.[58] Moreover, it does also provide a definition of John Cowper's own art as a novelist. Perdita, listening to Jerry Cobbold at the piano, asks herself the meaning of what she hears, and answers for her creator as she does so. 'Is it ... some modern musician imitating the old style? No, no! This is no imitation. This is life itself, life filling out the patterns and rules that it has made, *as if they were sails*, to carry it beyond itself, over unknown seas!'[59]

4

Maiden Castle was written after Powys's return to England in 1934, and was in part the fruit of a stay in Dorchester before his removal to live in Corwen in North Wales. Alone among the later books it returns to the themes of the earlier novels; and its peculiar interest lies in the fact that it both brings the *Wolf Solent* theme to a specific conclusion, and relates it to the metaphysical speculations aired in the two novels that succeeded it. *Maiden Castle* is, as Wilson Knight observes, 'a transition work'.[60]

It is perhaps the most Powysian of all the novels, the one in which the influence of other writers is least apparent. Here another of John Cowper's boyhood homes is the scene. Dorchester, with its memories of the Roman legions, a bustling county town very different from the dream-haunted religio-commercial Glastonbury, is described as

57. *Weymouth Sands*, p. 494.
58. ibid., p. 506.
59. ibid., p. 211.
60. G. Wilson Knight: *The Saturnian Quest* (Methuen, 1964), p. 49.

the scene of, and the means to, a man's awakening to reality. The novel is the author's most considered treatment of the theme of impotence, both sexual and emotional. The plot is less elaborate than that of *Wolf Solent*, but both its characters and events are more eccentric. The hero—or anti-hero—is called Dud No-Man, a name invented by himself and one which fits. He emerges from his self-enclosed world to a certain extent only, enough to realize his personal inadequacies but not enough to overcome them. Settled in Dorchester to write a historical novel, he befriends a young circus rider called Wizzie Ravelston, 'buys' her from her employer (both Powys, and Hugh Walpole in *Rogue Herries*, were guilty of plagiarizing *The Mayor of Casterbridge*), and sets up house with her. His deliberate refusal or nervous inability (it is never wholly clear which) to consummate their union, and his bachelor self-sufficiency and inward solitariness prove too much for her, however, and she leaves him, going to America with a young girl painter called Thuella Wye. Bewildered and half-defiant, Dud settles down again to wait for her return. In the intervening time he has discovered that his father, hitherto unknown, is a Welsh eccentric called Enoch or Uryen Quirm, who is seeking to revive the power of the old gods formerly worshipped at Maiden Castle, the great earthwork that rises outside Dorchester. Uryen is endowed with strange semi-magical powers, but when he loses faith in himself they forsake him and he dies. In these two aspects of the novel, the story of Uryen and the story of Wizzie and her lover, are to be found its twofold nature. It is a drama about self-enclosure and the impact upon it of another person; and it is a portrait of the human desire for power.

Dorchester is vividly present throughout the book as a symbol of the continuity of civilization, its atmosphere as is usual with Powys evoked less through sights than through sounds and smells.

Like the balmy air of a placid valley drifting over the grazing backs of the multitudinous cattle ... the combined scent of foliage and flowers, of dust and chimney-smoke, of sun-warmed masonry and mossy walls, came forth to meet them. But it was as if this 'Sunday smell' of Dorchester contained something quite beyond all these familiar scents. It seemed to bring with it—as if the whole ancient place had been one deep vase of thick-pressed *pot-pourri*—a subtle perfume that was like the sweet dust of long-buried generations, a consecrated secular dust from which all that was foul in mortality had long since evaporated, leaving only a thrice-purged residue, a holy deposit, the dust of what was inviolable in ashes, indestructible in embers, destined to perish only with our human senses.[61]

61. *Maiden Castle* (Macdonald, 1966), p. 390.

Dorchester's Roman past sounds repeatedly through the book both in the descriptions of the ancient ramparts and the great earthworks of Maumbury Rings and Poundbury, and in the more diffused evocations of Roman order and activity, that practicality which alone can assure the future. Maiden Castle itself is described with the kind of power which Powys shares with Hardy and Lawrence. It exerts a strong influence on the inhabitants; and in the magnificent chapter called Midsummer Eve, becomes the place where truth, both about personality and about relationships, is brought to light.

Names play an important part in the book's texture, especially nicknames. At the centre is Dud No-Man, a bastard who, on discovery of his bastardy, adopts this name of his own invention as an expression of his loss of identity. The search for his identity is furthered through his relationship with Uryen, Wizzie, and her own bastard child Lovie—he discovers, that is, the necessary human relationships of father, mate, and child, even though he eventually loses all three. Before meeting Wizzie his life is dominated by his Welsh mother and his wife Mona, both of them dead.

He had decided to come to Dorchester for several reasons, but as he pondered over his motives now, he tried to idealize them into a longing to solve, if he only might, on the spot where his own dead lay, the ultimate meaning of death itself. The phrase 'where his own dead lay' was already a pregnant one to No-man, for living as he had done for the last ten years almost entirely in the thoughts about these two women he had come by degrees to link up his whole conception of our dim human chances of immortality with their two figures.

If our survival of death, he had come to feel, depended on the intensity with which we lived our individual life, the intensity with which we grasped life's most symbolic essences then it was 'the Woman from Wales' who was more likely to dodge annihilation; whereas if our chance depended on the power we develop for sinking our individuality in others' lives, why then it was the dead Mona who had the better start.[62]

Here is the kernel of the novel. Dud's life with Wizzie is shipwrecked in part upon that very capacity to enjoy life's essences by himself which he inherits from his mother; and yet it is Mona, to judge from the strange incident at Hardy's statue which closes the Midsummer Eve chapter, who has the last word. There Dud, as if in trance, scrawls her name across the sketch of the figure of the stone goddess unearthed at Maiden Castle, the statue of one of those ancient powers who, according to Uryen, are the keepers of the ultimate secrets. At the end of the novel Dud is left alone with his solitary sensations; but he is wiser for his life with Wizzie, and

62. ibid., pp. 20–1.

aware that society as much as solitude is necessary for his well-being.

Dud's search for identity is bound up with his feeling for the past. His attitude to novel-writing is that of a medium: he feels himself to be in psychic contact with his heroine. Similarly he is dominated by his relationship with his dead wife, to whom he has made love in his mind nightly before meeting Wizzie. And it is always unconsummated love, an aspect of his self-enclosure and indicative of the sterility of his inner life. Uryen and Wizzies' seducer, the repulsive old circus manager Funky, repel him by their earthiness as much as their ugliness. His obsession with the town's past constantly excludes Wizzie; while his mythologizing habit of conferring nicknames on their acquaintances is a withdrawal from reality and the imposition of his own personality upon theirs.

Dud is indeed the fullest piece of sardonic portraiture in Powys's fiction, a development from Wolf Solent and from Magnus Muir. His inability to lose his temper, to be what Wizzie calls 'a man'; his small personal oddities and habits; his internal colloquys, are all described with wry humour but never sentimentalized, so that he retains our sympathy. The numerous scenes in which he quarrels with Wizzie are portrayed with poignance and realism, and are notably convincing in their demonstration of the differing tempos at which two people can live together; but they also serve to keep Dud in focus, and therefore make it easier to remain in sympathy with him. The story is an ironic one: when Dud finds a real as distinct from an imagined past in the person of his father he does not relish it. But Uryen prophetically miscalls him 'Mr. Newman' on their first meeting. Dud finds the present in the person of Wizzie, only to lose her. He is left alone, confirmed though chastened in his life-illusion. Some kind of balance has been struck.

Maiden Castle is more ostentatiously designed as a portrait of contending forces than is *Wolf Solent*. Neither Dud nor Wizzie is among those who can settle down and blend their individual lives with that of another person: the creative faculty is too strong in both of them. But they are both released for a purposeful existence: through Dud, Wizzie discovers her real devotion to her profession, and through Wizzie, Dud is brought out of a world of private fantasy into a life in which he learns to use his idiosyncrasies creatively. The subordinate characters are grouped around them, and each one has symbolic connotations. Of the men, two are contrasted to Dud in their philosophic outlook—the old Platonist Teucer Wye and the communist Claudius Cask; and both these men are presented as sterile life forces. The two others, Uryen and Funky, have affinities with pagan earth magic and fecundity, and Dud is afraid of both of them. At one point old Funky is likened to a rain-goblin, reminding us of the sinister part played by rain in *Wolf Solent*. The cleanliness of Wye and Claudius is stressed (Wye is also something of a dandy) as against the dirt and physical repulsiveness of the other pair. Dud, like Wolf, has to learn to accept without wincing the ugly and excremental elements in life. Powys, himself an extremely fastidious man, was aware of the dangers of hyper-refinement.

The contrast between the orderly social atmosphere of Greece and Rome, and the primitive magic of Wales (made palpable in the shape of Uryen) is paralleled by the contrasted influences of Dud's wife and mother; and the struggle between his need for Wizzie on the one hand and for his life of romantic dreaming on the other is a further aspect of the conflict between Rome and Wales, as indeed are the roles of all the women. Wye's two daughters represent the intellectual, physically sterile forces. Jennie, the elder, in her refusal to surrender to Claudius's desire for her, incarnates a fear of the physical which is an aspect of Dud's dilemma; while Thuella is another boy–girl figure of ambiguous sexual tastes. There is a remarkable and characteristic scene in which she and Dud, sitting beside a stagnant pond, indulge in a kind of arrested erotic frenzy without actually touching each other. Powys is in this novel especially concerned with sexuality in its repressed or cerebral forms. The other two main women characters, Funky's old wife Grummer, and Uryen's wife Nance, are both of them 'earth women', the one sinister, the other kindly. Nance's warm sexuality is contrasted with Jennie's hardness; both Grummer and Thuella are attracted to Wizzie—there is a most elaborate network of relationships, each one of which illuminates the central contrast between the life of mental day-dream and the life of bodily love and personal commitment. It is Powys's strength that while demonstrating the necessity of normal sex and worldly wisdom he does full justice to the more unbalanced and extravagant aspects of human nature and its desires.

As a portrait of man's longing for power and fulfilment the book is also elaborately organized. Power is related to desire, mental and sexual, and to desire frustrated and desire fulfilled. Powys, a man singularly lacking in worldly ambition and conscious of a reservoir of spiritual energy within himself, was especially interested in those men who, without much practical ability, were gifted with oratorical or therapeutic powers, and he has created a memorable number of them. John Geard and Sylvanus Cobbold are two very different specimens of the type; and Uryen provides a third variant. He is a less sympathetic figure than his predecessors. Powys has a remarkable capacity, nowhere more evident than in these 'magician' figures, for combining the extravagant and the fantastic with the brutally realistic. Uryen's speech to Dud about his inmost beliefs strikes the first note.

'I became convinced, not from any revelation, you understand, but because of this *necessity* I'm under of bearing the pain of the world, the pain of what beats against the wall, that in one incarnation after another I've been the same Power! ... I've been the Power that's older than all these new gods, the Power that's deepest of all, for it's got Death in it as well as life. It's this Power ... that beats in its pain against the wall of the world. You can cry out, lad, if you like, that it's all fantasy and illusion, you can cry out that your excavations set it at nought; but I tell you that sooner or later you'll know it as I know it! I tell you it's in all the pain of the world where love turns to hate and beats against the wall! It's in the despair of all the sterile love that's ever been since the beginning! Don't you see, what force there is in sterile love? Why, my dear boy, it's the strongest force there is! Rampant desire unfulfilled—why, there's nothing it can't do! Stir up sex *till it would put out the sun* and then keep it sterile! That's the trick. That's the grand trick of all spiritual life.'[36]

This is in fact a dramatizing of elements already in the novel, such as Dud's own love-making and his trance with Thuella, which gives him a delight that seems to raise him to some superhuman state, and which is related to his cult of aesthetic sensations. As he tells his companions in his own turn,

'when ... I come on a patch of green moss on a grey wall, or catch the peculiar scent of trodden grass, I get a sensation that's more important than what you call "love" or anything else, nearer the secret of things too! It *is* "love" in a certain sense; but it's love of life itself and of something that comes to us through life!'[64]

This 'something that comes to us through life' is what Powys has been hinting at in Adrian Sorio's book about destruction, in Betsy Cooper's Cimmery Land, in Wolf's mythology, and, in *A Glastonbury Romance*, Mr. Evans's beliefs about Merlin's mysterious 'Esplumeoir'. In *Maiden Castle* Powys subjects these mystical intimations to a closer scrutiny through the confrontation between Uryen and his son. Uryen cannot survive the publication of his beliefs in print: 'by publishing his life-illusion' he has 'killed his heart'.[65] It is Dud who, at the end of the novel, voices his own and Uryen's attitude to his life.

63. *Maiden Castle*, pp. 251–2.
64. ibid., p. 365.
65. ibid., p. 482.

'We both live at a somewhat different level from most people ... with us ... the actual substance of our planet down to the centre of the earth, with all the elements that work on it out of space, is something—its mystery, its power for good and evil—that we can't take, as most people do, just for granted! We think of it all the time ... and to him it always meant—this vast weight of matter – something separating us from the real reality.'[66]

Dud himself, while living in this awareness, refuses Uryen's romantic quest. 'He could *not* live, as this dead man had done, in a wild search for the life behind life. One life at a time! But neither would he close one single cranny or crevice of his mind to the "intimations of immortality" that in this place and at this hour were so thick about him.'[67] Powys's own scepticism speaks here: he saw, and puts it on the lips of Christie Malakite, that all philosophies were intellectual expressions of emotional responses, that they were to be used for the practical purpose of maintaining man's sanity in an existence which by its very nature was a threat to his identity. To enjoy life, to respond to his utmost to his own living consciousness, was the fundamental rule of life without which all social contacts would prove sterile. And fulfilled desire is as much a part of this as unfulfilled desire: Wizzie's departure to follow her vocation is a protest against Dud's kind of sexual love. (Powys uses her circus horse as a symbol of fulfilment, much in the way that Lawrence might have done, though more sparingly.) Even the repulsive old Funky has his value: despite his rape of her he represents something positive to Wizzie, a force of life itself.

Dud's revulsion from Uryen and his hatred of the fact that Uryen is his father are uncomfortably convincing: Powys here succeeds in presenting a relationship that is at once psychologically credible and suggestive of something permanent in human nature. His boldness in handling the grotesque, and his precision in catching the precise nervous reaction to it, are well illustrated in the description of the two men sitting on the slopes of Maiden Castle while Uryen tells his son why he has changed his name from Enoch.

[Dud] noted that under his father's haunches lay a daisy, whose brittle stalk had been crushed, but whose rose-tinged petals emerged quite intact. In the process of fidgetting about to make his position comfortable, Mr. Quirm had got the bottom of his coat rumpled up above the seat of his trousers, and these little rose-ringed petals peeped out from beneath his rump in a manner that was distressing to No-man.

Dud did not go so far as to entreat his parent to move, though the

66. ibid., p. 495.
67. ibid., p. 496.

phrase: 'Excuse me, sir, but you're sitting on a daisy,' hovered on the tip of his tongue, but the presence of the daisy in that position did something to increase his nervous revolt. He had a sensation as if he could actually feel the man's huge, dusky, smouldering soul heaving and labouring there, in the centre of that hot mass of ill-smelling, sedentary flesh and blood, and in the intensity of his reaction against the seed that begat him now he thought to himself: 'I'll get up and make him come on *before he's got it out*; and every time he tries to tell me about it, every time he mentions this damned word "Uryen" I'll change the conversation.'[68]

And yet Uryen remains an impressive, haunting figure: his mad quest may have its ludicrous side, but he has more vitality than his opponents: indeed it is the major weakness of *Maiden Castle* that the supporting characters are so unreal, Claudius and Teucer's son Dunbar especially existing more as mouthpieces than as living people. The vitality of the book resides at the centre, in the finely observed relationship between Dud and Wizzie. Despite its outlandish beginnings this is a most convincing study. Their quarrels have the ring of truth; and still more touching are their bewildered attempts to make contact with each other, attempts which nearly always fail.

She looked steadily at him and their eyes clung to each other . . . Neither of the two seemed to wish to be the first to look away; but the girl didn't feel as if either of them were thinking solely of the other. They each seemed to be looking *through* the other, down some long receding vista of future days.

Almost as instinctively as if No-man had been Lovie, the girl suddenly put out her hand to straighten the collar of his coat. There must have been something about this natural gesture that struck the man as unusual; for the character of the expression in his eyes completely changed and in its changing caused a change in hers, too. They no longer looked through each other, thinking of their own lives. They looked *at* each other, wondering, confused, embarrassed, and with a sort of tentative shyness.[69]

Such small details go almost unnoticed in the sprawling body of Powys's work; but *Maiden Castle* is full of them. For if Powys does not as a rule show us people interacting dramatically in terms of character development, he is none the less supremely realistic when it comes to depicting the shock and suffering of conflicting egos, fixed in their own self-sufficiency. Dud, who is described at one point as 'a malicious scapegoat', gets on everybody's nerves; and the same impulse which led Powys to castigate himself in the *Autobiography*

68. *Maiden Castle*, p. 245.
69. ibid., pp. 344–5.

seems to lie behind the abuse hurled at Dud by the frantic Jennie.

'You thought only of your own selfish sensations when you first brought Wizzie here ... It was nothing to you that you took her life away from her ... Nothing to you that you broke up her career and spoilt her natural self-expression for ever ... as long as you can hoist a woman up into your own romantic fancies, you think you've done all that's necessary ... You're too selfish, or too depraved, even to give her a child ... You get round her by your damned "sympathy" and your romantic talk, and then go and keep her shut up like a common tart ... The truth is, my good staring friend, you don't know what real feeling is!'[70]

The cause of this outburst is in part Dud's appearance, with his 'mouth open and ... a tiny dribble of saliva ... descending his chin', and with his 'unruffled air of martyred helplessness that seemed to be murmuring "Hit me! Hit me!"'[71] This is indeed a novel which explores the whole nature of nervous tension. Thuella and her father do, in a sense, complement the relationship between Dud and Wizzie, an enforced family relationship taking the place of the others' free association. Powys succeeds brilliantly in conveying just how irritating an old man can be, and at the same time catches a note of authentic domestic anguish in Teucer's cry, 'You've put your cold cream on my shelf, *next to my books!*'[72] The whole of the Glymes passages are a chilling portrayal of two people living on each other's nerves. And the suppressed irritation of Thuella and her father, Thuella's own repressed eroticism, the emotional frustration of Jennie Dearth, and Dud's own sterile love-making are all of them examples of that restrained energy which was, for Uryen, the source of real spiritual power. Just as the old gods lie buried under Maiden Castle, so do the passions lie buried in the people of the novel. Uryen's beliefs are in the end neither denied nor confirmed: they exist as a pointer, as a way of putting into a certain perspective an element in human consciousness that today would have a specifically psychological reference; and they are revealed as the logical extension of Dud's own self-centred world.

To say this is to indicate where the peculiar nature of these Wessex novels makes itself felt. They are psychological myths, romances of much outward circumstantiality and realistic detail about certain states of mind and their interaction. They project a world of their own which corresponds to feelings and perceptions deep within the human mind. Outwardly implausible though much of *Maiden*

70. ibid., pp. 266–7. 71. ibid., p. 266. 72. ibid., p. 182.

Castle may be, it takes on a hypnotic reality in the encounters between its leading characters. *Wolf Solent* and its two successors, although full of anachronisms, have clear links with some recognizable outward world; but *Maiden Castle* is more like an abstract of life. This is not to say that it is not life-like; but its truth is the truth of poetry rather than of prose.

CHAPTER FOUR

The Welsh Novels

1

JOHN COWPER POWYS was sixty-two years old when he moved to Wales, but almost thirty years of life and writing still lay before him. The labours of the last five years might well have proved sufficient for a lesser man; and indeed the *Autobiography* and the Wessex novels are an achievement sufficient in themselves to validate his claim to greatness. Nothing is more remarkable about this most remarkable man, however, than his abiding and continuing vitality. The return from America was a return to roots; it was not, however, to the roots that might have been expected, the Dorset and Somerset countryside, but to far older ones, to the country from which the Powyses originally sprang, and which had, as he himself records, exercised a spell upon his imagination ever since he was a young man. But the move to Wales was not a withdrawal to some sentimental dream-world. Powys took an active interest in Welsh affairs, made friends with his Welsh neighbours, set out to learn the Welsh language, and plunged into an exhaustive study of Welsh history and traditions. What the landscape of Wales meant to him the reading of his novels will show. A whole new life had started; and with it a second novelistic career. His vigour was unabated, his power of imagination as intense as ever; and if the contemporary world seemed to recede from his vision this was not, as the *Letters to Louis Wilkinson* make clear, because he lost interest in it, but because his mind, always alert to the supra-temporal aspect of things, found in Welsh fable and mythology a more satisfying vehicle for his view of life. In choosing to write about Owen Glendower and Merlin he was choosing a world which was contemporary with himself, and a more appropriate way of expressing the self he really was.

Powys's first novel of his 'second period' stands out, even in a body of work like his, as something of an oddity. *Morwyn: or The Vengeance of God* is a strange blend of fantasy, mythological lore, and personal testament. It was described by the author himself as 'my anti-vivisection romance'; but although denunciations of vivisection take up much of its space, it is a good deal more than a tract. It forms, rather, a prelude to the two great Welsh novels; and, like

Maiden Castle, it clarifies and develops philosophical and personal attitudes explored in the earlier books. It is told in the first person, the narrator being an obvious self-portrait; and the book is in some ways the most lucid and succinct account of his philosophical position. One says 'succinct' advisedly, since, although Powys was to write other fantasies, *Morwyn* differs from its successors by its greater coherence and economy. It is the swiftest and most simple of the novels.

Beginning in the Berwyn mountains at the back of Powys's home at Corwen, the story tells of a descent into hell. The narrator, a rather unconvincing half-pay captain (he never really shows any signs of his alleged military past), is precipitated by a meteorite into the lower regions of the earth, together with his dog, the spaniel Black Peter, the Welsh girl Morwyn, and her father, who is a vivisectionist. They find themselves in a cavernous region peopled by the shades of all those guilty of sadistic cruelty in their earthly life. The vivisectionist has been killed in the fall (his new ghostly body is ingeniously described) but his spirit continues to accompany Morwyn and the narrator as they try to escape from the underworld.

They are speedily joined by the shades of Torquemada and the Marquis de Sade, and later by those of Calvin and the Emperor Nero. This level of hell is peopled by lost spirits, who are now allowed to do whatever they like, one favourite occupation being the watching on television of vivisectional experiments. It is not a place of punishment, but a self-created world cut off from the rest of life or afterlife; and within this world the shades have the power to do mischief to the living, to the extent at any rate of frightening them into madness. Much of the story deals with the attempts of Morwyn and the narrator to escape from them, hampered in part by Morwyn's continuing loyalty to her father. Their escape is finally engineered by the Welsh bard Taliessin, the traditional mouthpiece of Welsh bardic wisdom and inspiration, who is the only human being who has ever entered hell for reasons of simple intellectual curiosity. (He is to reappear in Powys's fiction in a very different guise, in *Porius*.) In Taliessin's coracle a descent is made into the abyss of hell itself, where, in a powerfully described desolate sea-landscape, the travellers come upon the twin horrors of the gods of religion and science, erected in the first place by men, and enlarged continually by men's dreams of fear and cruelty. The landscape suggests something primeval, and monsters like those of the Jurassic age are sporting in the 'dark, oily water'. Far out in this sea two monstrous leviathans for ever rend each other with horrific cries and a noisome stench. Powys here pictures a struggle at the heart of the creative process, the horror out of which love and beauty must be born. The fact that the narrator finds a certain ecstatic fascination in what he sees suggests that this is a kind of stage in human development, a fundamental strife that lies beneath the more overt forms of cruelty. It is the second level of hell.

But below the abyss there lies a greater secret—the mysterious place where Saturn and Rhea sleep until the return of the age of gold, on the threshold of which Merlin too lies sleeping in his 'Esplumeoir' or secret hiding-place. Hope is hidden in a place below or beyond hell. Here the magic of Merlin has the effect of turning the torturers into their own victims: in his treatment of retribution Powys always portrays it as a law, not as something to be inflicted, but as something inherent in nature. The golden age may lie sleeping but it is at the heart of things. However, even in this holy place Powys's irony and sense of bathos do not desert him: the great judge Rhadamanthus is presented as a pitiable figure (justice, human justice, has no real power over evil) and the torturers can even penetrate the sanctuary. But justice has the power of forgiveness: the giant Tytyrus is eased of his hurt (though the narrator receives a mysterious wound in the groin), and against the mocking laughter of Democritus a way of escape is found whereby Morwyn departs on a mission of conversion into the New World (though not much success is predicted for this) and the narrator returns home to Wales, receiving on the way a vision of the Elysian Fields, where he is comforted by Powys's supreme master, Rabelais.

'You are going back into your own world, dear cod,' he said gently, 'and may that Intellectual Sphere, whose Centre is everywhere and Circumference nowhere keep you in His Almighty Protection. *He* is the System-of-Things, my honest friend, and *not* these false gods. He works slowly, but He works surely, for His ways are not the ways of power and force, but the ways of mercy and pity. Beware of those who look only to the future; for all true advance is also a return. The sleeping-place of the Age of God is in the depths of every human heart; and to this must all revert. Bloody religion and bloody science are not forever. At the bottom of the world is pain; but below the pain is hope. Be of good cheer, dear cod, He is overcoming the world. There is knowledge; but He is not in the knowledge. There is religion; but He is not in the religion. Wherever a man refuses to do evil that good may come, wherever a man is merciful and pitiful *even unto his hurt*, there and there only is the great and true God, who is below all, and above all and in us all!'[1]

Powys nowhere expressed his message and beliefs more simply or movingly than here. His humanism is of the most traditional kind,

1. *Morwyn: or The Vengeance of God* (Cassell & Co., 1937), pp. 320–1.

but what makes it so impressive is the thoroughness with which it is grasped. Reverence for all life is at the heart of it, and a belief in the rights of every single entity. It is before this conviction that 'everything that lives is holy' that all scientific investigation, all religious belief must be judged. Powys, although he rarely mentions William Blake, is of Blake's world, and in the great tradition of the seers and visionaries.

What is especially notable about *Morwyn* is its coherence. Powys's narrative method is always leisurely and repetitive, but this is less noticeable here than elsewhere; and the adventure has a logical development. The attacks upon vivisection, while too reiterated to be effective, lead up to the final affirmation of Rabelais. Throughout the book we are made aware of a kind of dialectic of creation; and there is a real honesty about it, a seriousness of concern that overrides its eccentricity and extravagance. It is informed from start to finish by a spirit of questing curiosity, mediated half-humorously through the psychological reactions of the narrator. The marvels are all part of a greater marvel that includes the author's own mind and temperament.

Nevertheless *Morwyn* fails to realize Powys at his best. The descriptions of hell, though careful and meticulous, are not without monotony. The character drawing is perfunctory, and the historical shades are given no distinctive personal colouring. Morwyn herself is simply an idealized embodiment of the sylph-like figures of whom Powys writes more interestingly elsewhere. The most vivid person after the narrator is Black Peter, one of the best-observed dogs in fiction. He provides a touchstone of reality at every turn.

Morwyn is an outline of John Cowper Powys's vision in its fullness. It demonstrates the mystery of cruelty in the heart of the creation; the power of the imagination to shape reality itself; and the paramount importance of the Rabelaisian Tao. It reflects Powys's lack of dogmatism, his realism, his compassion and feeling for the inanimate. More notably it illustrates his faith in and his feeling for the mystical significance of sex. And all this is mediated through the Welsh myths and his own devotion to the great masters of the Greek and European traditions. His final conclusion is that what may be called the magical view of life is wiser than the scientific. It is a pity that his vehemence should be so one-sided. He is less concerned to be fair to the scientist than to the priest, and his references to scientific work are lacking in his usual balanced sanity. He loves more wisely than he hates.

2

Powys's command of narrative, so evident in *Morwyn*, supports with ease the vast chronicle of *Owen Glendower*, a chronicle only a little shorter than *A Glastonbury Romance*. This is the most detached, the most relaxed, the most Olympian of the novels, and the most entirely satisfying. In Welsh history Powys had found the perfect vehicle for the expression of his philosophical viewpoint and dramatic gifts; in it his imaginative world was able to take unfettered shape.

The novel is at one and the same time a factually accurate account of Owen's rebellion against the English overlords, and an account of the fortunes of the romantic spirit in the hazards of daily life. In the first respect it is an amazingly vivid creation. The whole background of fifteenth-century Wales is presented with unobtrusive artistry. Not only are the descriptions of clothing, food, buildings, furnishings, and all the outward apparatus of civilized living precise and yet casual, but the ways of thought, the mental perspective of the time are brought before us and related to our own. Thus at one point the Thomist Father Pascentius remarks that

'Every age ... feels itself to be worse and more wicked than the preceding ones. Our age does, as you say, suffer from breaking down of faith and chivalry and from the grievous imputations implied in the mere existence of the anti-Pope; but you must remember that all great virtues carry their defects, I might say their *curse*, with them. Things were done under the urge of faith that sicken us in these enlightened days. Between ourselves, my son, I think the worst aspect of *our* age is the *intelligence* of its cruelty. King Hal, for instance, in his burning of heretics, is influenced by no old-fashioned wrath against blasphemies. It's a pure political move, to gain favour ...'[2]

Here Powys is using the past to speak prophetically of the present, and at the same time asserting the contemporaneity of every age. This is done in a variety of ways throughout the book, as when another of the characters 'could remember catching sight of the old-fashioned, brown-robed begging friar under a heavy Norman arch amid the flamboyant modern buildings and thinking how much and more simple, more honest, more close to Nature life must have been in the old days'.[3] This novel, like Powys's whole output, is a corrective to false notions about the nature of modernity. On the other hand it may be argued that in their interior monologues and re-

2. *Owen Glendower* (John Lane, The Bodley Head, 1942), p. 624.
3. ibid., p. 88.

actions the characters are more Powysian than fifteenth century; but this is only to pinpoint the fact that Powys is using the fifteenth century, just as he used 'contemporary' Glastonbury or Dorchester, to present his own picture of human existence and its dilemmas. His use of the past is functional, not merely informative or aesthetic.

In two essays in *Obstinate Cymric* he speaks of his interest in the Welsh aboriginals, and in the ancient traditions of the people. What he found in Wales was

a link between the spring-time of christendom and our modern age; a link which the potent centuries that come between have buried so deep. There are worshippers of the flow of time to whom such a living link between past and present means nothing; but for those of us who refuse to pay to time such unphilosophical tribute it means everything.[4]

In another essay in the same collection he brings his understanding of the Welsh to the question of the relation of oppressors to oppressed which he had first raised in *Wood and Stone*.

If ethnological professors find alive today in Wales people with skulls whose shape reverts, in a steady father to son ascent, to the paleolithic era, it seems probable that no race in the world, except the Jews, have felt the iron enter so deeply into their souls, the *literal iron*, of being domin-ated by the more cruel weapons of races that mentally, emotionally, and spiritually they felt to be inferior to themselves.[5]

It is easy to understand from this how Powys, with his instinctive fellow feeling with the downtrodden and defeated, should have felt himself to be among a sympathetic people. Their very history as well as their mythology provided the perfect objective correlative for his own subjective philosophy.

The very geography of the land and its climatic peculiarities, the very nature of its mountains and rivers, the very falling and lifting of the mists that waver above them, all lend themselves, to a degree unknown in any other earthly region, to what might be called the *mythology of escape*. This is the secret of the land. This is the secret of the people of the land. Other races love and hate, conquer and are conquered. This race avoids and evades, pursues and is pursued. Its soul is forever making a double flight. It flees into a circuitous *Inward*. It retreats into a circuitous *Outward*.[6]

The vast age, too, of this civilization held an attraction for him, and in *Porius* he was to plunge into the tangled world of Welsh myth-ology. In *Owen* too the mythological element provides a kind of

4. *Obstinate Cymric* (The Druid Press, 1947), p. 47.
5. ibid., p. 83.
6. *Owen Glendower*, p. 889.

continuous undertow. But for the most part it is the outward action
which carries the message of the tale. What had been expressed in
terms of dramatic psychology and analysis in the earlier novels is
here presented mythologically in a story. Wales and the Welsh
become symbols of the human spirit. 'Owen is Owen still! ... They
can out-sail us, out-fight us, out-trade us, out-laugh us—but they can't
out-last us! It'll be from our mountains and in our tongue, when the
world ends, that the last defiance of man's fate will rise.'[7]

In *Owen Glendower* there is far less authorial comment and digres-
sion than in the earlier books. It is Powys's most objective work.
The saga of a defeated nation, it also examines the nature of defeat
in relation to its two principal characters, Owen himself, and his kinsman Rhisiart.

In both of them we are presented with aspects of the romantic
vision. Rhisiart, the young Welsh–Norman clerk from Hereford is
filled with aspirations to personal glory and achievement, desirous
of redeeming the record of an ancestor who long before had treacher-
ously handed over to the English the fortress of Dinas Brān. Dinas
Brān, by now a stark ruin on an abrupt hill at the entrance to the valley of the Dee, is for Rhisiart a symbol of the romantic vision, its
foundations sunk 'in that mysterious underworld of beyond-reality
whence rise the eternal archetypes of all the refuges and all the sanc-
tuaries of the spirit', the place which he feels to be his destiny. But in
the event Rhisiart fulfils his dream in ways totally beyond any that
he could have imagined. His only contact with Dinas Brān is when
he is imprisoned there for a while as a hostage; his destiny is to serve
his kinsman Owen. And his first sight of Owen drastically modifies
his romantic ideas: he feels 'an upwelling of fierce protective pity'.

Owen's presence affected him with the tremulous heart-beating feeling
such as a young savage might experience who finds that the god of his
race—upon whose rough image he had long cast a negligent and even
critical eye—has suddenly appeared to him in the wistful and helpless
beauty of his real identity out of that familiar and neglected shrine ...
Rhisiart never again got quite the impression he received that midsummer
afternoon, and there came moments when its memory grew blurred. But
it never altogether left him; and the Owen he saw that day took his place,
easily, naturally and with a fatal inevitableness, on the ramparts of Dinas
Brān and gathered into himself their mystic enchantment.[8]

Rhisiart becomes Owen's secretary and right-hand man, ending up,
ironically enough, though quite consistently with his character, as
an English judge. He is signally unwarlike, though capable of a cer-

7. ibid., p. 781.
8. ibid., p. 122.

tain bravery when transported out of himself; he has a sadistic streak, and is an ineffective lover. His relationship with Owen's daughter Catharine is beautifully observed. He finally marries Tegolin, 'the Maid of Edeyrnion', whose devotion to the mad Friar Hugh has made her something of a local saint. Tegolin is a more shadowy figure than Catharine, but her close, almost sisterly, relationship with Rhisiart is presented as something stronger than romance.

The only woman whose body had ever lain by his body in the magic bonds of sleep was the woman now by his side. The Maid had known all the while the mystery of this bond, the fusion of their souls on that Midsummer night beneath the sub-rational, sub-passionate under-tides of sleep.

He had been oblivious of this. But it was this, and nothing less than this, that gave to his possession of her now this incredible feeling of recurrence, as if they were only returning, easily and naturally, to a link that had existed between them time out of mind.[9]

Again the stress is laid on the archetypal world of images, on a reality envisaged as subsuming rather than overarching the one we usually know.

This physio-spiritual identity manifests itself also in Rhisiart's relationship with Owen. At a particular crisis he saves Owen's life by sucking his blood from a poisoned wound, and swallowing it. This taking of Owen's life into himself is reflected in the novel by a transference from Rhisiart to Owen as the central point of consciousness, an unusual and imaginatively persuasive technical device. This is Rhisiart's finest hour; his darkest is when, in the spirit of Shakespeare's Claudio, he accepts his life at the price of his wife's dishonour. The pathos with which this is treated, as well as their later reunion, is very characteristic of Powys. Rhisiart and the Lollard Walter Brut are in prison awaiting execution. But Tegolin has procured means of remitting Rhisiart's sentence to one of imprisonment.

... the truth was that Rhisiart from the first time they met had been conscious of something in Tegolin that was stronger than himself; and upon this stronger power he had always unscrupulously leaned. And this leaning upon her had reached a sort of culminating ecstasy as he longed just now, in his weakness and his pain, to go to sleep forever upon her breast.

Thus when she talked of 'giving herself' to armourer Shore, this 'giving herself' didn't call up any image of his actual Tegolin, with her red braid pressed between her white shoulders and a strange bed, submitting to the final outrage. It rather called up a comfortable vision of Master Dickon's hearth with a great bowl of venison stew ... the images created

9. *Owen Glendower*, p. 715.

by hunger—and with the lively Julietta, of whom he'd heard Nance talk, keeping a place for him too at the table: and only a dim benevolent cloudy *blur*, resembling God the Father, to show that Tegolin had 'given herself' to anyone!

It was the weakness of his famished body that formed these dishonourable visions; and it was the escape from the barrels of tar and the red-hot prongs, and from the time it took to get it done, for he'd seen it at Hereford as a child, that made him sink into her strength as a tired sea-gull into an ocean-wave.

And as he looked at this beautiful being upon whom his life depended, and who was prepared to give him his life, he felt as if he were absolved by those soft breasts and by those white arms from the whole burden of choice, from the necessity of any decision at all! A deep in-sucking tide of infantile gratitude drew all the manliness out of him; while the expression in his eyes made so great a contrast to his hollow, emaciated cheeks, his straggly beard, his pinched hawk-nose, his narrow forehead, that the girl began to feel as if a Rhisiart, younger even than the one who had allowed her to kiss his crusader's sword and had teased her about her page's dagger, was begging her to take him on her lap, to hold him to her breast, to save him from the wolves!

Without a quiver of his mouth or a movement of his manacled limbs, the big tears of absolute weakness began to form in his eyes and to trickle down upon his beard; and she knew that whether he understood or not the price she'd paid he accepted the life she'd given him.[10]

This passage is a remarkable development from Powys's earlier work. The quietness of the style, the precision of image (for example, the appropriateness of the sea-gull, ocean-wave simile in relation to the rest of the passage), the realism of the whole approach, that yet lacks nothing in dignity, are representative of John Cowper's achievement at its very best. In a lesser writer Rhisiart's decision would be matter for bitterness or cynicism; but Powys is wise enough and fair enough to portray the whole situation in the round, and even here with a light dusting of compassionate humour.

Owen, on the other hand, is the man who finds romance thrust upon him. At the time of his coronation he destroys the crystal which he had used to determine the future, and thus symbolically resigns himself to fate. Indeed his role is for the most part a curiously passive one. He is shown as being half-sceptical of his magic powers, and these are seen to reside in a capacity for a trance-like self-detachment in the course of which he draws power from the spiritual energies within him. Believing in his own power to control events he is as disillusioned in this as he is in the failure of the expedition led by the Maid of Edeyrnion. Belief in himself is matched with dis-

10. ibid., pp. 837–8.

belief in other people's valuation of him. His failure to win a victory
in England springs from his failure to do violence to his own prin-
ciples, or more strictly to his life-illusion, by unnecessary bloodshed.

One night he awoke just before dawn . . . and he had a vision of besieging
the King and his heir, however long the siege might last, till he starved
them out! But . . . something in his own nature had balked. He thrust his
hand under his pillow of rugs and touched the rusty bronze that had been
the death of that old peace-maker of Dinas Brān; and as he did so the
impression came over him out of that vast stillness, a stillness unbroken
even by a sentry's tread, that he and his people *could afford to wait*, could
afford to wait till long after his bones were dust and Henry's bones were
dust. He knew how his own soul could escape, escape without looting
cities and ravishing women.[11]

Owen's character is singularly complex. Cruelty and magnanimity are
strangely intermingled. He can surrender the Maid to Rhisiart, and
yet cold-bloodedly consign an enemy to a lingering death. He is an
elementalist of the kind pictured in so many of John Cowper's novels,
but his powers of contemplation prove fatal to his hopes of delivering
Wales; and as a result 'there had been a curious gulf between his
feeling *about* what was happening and what actually *was* happening'. The tragedy of the book lies in the fact that 'he had carried
down with him, as in a doomed ship, every human creature he
loved'.[12]

But the final ending is not tragic but inspiring. Owen becomes a
myth, even in his lifetime. The last chapter of the novel, perhaps the
finest piece of writing that Powys ever achieved, shows him at the
moment of his death extending his life into the very air and spirit
of Wales itself. He becomes almost a part of the physical landscape,
his personal ideas, like his psychic powers, being lost in something
greater—as the priest senses in his dying cry.

. . . Glyn Dŵr still had his arms outstretched. 'Prince of Powys—Prince of
Gwynedd—Prince of Wales——' and then in a tone that made the boy
stop crying and made even Lord Talbot cross himself, 'Prince of Annwn!'
    A deep silence followed and Father Sulien said to himself: 'He was
dead before he spoke. *A spirit spoke through him.* They're holding up a
dead weight now.'[13]

The invocation of the lost world of Annwn links Owen to the golden
age of Cronos. It is typical of Powys to make his hero deficient in the
traditional heroic qualities, but to see in his life-illusion a medium

11. *Owen Glendower*, p. 821.
12. ibid., p. 562.
13. ibid., pp. 925–6.

for a dimension of life that can still be apprehended through contact with the physical. The struggle for Wales is emblematic of a more universal struggle in the human spirit; history has become a myth.

The novel thus exists as a narrative first and foremost, and is not, like most of the other books, conceived pictorially. Its numerous characters accompany the action rather than control it, however: one is perpetually conscious of the impersonal tide of events, chance, or destiny whichever way one chooses to view it. The historical events are for the most part refered to obliquely, and are secondary to the sense of the continuing undercurrents of daily life.

A silence fell upon the three of them now, a silence through which they could hear all manner of faint sounds. The silence seemed to mount up from the sea and sink down from the sky. It flowed around and around; buoying up the sounds that floated upon it, as if they'd been relaxed swimmers on a smooth tide; and the silence mingled with the sun-sparkles, too, that were rocking on the in-coming waves, and with the rare sea-scents that kept entering that turret window. But the sounds were what the silence loved best of all; and *they* rose from all manner of different directions.

They were casual sounds, drifting sounds, accidental sounds, without order and without cohesion. But they were the music of life. Some came from fishermen drying their nets on the rocks, some from seagulls along the walls of the jetty, some from cattle and sheep in the castle-meadows, some from horses and hounds in the castle-yard. They were fainter, more volatile, more ethereal than the living things that uttered them . . .

Fused together, these isolated sounds evoked a sense of the continuity of life by sea and land, a continuity simple, tranquil, universal, detached from individual hunger or desire or pain or joy.[14]

It is this constant sense of the continuity of life that gives Powys's narrative its grandeur; each event is seen in its total physical context. The ordinary and the everyday are continually present, and there is a masterly balance between the heightened moments of epic grandeur, such as the crowning of Owen or the Maid setting out for war, and the domestic littleness of every day.

Two episodes are good examples of this. Powys's basic position is clearly illustrated at one of the heightened moments of the novel when the sadism latent in Rhisiart is stirred up by the attentions of Tegolin's mother, the beautiful and perverted Lowri ferch Ffraid. He is both terrified and stirred by contact with her; but all other thoughts and feelings are driven out of his head by a pressing need to urinate. Powys adverts amusingly on this phenomenon in the

14. ibid., pp. 685–6.

Autobiography remarking that 'It presents itself to me as a *sine qua non* of any honest recital in this kind that it should at least not totally rule out the intimate miseries and reliefs of this diurnal passing of matter through the body'.[15] For Rhisiart the lesson was that 'Nature comes first ... before all good and evil, before *everything*!'[16]

More complex in technique is the moving episode when the peace-loving old Seneschal of Dinas Brān, Adda ap Leurig, arrives at Owen's Snowdon refuge with the sacred sword of Eliseg thrust through his buttocks by the scornful English. As the old man lies on the ground in the midst of Owen's court 'not mortally wounded but dying from pain and shame, his thin form in its grey clothes made with the sword that pierced him the shocking image of a bleeding cross'.[17] The shame is greater than the pain : he has fouled the sword. No Christian rite can comfort him, nor can the exhortations of the Lollard. The power of healing is conveyed by Broch-o'-Meifod, the giant miller from the sacred site of Mathrafal, who is Owen's closest companion, severest critic, and most faithful follower.

'Bronze and rust, that's all it is. A man's dirt and a man's blood are more precious than rusty bronze! And the belt—an old piece of saddle-leather! And Eliseg—rest his bones under his pillar—foxes and crows have vented on *him* time out of mind! Men in after ages, Master Adam, will think less of swords and belts than of blood and dirt. Is Edward of Carnarvon a laughing-stock because they killed him with a red-hot clyster? No! No! *He* died for Gaveston, his darling, and *that's* their tavern-jest, if there is any!'[18]

This anal imagery recurs in Powys's work. The murder of Edward II is referred to again in *The Brazen Head*, where it becomes the symbol, as well it might, of the ultimate in pain. The vision of Holy Sam in *Glastonbury* will be recalled, and the giving of the enema to old Abel Twig : it is as if Powys is insisting that mystical illumination cannot be divorced from the most despised physical processes. In *Owen Glendower* the pathetic outcast whom Rhisiart meets at Valle Crucis Abbey, and who 'had been caught making love to a plough-boy', and whose 'abasement was so complete that it was beneath humility',[19] turns up at Harlech castle as the sin-eater, devouring bits of bread and meat off the bodies of the dead, and in so doing taking their sins upon himself.

Powys's treatment of homosexuality is closely allied to this vision of the transformation of the rejected. Although not a homosexual himself ('I would shamelessly confess it to you reader, if I were!' he

15. *Autobiography*, p. 148.   16. *Owen Glendower*, p. 251.
17. ibid., p. 491.   18. ibid., p. 494.   19. ibid., p. 252.

remarks in the *Autobiography*),[20] he was drawn, as he confesses in the same book, to the boy-like type of girl; and these faintly herma-phroditic figures have, as has been seen, a special significance in his work. They look forward to the golden age when all that lives will be looked upon as holy, just as the dying Adda sees 'the blood and excrement of the whole world' become holy in the eyes of Broch-o'-Meifod. And so, appropriately enough, it is the boy–girl Tegolin who gives Adda his farewell kiss, covering his face as she does so with her red-golden hair, so that 'it seemed to Owen that from the head of that living cross on the floor there had blossomed a great fiery flower'; he sees Yeats's mystic rose, now

> Love has pitched his mansion in
> The place of excrement.[21]

What is so remarkable about Powys's imaginative world is its con-sistency and coherence. The same vision informs all the novels, how-ever variously embodied.

The narrative of *Owen Glendower* is maintained for the most part with consummate ease, and nowhere is Powys's sheer story-telling power more evident than in the first portion of the novel, that des-cribing Rhisiart's adventures until his release from Dinas Brān. This occupies three months out of the time-span of sixteen years, but no less than one-third of the novel's total length; and yet it is this early particularity which gives perspective and poignance to the saga as a whole. These scenes in the Dee Valley round Llangollen and Valle Crucis are recalled constantly, and give an impression of temporal depth and historic substance to the rest. Subsequent chapters are grouped round specific places—Owen's Snowdon stronghold, where the atmosphere is full of uncertainty and menace; the English border country where takes place the battle at Bryn Glas, with its horrible aftermath when Lowri and the other women mutilate the bodies of the English dead; the forests of Twywn, which form the melancholy misty background of trees and wetness for Rhisiart's tragic love for Catharine; Harlech where the extremes of light and darkness, freedom and cruelty, meet in the shape of the castle and the sea; and Corwen, with the great prehistoric fortress which was to figure in the next novel, *Porius*, for the final scene of Owen's death. In the penultimate chapter, where the scene shifts to South Wales and England, there is a certain flagging of pace; but here too we have the great prison scenes and the unforgettable introduction of the sleepless king. Powys makes interesting use of Shakespeare in this

20. *Autobiography*, p. 426.
21. *Collected Poems of W. B. Yeats*: 'Crazy Jane Talks with the Bishop'.

book, and even introduces some of Hotspur's words from *Henry IV* as the language of a spirit.

The supernatural element in the book is presented with Powys's usual blend of credulity and scepticism. At magic he looks askance; but the presence of spirits in the shape of embodied beliefs is as prevalent here as it is in *A Glastonbury Romance*. Only in the strange and unexplained sounds heard by Rhisiart in the Gorsedd mound at Glyndyfrdwy does the preternatural make itself felt, though the use of indirect narration as in Elphin's account of the murder of the strange half-heathen prophet, the Scab, at St. Derfel's shrine, can produce an eerie effect. More pervasive is the presence of aboriginal tradition and beliefs, of which the lost city of Mathrafal is the symbol. Owen, riding through its buried ruins proclaims that

'these first people must have known secrets beyond the understanding of our fathers. But our fathers were bards as well as warriors, and though they understood not the hidden meaning of the words, and though the words seemed to them like the motions of winds and motions of waters, they gathered up their ignorance into the most magical names ever invented by man ... Our fathers flung into this name all their beating against the gates of the mystery that bowed them down, as it bows us down!'[22]

Here Owen, like Uryen in *Maiden Castle*, equates spiritual energy with protest and frustrated passion; and it is this, rather than formal theology, which for Powys is the essence of religion. The differences between the various religious beliefs are constantly emphasized, as if to highlight the necessity for individual vision. The whole novel is preoccupied with the romantic ideal.

But these various religious and philosophical positions are always related to the novel's developing action, and are evaluated by it. Thus Father Pascentius and Broch-o'-Meifod, although allied in their opposition to the vivisectionist cruelty of the French Ambassador, are powerless to meet Owen's extremist need. Broch, with his fatalistic, death-loving nihilism is too detached; while Pascentius as Rhisiart says of the Monks of Caerleon is 'so much *on the inside* of the supernatural that the little accidents of daily life, the harshness of a superior, a hole in somebody's sandal, the substitution of wine for beer, a chilly draught in the choir-stalls, a leak in the gutter pipe, caused [him] more actual worry than any glimpse into the dark vistas, full of howling devils, of death and pain'.[23] Thus are both atheism and religious orthodoxy found wanting. In Mad Hugh we have a

22. *Owen Glendower*, p. 413.
23. ibid., p. 24.

variant on the religious life of Sam Dekker, with the dead King
Richard as his Christ. And as in *A Glastonbury Romance*, all these
beliefs, the Catholic, the devil-worship of Derfel, the magic and
astrology of Owen and of Hopkin, the prophet from Gower, and the
prophesying of Lowri's mother, Ffraid, are set against the men of
action but no imagination—men like King Henry, denied the gift of
sleep until promised it by the mad Friar Hugh. And there is a real
inner logic in events. The Scab is slain by his own magic: his religion
plays on the sadistic eroticism of the girl Efa, so that her provocative-
ness leads him on to make the assault which brings about his death.
Again, Hopkin prophesies 'the most startling events, from the crowning of a Welsh prince in London to the anointing of a great king by
a girl in armour'.[24] These prophecies are indeed correct; but Owen,
fatally misapplying them to himself is led on by them to plan his
disastrous invasion of England with the Maid of Edyrnion at the
head of his armies—a brilliant and inventive stroke of irony on the
author's part. The final conclusion, echoed in Powys's last novel, *All
or Nothing*, is that the ultimate secret rests in our own hearts—as
he makes Rabelais point out in *Morwyn*. It is Owen's dependence
on the French fleet, his drift into fatalism, which proves his undoing
in a temporal sense.

Though religious matters are dealt with in a dramatic manner,
the characters of the novel lack the interior vividness of those of the
earlier books or of *Porius*. One becomes familiar with their presences
rather than acquainted with their inner selves. But those presences
are haunting: Owen's solid matter-of-fact wife; the wily but kind
and lonely Father Pascentius; Mad Hugh; the bland and tactless
Lollard. In Broch-o' Meifod, we have another, and the most remarkable, of Powys's giants, a dour, bald, almost elemental figure, whose
deep heathen wisdom is in perpetual counterpoint to Owen's romantic
mysticism. In antithesis to Broch is the weird sado/masochistic
relationship between Lowri and her husband Simon. Lowri comes
nearer to the actuality of sadism than does Mr. Evans but she remains a somewhat melodramatic figure and recalls Maulfry in Hew-
lett's *Forest Lovers*. The dwarf Sibli, on the other hand, in whom we
find a similar vein of cruelty, is worthy of the imagination of Sir
Walter Scott. She is a remarkable creation, never sentimentalized, at
once grotesque, touching, and alarming.

There are a myriad smaller details that fill out the narrative and
give it body and humanity—the gallery of animals, from Rhisiart's
horse Griffin to Owen's cat and the hound Corbyn; the two old
nurses; the boy Madoc, whose death is described with such ruth-

24. ibid., p. 637.

less casualness; the pages and waiting women; the Wessex soldiers; and the various children whose appearance keeps lightening the narrative. Most memorable of these, perhaps, is Julietta, the daughter of the man who saves Rhisiart's life in prison—at the price of Tegolin's body. 'They're going—to put—*my* one,' she sobbed, 'into the fire—because he won't say his "Ave, Maria". Father told me *that* —when I wouldn't say mine because there was onion in my broth! I hate onion, don't you?'[25]

An intensely felt physical actuality informs this world, sustaining it and making it as real as the one we know, while being transformed repeatedly by the illuminating detail. Thus, describing the corpse of Owen's captain Rhys Gethin, Powys observes that

> the skin of Gethin's face wasn't only whiter than is usual with the dead but there were drops of death-dew still upon it that normally should have dried. In the second place the women who 'laid out' this obstinate corpse had not been able to close the eyelids completely, so savagely had they been fixed upon the sight that killed him; and in the crevice, out of which the eyeballs peered, certain excretions of rheumy glue had formed themselves, that now, catching the light of the candles, gleamed like fragments of sardonyx.[26]

Such a touch is typical of many. Throughout this enormous narrative the author never loses hold of what has gone before, referring back to tiny details and slight events in a manner that shows a total acquaintance with his world. As a feat of memory and imaginative control alone the work is an astounding achievement for a man of nearly seventy.

But the supreme value of this magnificent novel is the spirit and vision which fills it. It embraces cruelty and passion and ambition and beauty, is soaked in the recurring atmosphere of the seasons, of the Welsh weather, and the magic of the landscape. Above all it combines tenderness with grandeur. One final quotation may serve to illustrate this. At the very end of the book Owen's unknown grandson comes across the hidden leader close to the ramparts of the prehistoric fortress of Mynydd-y-Gaer. Brokenhearted at being sent away to play by himself, he wanders about recalling the tale told him by his grandfather long ago about the magic of Gwydion the son of Don who slew the son of the king of Annwn.

> 'They sent me away,' his heart kept repeating, . . . 'They sent me away. I'm nothing to them. I'm nothing to anybody. *They've sent me away!*'

He uttered this last lament aloud; and for a second he thought that

---

25. *Owen Glendower*, p. 831.
26. ibid., p. 765.

some tremendous echo had caught up his moan and was repeating it, and the strange thing was that when he lifted his head and saw the tall tottering figure coming out of the wood towards him the remembered feelings of the child merged so completely into the present feelings of the boy that all fear, all amazement, even, was swallowed up. A vast indescribable sense of refuge, of escape, of sanctuary, lifted him up and drew him forward; and long before he was in the Prince's arms his tears of desolation had been transformed, as if Gwydion's magic had been undone, as if the cold snouts of the recovered herds were all about him, as if the lost hero were alive again, into the sobs of one who out of a long darkness finds himself on the threshold of his home.

'*They've sent me away*,' his grandfather repeated as he hugged Catharine's first-born to his heart. 'They've sent both of us away; they've sent all of us away.'[27]

Here is the true heroic note, eloquent, visionary, and yet precise— those 'cold snouts' are the mark of Powys's grip upon his world. And *Owen Glendower* creates a world, a world full of mental spaciousness and reverence for life, a world of sanity and colour, of scepticism, exuberance, and charity. It is Powys's definitive and crowning work.

3

A gap of ten years separates the publication of *Owen Glendower* from that of *Porius*, a comparatively unproductive decade for Powys compared with the ones that preceded and followed it. He wrote his studies of Rabelais and Dostoevsky, and what are perhaps the two most readable of his philosophical books, *Mortal Strife* and *The Art of Growing Old*; but much of the time was devoted to the loving composition of his 'Romance of the Dark Ages', that 'buggerly great book' as he described it to Louis Wilkinson. 'It suits my weaknesses, badnesses, all my whimsies and quimsies and de quincies, all my superstitions, prejudices, blasphemies and blissphemies, my hoverings round and my shootings off, my divings down and poppings up— and so ... I shall finish the Best Book of My Life by October 8 1945 when I'll be only 7 years off 8o!'[28] In fact he was still at work revising it as late as August 1949. Over no other of his novels did he take so much trouble, and it was clearly designed to be a crown to his life's work. And so in some respects it is. But the book as we now have it is not the one that Powys originally conceived. It was extensively cut and rewritten to satisfy an interested publisher who did not in the end accept it. *Porius* is one of the great casualties of literature. (See Appendix.)

27. ibid., pp. 880–1.
28. *Letters to Louis Wilkinson*, pp. 142–3.

If *Owen Glendower* is the novel from which Powys stands most detached, *Porius* is the one which reflects most fully his inner world. Not only is its central message spoken with a sense of passionate personal involvement, but also its landscape perfectly reflects all that Powys responded to in Wales. He interprets the Welsh spirit in terms of the way of life in which he had come to believe; and wrote that

a race as ancient as this—whose ways and customs still retain memories of the Golden Age when Saturn, or some megalithic philosopher under that name, ruled in Crete, and the Great Mother was worshipped without the shedding of blood—must have some secret clues to the mystery of life, some magical ways of taking life, *simply from having lived so long in the same hills and valleys*, such as have not been revealed, and could not be revealed, to more recently arrived peoples.[29]

The whole of *Porius* is soaked in the atmospheric spirit of those hills and valleys; and the numerous descriptions of their special climatic conditions all serve to indicate the nature of their inhabitants. Thus, at the very beginning of the novel Powys gives us one of his characteristic descriptions of the mist.

Wavering and fluctuating in its advances and retreats, and only tangible to the sensitive skin by a faint impact of wetness and chilliness, the mist rises, it would appear, by its own volition, or by the will of the divine water, straight out of the river, and unaffected by wind or sun assumes, weak creature as it is, the dominant and mastering control of a whole unreturning day. This rape of a day by the weakest of her children was more significant of that spot than any other of Nature's methods.[30]

The tone of this is noticeably more animistic than in earlier books: we are already entering the world of Powys's final phase, in which animate and inanimate alike form a part of a single overriding consciousness.

Porius reverts in form to the panoramic method of *A Glastonbury Romance*. It is conceived on a vast scale (it is the third longest of the novels) and has a complex body of themes; but the themes are not related to each other dramatically, and the presentation is curiously static. The central issue is the autonomy of individual human choice and vision over every creed and pressure from without, and 'the holiness of the heart's affections'. Thus Brochvael, one of the central characters, feels within him 'something beyond and outside his physical body, ... powerful and strong, free of all ... compulsions, the inalienable independence of his own personal spirit'. Similarly his daughter Morfydd vows that 'henceforth, whether loved or

29. *Obstinate Cymric*, p. 83.
30. *Porius: A Romance of the Dark Ages* (Macdonald, 1951), p. 5.

unloved, whether secure or insecure, whether lucky or unlucky, whether deciding right or deciding wrong, she would sink into her spirit and remain strong and intact, there, however much she betrayed herself elsewhere'.[31] For Powys it was the aboriginal Welsh who best embodied the art of keeping such a vow.

The central incident of the novel is the invasion of the Vale of Edeyrnion by a body of Saxon raiders between 18 and 25 October A.D. 499. This invasion is not portrayed directly, however, but is related almost entirely by rumour and indirect narration. The author's real concern is with his characters' inner thought and more obscure sensations. The entire world of *Porius* is mediated through a web of sense impressions, and there is very little emotional tension. The whole presentation is undramatic: indeed, this might not unfairly be described as an *anti*-dramatic novel.

Its spatial deployment is clearly marked. The central point of reference, the quiet heart of the struggle, is the earth itself, together with its primitive inhabitants, those 'forest people' who are worshippers of the earth-goddess and attuned to all that which the bloodless worship of the Great Mother, invoked at the end of both *A Glastonbury Romance* and *Owen Glendower*, may be said to stand for. The forest people remain invisible throughout the novel, but we are constantly aware of them. Their mouthpiece is Myrrdin Wyllt, or Merlin, last, greatest, and ugliest of Powys's formidable gallery of grail-bearers. Modern treatments of the Arthuriad may be distinguished by the different ways in which Merlin is presented. There is the engaging, intensely human, half-comic Merlin of T. H. White's *The Once and Future King*; there is the lofty, passionate, enigmatic Merlin of Charles Williams's *Taliessin Through Logres*; there is the earthy, rough, and primitive Merlin of C. S. Lewis's *That Hideous Strength*. John Cowper Powys's Merlin, as might be expected, is totally original. Dressed like a common herdsman he speaks 'in a low, hoarse, guttural whisper, like someone who had given up for long years the use of human speech'.[32] He exudes a strong smell of fungus, has 'a crop of coal-black hair' and enormous ears; his eyes are set close together. His role is passive: he exists as a medium for forces stronger than himself, and recapitulates within himself the entire evolution of humanity from the vegetable kingdom—an embodiment in flesh of Wolf Solent's vision of the Glastonbury plain. He is a lord of the animal kingdom, and is constantly surrounded by the beasts of the forest. He is the 'latest incarnation of the god of the Golden Age'; and in answer to his page's query, 'What turns a god into a

31. ibid., p. 468.
32. ibid., p. 54.

devil, master?' he voices the anarchic gospel of Powys's own old age.

'Power, my son. Nobody in the world, nobody beyond the world, can be trusted with power, unless perhaps it be our mother the earth; but I doubt whether even she can. The Golden Age can never come again till governments and rulers and kings and emperors and priests and druids and gods and devils learn to un-make themselves as I did, and leave men and women to themselves! And don't *you* be deceived, little one, by this new religion's talk of "love". I tell you wherever there is what they call "love" there is hatred too and a lust for obedience! What the world wants is more common-sense, more kindness, more indulgence, more leaving people alone. But let them talk! This new Three-in-One with its prisons and its love and its lies will only last two thousand years. The thunderer I begot—and I'd have swallowed him if his mother hadn't given me a stone instead—lasted for ten thousand years. But none of them last for ever. That's the hope of the world. The earth lasts and man lasts, and the animals and birds and fishes last, but gods and governments perish!'[33]

The robust and casual aside about Saturn's attempt to eat his own children is typical of Powys.

The wisdom of Merlin is associated with the feminine principle, and towards the end of the novel he performs his one act of overt magic—he re-endows the owl Blodeuwedd with the body given her by the enchanter Gwydion, the body made out of the blossoms of the broom, the oak, and meadowsweet, of which she was deprived because of her faithlessness to Llew Llew Gyffes recorded in the fourth branch of the Mabinogion. And the restored Blodeuwedd is a symbol of the elemental freedom of every being by virtue of its inheritance in the natural order.

Certainly while this newly created Being remained for a moment or two poised on her feet, ready to use her arms as wings for her restored and reconstituted flights, back and forth, in defiance of the vengeance of Gwydion and of the Church that had accepted such vengeance as its own, over the valleys that were now hers once more to delight in ... Morfydd felt a strange out-rush of sympathy for her, of sympathy so strong that she never forgot it all her days. The creature was beyond all words beautiful, in that wild-tossed torchlight under that far-flung moonlight. Her form hadn't only taken into itself the spring-time blossoms of its first engendering, it had taken into itself all the moss-deep unfoldings and unsheathings of the loneliest places, all the fibrous disentanglings of velvety filaments from the under-sides of silvery-veined boughs, all the tangled growths that hide the secret processes of new life between the dark retreats of marsh-waters and the still darker retreats of ancient forests.[34]

33. *Porius*, pp. 676–7.
34. ibid., pp. 656–7.

This total identity between human spirit and earthly substance is the end-vision of Powys's progress through romanticism, his final identification of the weak, downtrodden, and oppressed with the permanent and the enduring. And this is the revelation of Merlin. In his strength and helplessness he is one of Powys's supreme creations, and his deliverance from his tomb on the top of Snowdon is a fitting conclusion to the vast narrative and one which shows where its true purpose lies.

The world of Merlin and the forest people is, however, the centre of a continuing political and ideological struggle. On every side of the forest people we find religious and racial forces all pulling against each other. There is, for instance the dwindling power of Rome, now only the ghost of itself. The present head of the House of Cunedda, which rules Edeyrnion, is married to the daughter of a Roman patrician; and both this old soldier, Porius Manlius, and the Princess Euronwy embody the virtues of orderliness, pride, and self-discipline, virtues which are vital to any continuing civilization. Euronwy is also the cousin of the British leader Arthur, who is waging war against the invading Saxons; and it is in its Arthurian aspects that *Porius* is most surprising. For the figure of Arthur has very little glamour about it. He is presented as a professional soldier first and foremost, and not a hint of the Arthur of later legend is given; moreover his court consists mostly of raw and pitiful young officers. The treatment here is not only anti-dramatic, but anti-romantic as well. The House of Cunedda itself, the rulers of the native Brythons or Celts, has intermarried not only with the Romans but also with the forest people and even with the aboriginal giants of Cader Idris— a factor of immense importance to the inner world of the younger Porius, son and heir of Prince Einion, and hero, if hero there be, of this complex chronicle. The house of Cunedda stands for the civilized norm in a confused world, and its marriage links make it a kind of balanced centre in the region, necessary for the well-being of the people, a fact epitomized in the marriage between Porius and his cousin Morfydd. The forest people owe their real allegiance to their matriarchal rulers, the Modrybedd (or, as Powys engagingly calls them, 'The Three Aunties') who are the last of the line, elderly princesses whose betrayal of the forest people when they invoke the violent Saxons against the power of the house of Cunedda precipitates the tragic action. There is for Powys a tragic element in the failure of the matriarchy, for beneath such peaceful primitive societies he perceived the continuing survival of the Age of Gold.

Indeed it is the women who are the active ones in the book: the men are comparatively powerless. Porius himself, for all his giant strength, is a typical Powysian elementalist, a dreamer, slow-moving and introspective; and his cousin Rhun, the soldier of Mithras, is of a similar type. Prince Einion is too cynical and detached to be effective, his brother Brochvael, the most attractive character in the book, too much of a scholar. Merlin is passive and relatively helpless by his very nature. But while the men are always talking and speculating it is the women who act. Morfydd, and Euronwy, the Aunties, even the Gwddl-Ffichti girl Sibilla and her daughter Gunta affect events either by deliberate plotting or, as in Sibylla's case, by sheer waywardness. Merlin deliberately submits himself to the enchantress Nineue —another of Powys's 'sylph' figures, this time with distinctly sinister attributes. But Powys's handling of her character is uncertain, and her precise significance therefore hard to determine.

This inversion of the usual sexual roles (in keeping with one of the leading motives in the book, the deliverance of both Porius and Brochvael from long-inherited presuppositions and prejudices) is further underlined by the ambiguous attitude to savagery. On the one hand we have the deliberate cruelty of the Saxon invaders, as typified in the desecration of the corpses of the Princess Tonwen and her elderly lover; but also present in the book is the continuing influence of the Cewri or aboriginal giants, one of whom, Rhitta Gawr, had once ruled in Mynydd-y-Gaer, the hill fortress portrayed in its ruin in *Owen Glendower*, but here as the centre of rule for the entire valley. Another giant has married Porius's great-grandfather, and a few last remnants survive on Cader Idris. They are the original inhabitants of the land and are introduced into the story horrifically enough, though without sensationalism, as devourers of the dead. And yet for Porius there is a magic about them, and he yearns to know them, to renew contact with his primitive origins. In previous novels these giant figures have been repositories of wisdom, symbols perhaps of the rejected powers of the buried self; in Porius they are confronted as they really are in all their awesomeness, and yet clearly, in the light of day. Porius's mating with the young giantess is followed by the death of both her and her father in a mountain lake; and, for all the fact that this is the saving of his own life, Porius can only feel a heart-broken regret. Something rare, mysterious, and precious has departed from the earth, and even at the height of the vision on Snowdon top of Merlin's plan for a second age of gold he recalls 'the floating blood and the strewn hair and the green water in those foot-hills of the Cader'.[35] Powys here seems to be asserting, under a figure, the need to return to roots, to the essential animality of man, to acknowledge his part in the natural order.

35. *Porius*, p. 681.

This theme is further developed through the conflict between Christianity and paganism. The former is most unsympathetically presented in the person of the bigoted priest Minnawc Gorsant, though he is also at times a figure of fun, as when in a sly aside Powys depicts him as 'invoking what was visible of the sky at the expense of the man at his feet',[36] and it is the heretic Pelagius who is Porius's real source of inspiration. Brochvael's hero is the emperor Hadrian, and he invokes the Roman's presence as he sits in the secret underground retreat of the last of the ancient Druids.

More than any other recent figure within these confused and chaotic modern times, this great ruler had always possessed a peculiar attraction for him. And now in this murky and mystical hiding place, now in this citadel of all he most instinctively detested, of all that was occult, obscure and treacherous, of all that was obscene, unclean and barbarous, his mind turned to this sceptical and civilized ruler of the world with incredible relief and comfort. Here was an emperor who took religion and piety and patriotism and morals *as they ought to be taken*, with indulgent and humorous common sense. Here was an emperor prepared to number Jesus among the gods, and yet prepared to build a temple to Venus on Mount Calvary! Sceptical and indulgent, believing in nothing, yet believing in everything, the elegiac celebrant of his own pale and bewildered soul, the mere idea of Hadrian always gave Brochvael a reassuring sense of the triumph of wisdom over folly and of tolerance over intolerance.[37]

The sceptical balance of Hadrian's attitude to life is contrasted with the ruthless, ultimately sentimental demands of Love—love conceived as a metaphysical absolute. Porius reacts violently against the homage of Drom, another bisexual figure, who is a convert from Druidism to Christianity.

There was no treachery, no cruelty, no hypocrisy about Drom's kiss. It was worse. It took away a person's ultimate right—the abysmal *right to choose*, to choose *not* to love Drom, or any other living creature, the right to live alone, and finally to choose death if a person preferred death to life ... It was the kiss of rounded identity, of perfect balance, of the reconciliation of all opposites, the kiss of everlasting peace, the kiss of unutterable sameness, the kiss of pure divinity, the kiss of anti-*man*.[38]

This theme is also touched on with regard to Merlin. With one of his historical ironies, comparable to his treatment of Hopkin's prophecies in *Owen Glendower*, Powys declares the tale of Merlin's imprisonment by Nineue to be a deliberate hoax of Merlin's own, sedulously recorded by the Henog or historian. Merlin discusses this with his page Neb ap Digon.

36. ibid., p. 304.   37. ibid., p. 256.   38. ibid., p. 599.

'Do you know why I want the Henog of Dyfed to tell posterity that
Myrrdin Wyllt was helpless in the power of Nineue ferch Avallach?'
Neb gave his master another impish wink.
'You *do*, little one? Well, on my soul, I believe you do!'
'Because as long as the Three-in-One rule in Heaven, cruelty and love
and lies rule on earth.'
The counsellors green-black eyes seemed to sink inwards into his skull,
and, as they sank, the bridge of the nose dividing them seemed to sink
away also, so that as they increased in depth they not only increased in
size but displayed a tendency to coalesce and become cyclopean.
'Did you hear me say that?'
Again Neb nodded.
'Tell me, little one, what is it that makes you serve me as you do?'
Never had Neb's face looked so grave.
'Because you were God before the Three-in-One conquered heaven; and
you made people happy before cruelty and love and lies ruled the earth.'[39]

Later on, Merlin tacitly allows Neb's attribution of his divinity.

'And now, little one, I want you to see how I have a real right to break up
the image of one god at least. You mustn't be frightened if I show you
how my pet snake—it has to be a little one because real snakes are rare
round here, and this was the only one near enough to hear me whistle—
twines itself round my wrist and tries to put its tail into its mouth. A
slow-worm can act unending Time as well as a sea-serpent. You won't be
afraid, Neb ap Digon?'
'No, master!'
And the small creature really did show no sign of uneasiness as the
Being who declared he had been buried on yr Wyddfa revealed his wrist
with the slow-worm twisted round it so tightly that its tail did give the
impression of entering its mouth. But the counsellor now began murmuring something in a language that was apparently more difficult for his
human listener to understand than for the slow-worm, for that intelligent
reptile promptly untwisted itself from his wrist, glided across his beard,
and crawling along one of his legs made its way silently and rapidly into
the open air.[40]

But the image of the snake is used elsewhere in the novel with a
rather different reference, though one still applicable to Merlin's
action. Porius sees on the face of the Emperor Arthur's nephew
Medrawd or Mordred an expression that reminds him of

a rough clumsily painted Byzantine picture that hung in his mother's
bed-chamber. It was a picture of the Infant Jesus playing with a snake.
The little Jesus, a comically plump babe, was lovingly and obstinately
thwarting the one supreme desire of his dangerous plaything, *the desire*

39. *Porius*, pp. 274–5.
40. ibid, p. 277.

to escape. This desire had smouldered into such a recoil of tragic desperation that even as a boy Porius had read in the one small saurian eye which alone was visible the shuddering resolve, *sooner than not to escape to drag the world's hope of redemption down with him!*[41]

The single eye looks forward to Merlin's Cyclop eye, which has in any case already been noted in an earlier passage in the book; and the plump and bland little Jesus relates to the kind of smug indifference of 'love' denounced in the passage about Drom's kiss, where the right to choose death, to escape, is regarded as an inalienable right of man, a right which Merlin tacitly recognizes when he releases the snake of unending time. This is but one example of how Powys uses imagery in this enormous book: never ostentatiously, never underlining his pointers, however much he may underline his sentences; but working always out of some reservoir of unconscious imagery that his imaginative instinct dives into unerringly as his themes develop. Merlin is himself an image of that reservoir of power and it is he whom at the end of the book Porius, having released him from his Snowdon tomb, chooses for his God. And that deliverance is itself a result of chance. Nineue attempts to seduce Porius from his task; but she chooses an erotic gesture which happens to be repellent to him. On such a small individual peculiarity does Merlin's release depend.

Or so it appears: in fact Merlin's stature by the end of the novel is such as to preclude any sense that his is not in fact the ultimate power. And it is the power of the oppressed and long-enduring, the power of the earth itself which outlasts all man's illusions. Powys never surpassed the grandeur of the prose in these final pages. It is writing on a scale unattempted now, musical, at once spare and noble, controlled and yet unselfconscious.

More and more strongly did Porius get the feeling that in his isolation on this peak of the planet by the side of this titanic creature of whose essential being he knew so little, and even felt disinclined to know more, he was re-living an experience he had had long ago when the world was young. He could still hear the far-away screaming of eagles but the sound had grown so faint that it seemed as if Myrddin Wyllt had been correct in declaring that those great Birds of Absolute Power had felt some *counter-bolt* whistling past their small, cruel, beautiful, imperial, exquisitely feathered skulls! And as he listened, watching the great beast-ears above him quiver like sails in that icy wind, he fancied he could catch moving up to that mountain-top a vast, indescribable, multitudinous murmur, groping up, fumbling up, like a mist among mists, from all the forests and valleys of Ynys Pridein, the response of innumerable weak and terrified and unbeautiful and unconsidered and unprotected creatures, for whom this first-born and first-betrayed of the wily

41. ibid., p. 138.

earth, this ancient accomplice of Time, this angulomeetis of subtle counsels, was still plotting a second Age of Gold.[42]

It is Porius who is most responsive to Merlin's spell, for, like Wolf Solent, he has his own interior spiritual rituals, which make him sensitive to the whole world of which Merlin is an embodiment. His equivalent of Wolf's 'mythology' is called by him 'cavoseniargizing'; and unlike Wolf's mythology it is free from dualism or self-dramatization. Rather it is a deliberate cult of sensuous enjoyment. It is pagan and non-violent, a spiritualizing of bodily sensations which lead to a heightening of personal self-awareness and detachment from immediate pressures. Porius finds that Nineue also practises this art; but, while she uses the power the practice brings her to dominate Merlin's helplessness, Porius uses it to serve him. A further example of 'elementalism' is provided by the poet Taliessin, with his self-identification with the inanimate, and his worship of the goddess of chance. His poems, besides being remarkable creations inspired by the surviving Bardic poems, such as those found in Lady Charlotte Guest's translations from the Mabinogion (one of Powys's favourite books), also serve to place such contemplation in perspective: to celebrate the significance of everything can be to assert the significance of nothing. And this problem remains unanswered finally in *Porius*. Powys is content with

> The 'Enough' that leads forward to no consummation,
> The answer to all things, that yet answers nothing.[43]

(It is worth noting that he was a much more original poet in his novels than he is in his own books of verse: the poems he attributes to Jason Otter, Edgar Athling, and Taliessin are both appropriate to their authors and impressive in their own right.)

Towards the end of the book the narrative becomes somewhat disjointed and incoherent, and this is the result of the cuts which, as was the case with *Wolf Solent* and *Maiden Castle*, were imposed upon the book, the original thirty-three chapters now standing at twenty-nine. *Porius* is a flawed masterpiece. It is more impressive as a whole, and in recollection, than in its separate parts. The prose becomes increasingly circular and repetitive, and the tone at times resembles that of an old man talking to children. Powys was to turn this to good advantage in the later fantasies; but in *Porius* which is only fantasy in part, the method becomes tedious. And the oblique manner of narration, the way in which most of the events are described at second hand through the observations of the characters,

42. *Porius*, pp. 680–1.
43. ibid., p. 418.

robs the heavy fabric of words and speculations of the necessary dramatic frame. All too often we are *told* that events are exciting without being *shown* that they are: a note of self-indulgence is struck. Powys declared in his letters that he enjoyed composing *Porius* more than anything that he had written, but perhaps for this very reason we move ever deeper into a private world. The final fantasies are the logical outcome of this process.

As in *Owen Glendower* we are presented with a long continuous narrative at the outset; but in this case the journey of Porius and Rhun to the tent of Merlin is not sufficiently interesting to supply the necessary emotional perspective of the passing of time; and in any case the action of the novel takes place within a single week. Another shortcoming of the book is that there is no controlling centre of interest. Porius and Brochvael are not sufficiently different for contrast or conflict. A few of the other characters stand out vividly— Prince Einion himself, the Aunties, the old serving man and woman, Gwrgi and Canna. But there is a remarkable absence of interest among most of these in what is going on.

The triumph of *Porius* lies not in its drama but in its total atmosphere, the way in which a view of life is projected through the detailed portrayal of the mental landscape of a bygone world. One says 'mental landscape' advisedly, since, although the physical landscape is all-pervading, it is not, any more than it is in any of Powys's novels except the early ones, directly presented or described. Rather it comes before us in a myriad small details, details that are in their turn related to the thoughts and feelings of the characters, so that we are made aware of the country from the inside and see it as it affects its inhabitants. Man and nature are portrayed as being one, and nature is the judge of man: in *Porius* the world of affairs is largely irrelevant. This makes it sound like an escapist novel; but in its imaginative coherence it relates to the contemporary world, its self-sufficiency providing its own justification.

The historical background is as unobtrusively presented as it is in *Owen Glendower*: indeed the book is even more remarkable than its predecessor in its power to evoke the actual quality of life at such a remote time and in such a remote spot: there is at once a feeling of primeval remoteness in time together with a sense of acute actuality in space. There are some memorable interiors—Brochvael's Stone House, the Cave fortress of the Aunties, and, most remarkable in its unexpectedness, the underground dwelling of the Druid, an 'absurdly childish hole in the ground with the water oozing through the cracks in the mossy stones'.[44] Accompanying these is a constant noting of

44. ibid., p. 243.

sounds and sights and smells: often one seems to be moving in the world of Edeyrnion with the senses of an animal. And in none of Powys's novels is there such a meticulous account of weather and effects of atmosphere, repeated accounts of mist especially, mist at dawn, mist at sundown, the mist rising upwards from rain-soaked leaves. It is almost as if the normal order of vision is reversed, the landscape being mediated against a background of human characters instead of the other way round. And yet, having said this, it remains to point out the almost wearisome meticulousness with which the characters' movements and sensations are plotted: Powys is totally immersed in the world he has created, and this slow-motion technique, irritating if one is trying to read him in a hurry, only serves to give his work an added depth. And if one were to try to illustrate the nature of that world and to capture the magic of the book's essence, one could hardly do better than turn to the account of the ride through the forest of the youngest princess and her aged lover on the great horse Brithlas.

The waxing moon, grown big between her silver horns with the burden of her own shapeless body, seemed to those two riders to shine upon them ever more weirdly and more ominously as they plunged deeper and deeper into that huge forest. Not a wolf, not a fox disturbed the silence, not an owl, not a night-hawk. Nothing was audible but the steady hoof-fall of the dapple-grey, thudding upon moss soft as sleep, upon grass fine as hair, upon marsh-sedge fragrant with water-mint, upon wind-ruffled drifts of dying leaves, upon muddy beds of last season's dead leaves; nothing but the old man's deep-drawn breaths and the sigh of the wind ... in the woman's long hair as it floated silvery-white behind her. Hour after hour seemed to be passing over their heads, charged with strange meanings; and they felt as if all the years they had been friends together were returning on soundless wings to reassure them, to let them know that in their supreme moment they were not alone, but that all their shared memories like guardian spirits were about them, risen up alive from their paer dadeni, the imperishable cauldron of re-birth.[45]

45. *Porius*, pp. 345–6.

CHAPTER FIVE

The Fantasies

THE novels of Powys's last years were written purely and simply for his own pleasure. He continued to write till very shortly before his death; and these works of his eighth decade have a character peculiarly their own. With the exception of *Atlantis* none of them asks to be treated with the same consideration as the earlier books; they are for the most part light-hearted in tone, extravagant in invention, and written in an increasingly limpid and simple style. They exhale an atmosphere of keen enjoyment. His imagination, always inclined to the grotesque and the preposterous, now allowed itself unfettered sway; he concerned himself less and less with narrative plausibility and wrote increasingly as the fancy took him. But if these later books suffer from a breakdown of imaginative and intellectual control they do manage to project a kind of nursery-tale world of constructive lunacy, and are still shot through with passages of insight, tenderness, and beauty. And they are richer in humour than any of the earlier books. They are not the best introduction to Powys's work, nor do they, *Atlantis* and *The Brazen Head* apart, enrich our understanding of his other work; but they have an interest of their own. They are the spontaneous fairytales of a Rabelaisian surrealist reenchanted with his life.

1

The first of them is *The Inmates*, published in the year after *Porius*. It is a very different novel from its predecessor, being comparatively short and almost entirely lacking in any sense of the poetic. It is indeed Powys's most prosaic and most baffling novel; but it is seriously conceived. The preface, so much more lucidly and better written than the book itself, shows that it was designed to be a kind of fable, using the concept of madness as a critique of accepted moral and social values. The scene is a mental home called Glint; and although the actual running of the place is eccentric to a Powysian extreme, its physical presence, as might be expected, is vividly realized. So too is the sense of confinement, and the alarmingly perpetual nearness to violence and repression. The story, what there is of it, concerns the incarceration of a mild sexual fetishist called John Hush and his successful plot to ensure the escape of a number of his fellow inmates in a ludicrously improbable giant helicopter. Powys uses these various inmates as mouthpieces for ideas and fancies adumbrated by him in the philosophical books and in the other novels, though the practice of vivisection is more lightly touched upon than in his treatment of Hell's Museum. At the end of the book the magical element is introduced in the person of a sketchily described adept from Tibet, who has the power of wielding a devolutionary cosmic ray that can destroy a man by reducing him 'from human to animal, from animal to vegetable, from vegetable to mineral, and so on down the scale to bodiless gasses and even, perhaps, to atoms and mesons'.[1] This is a negative aspect of Wolf Solent's and Owen Glendower's intimations of man's primeval origins.

At times the book is extremely funny, funny with a wild, almost Firbankian exuberance; but the serious elements in it, such as the love of John for Tenna Sheer, call for a closeness of attention which the farcical elements disturb. The leisurely development of the first two-thirds of the novel is succeeded by a confused scramble of events which does nothing to secure either the reader's attention or his respect.

The most memorable things in the book are the inmates themselves, both the lunatics and their keepers: indeed it is hard to distinguish the former from the latter, so pervasive is the note of mental extravagance. Tenna especially trembles on the verge of murderous outbreaks, and her character is most touchingly portrayed. What sanity there is in the novel is located in the person of the gardener, Mr. Frogcastle, an anticipation of Zeuks in *Atlantis* and in some measure a portrait of Powys himself in his old age—certainly of his own perspective as a novelist.

[His] eyes supplied the whole clue to the gardener's character. They were so wide apart that they appeared to focus in a completely different way from ordinary human eyes. Instead of concentrating on any particular point in what they surveyed, they seemed to take in the whole length, breadth, height and depth of the object. The object wasn't isolated from its surroundings but absorbed and included in all its peculiar relations to its position in the world, so that a considerable segment of the object's environment, together with a fair stretch of the causes and antecedents that had made the object what it was, were embraced in one glance by the unnaturally wide scope of Daniel Frogcastle's vision.[2]

Some such width of vision can be detected in such a blend of the serious and farcical as the following:

1. *The Inmates* (Macdonald, 1952), p. 279.
2. ibid., p. 102.

The impression of immemorial antiquity made upon him by this cold white light that seemed so much older than sun, moon, or stars was indeed an impression of abysmal disillusionment; but it was the disillusionment not of the created but of the creator. This prae-dawn light was the diffused sigh with which the original world-builder had lamented some huge catastrophic mistake and with little hope of redeeming it had obstinately set to work to start all over again.[3]

Powys's view of lunacy would seem to be one of sceptical import for the sane: the mad are society's victims, and fortunate are those who can choose with John Hush 'the path *by which I can enjoy, and as I might say devour, every change in myself and every change in what is happening to me,* without bothering about my character or about my reputation!'[4] Here again Powys is the champion of the loner soldiering on.

The Inmates is a good example of the difficulties of writing fantasy in a contemporary setting, for Powys's attempts at modernity only serve to make it seem more frivolous than it intends to be. The real trouble is that although his characters and events may be very real to the author, he does not take enough pains to convey them to his readers; so that in *The Inmates* we seem to be overhearing a tale, or getting fitful glimpses through a moving curtain of scenes that we are told of but cannot look at for ourselves. This makes it difficult to participate in the joke or to take seriously the contentions raised. The book fails through a lack of organization and proper imaginative discipline.

2

Atlantis on the other hand is the richest and most sustained of the final fantasies, and the last of his books to be written in a style recalling Powys's old grand manner. Critical opinion, even among his admirers, has been divided over it. Wilson Knight speaks admiringly of its 'unique fusion of ancient myth and contemporary thought',[5] but H. P. Collins in his *John Cowper Powys: Old Earth-Man* dismisses it as 'almost wholly whimsy'.[6] For Powys himself it came to replace *Porius* as his favourite book: certainly Homer, from whom the novel derives, was the favourite author of his last years. The main theme is the voyage of the aged Odysseus beyond the pillars of Herakles to visit the sunken continent of Atlantis; having done this he voyages

3. ibid., p. 181.
4. ibid., p. 252.
5. *The Saturnian Quest*, p. 101.
6. *John Cowper Powys: Old Earth-Man*, p. 182.

further to the shores of America. The Homeric atmosphere is captured not only in the book's characters but also in its continual familiar references to Greek mythology. The novel is written in a lucid, swift-moving, but leisurely prose of the utmost fluidity and grace, with the usual Powysian afflatus of Homeric adjectives and a constant repetition of descriptive phrases. The atmosphere is temperate and serene, with a deep-welling undertow of humour and an overflowing delight in material things. It is easily the most attractive of the novels.

As background to the adventures of Odysseus there is a break-up of the order of the powers that control the world, a revolt against the Olympians. This revolt is only presented to us by hearsay, but fundamentally it is a revolt of the feminine principle against the masculine, a reawakening of the age of Cronos involving a disturbance of the repressed energies of matter, symbolized by the Titans and the monsters. This revolt is not so much a part of the story as a constant commentary upon it; and the success of the revolt is made apparent in the triumphant issue of the voyage, the destruction of the sinister ruler of Atlantis by the club of Herakles; and by the marriage of the boy–prophet Nisos with Arsinoë, the victim of the siege of Troy. The values of the Age of Gold are present in the character of the farmer Zeuks, reputedly the son of Arcadian Pan, and in the overall mood of the novel. Thus Powys relates the themes of *Porius* and *Owen Glendower* to his own philosophy of life. Zeuks himself progresses from a belief in defiance as the best attitude to life's blows, to one in enjoyment and forgetfulness. The conclusion reached is the same as in *Wolf Solent*; and, as with the former book, it is reached through an awareness of defeat. Awareness, not experience: Zeuks undergoes no dynamic process of conversion. The revelation comes to him in a scene that only Powys could have imagined. Arsinoë, the daughter of Hector, has beguiled her captivity in Ithaca by carving a wooden statue of her father in a desolate and shunned part of the island, the haunted place called Arima; and furthermore has stolen from Odysseus' keeping the armour of Achilles which she has put upon the statue and keeps burnished. Zeuks, being an unsuperstitious and irreverent mocker of the Gods, has not hesitated to use Arima as a short cut to Odysseus' palace when required to act as escort to the aged Ajax; and they come full upon the armoured statue shining in the evening sun. The shock is too much for Ajax, and he dies. Zeuks props him up between the statue's knees.

The afternoon sun was now projecting such a blaze of light that the armour of Achilles reflected it from every curve, whether convex or concave. In fact the incredible and miraculous gleaming of this armour which the cajoleries of the sea-goddess had extracted from the smithies of the fire-god, was so dazzling that whether it flamed back from the closed eyes of the son of Telamon or from the golden greaves of the son of Priam it compelled Zeuks to bend down till his own head was as deeply sunk forward between the knees of the dead Ajax as the head of Ajax was sunk backwards between the knees of the image of Hector.

Thus were the three figures united, one a corpse, one a work of art, and one a living creature; and this uniting of life with death, and of life and death with a graven image of human imagination had a curious and singular effect: for there came into the already confused and naturally chaotic mind of Zeuks one of the most powerful impressions of his whole life. In embracing those dead limbs and in drawing into the depths of his being the bitter smell of the old hero's scrotum, and the salt, sharp taste of the perspiration-soaked hairs of his motionless thighs, Zeuks completely forgot the dead man's announcement as to his own paternity. What filled his mind now was a sudden doubt about the wisdom of his proudly proclaimed 'Prokleesis' as the best of all possible war-cries for the struggle of living creatures with the mystery of life.[7]

Once again we are presented with the identification of the unlovely and death-like with illumination; and here Powys portrays that illumination as being itself the product of a particular confluence of various mental, spiritual, and physical forces. The tragedy of Ajax's death and the realization of total defeat which accompanies it, coupled with the physical embracing of the fact of death by Zeuks, renders superficial any attitude to life beyond an acceptance of its tragedy and of the need to live in spite of it. Homeric resignation would seem to be the best description of Powys's final attitude. The magical associations of Arima and the supernatural heightening of the whole incident make of it something of a theophany.

The gods themselves, however, are treated with a certain wry humour. They are shown to be dependent for their existence on their worshippers, a sceptical attitude anticipated in *A Glastonbury Romance*, and endorsed in *Maiden Castle* when Uryen's power deserts him, after he has made his beliefs public and thus destroyed their intimate connection with his inner self. *Atlantis* clearly has a contemporary reference when it predicts the imminent death of the gods through human disbelief. The kind of endurance of life and acceptance of life practised by Zeuks is more than an adequate substitute so far as Powys is concerned. Here as elsewhere it is religious fanatics who are the enemy to human happiness. Zeuks denounces Enorches, the priest of the Orphic mysteries, as an enemy of life; while Nisos more acutely sees him as a being without a real identity of his own,

7. *Atlantis* (Macdonald, 1954), pp. 283-4.

seeking escape from the vacuum within. ' "When I think," the embryo prophet now told himself, "I think like Athene and like Atropos and like the old Odysseus, from myself outwards. But I have a revolting suspicion that, when this horrible Orpheus-man thinks, he thinks towards himself inwards." ' [8]

The story of *Atlantis* moves slowly, is full of false starts and divagations, especially towards the end, where the voyage across the Atlantic is notably skimped and unrealistic. But the book as a whole remains impressive from the same inner consistency of tone that we have noted in the other novels, and from the way in which the author appears to be quietly laughing at the marvels at the same time as he is describing them. As much as *A Glastonbury Romance* this book is a portrait of 'life's multiple dimensions'. Like the mythical book written by the ruler of Atlantis 'it is landscape superimposed upon landscape rather than rhythm upon rhythm that is the method of its message',[9] a fair description of Powys's own work in the way in which it relates temporal scenes to their source in some kind of subconscious hinterland. 'The great thing,' as one of the characters remarks, 'is always to have *two* lives going; one of them the life we share with our friends, and the other the life we enjoy with our own mind and with our own senses.'[10] Most novelists are concerned with the first of these lives, but Powys is concerned with the relationship between the two, inclining increasingly, however, in the later books towards the latter.

Odysseus himself is a fine blend of the man of action and of an intense inner life, heroic in his qualities of detachment and singlemindedness: he is a conqueror in every sense. Nisos, who turns out to be his son, is the book's central point of observation—an attractively youthful figure, and pleasantly less complex than his predecessors, informed by a spirit of wonder and curiosity rather than of introspection. This in part accounts for the book's singularly happy atmosphere. The role of the elementalist falls into the background: in the person of Telemachos he plays but a small part in the action, and his apologia is half-discredited: it is as if Powys were beginning to tire of his more intense earth-mysticism, and becoming more of a spectator of life. The priest Enorches is, like so many of the characters in the later books who represent a point of view that the author rejects, a faintly comic figure: certainly his fanaticism is not treated with the scorn and indignation reserved for the priest in *Porius* or the dogmatists in *Morwyn*.

8. *Atlantis*, p. 99.
9. ibid., p. 336.
10. ibid., p. 337.

The women are, for the most part, lightly sketched in, and the surprising appearance of Nausikaa towards the end of the book has the appearance of being an afterthought on the author's part. But the two young girls, Pontopereia and Eione, are delightful; Powys, in his own particular idiom, shares Trollope's ability to catch the tone used by young girls when talking among themselves. Innocence is beautifully caught when Pontopereia asks Eione if she has ever been made love to:

'I'm not sure whether I have or not,' she said simply. 'A boy who lives near us pressed me once very tight against him, when neither of us had much on, and I felt something—the thing they all have, I suppose, that makes them men—pounding and throbbing and beating against me like a stick with the pulse of a heart. But it didn't make me want him to do anything; and it didn't frighten me or disturb me. I just noticed it; that's all, and wondered what I'd feel if he did anything else, and whether I ought to help him to do anything else. And then somebody came—and that was all.'[11]

'And then somebody came—and that was all'—there is a world of poignance in the words. Sexual sophistication is amusingly portrayed in the person of Okyrhoë, who irresistibly recalls a screen vamp of the 1920s; but the real triumph of female portraiture lies in the old women, Orpheus' nurse Eurycleia, the midwife Pentaia, and above all the elderly dryad Kleta.

It is in its portrayal of the mythological world that the peculiar beauty of *Atlantis* lies. In it for the first time Powys gives full imaginative play to his animism. Not only do gods and goddesses take part in the action, together with monsters and beasts of fable like the great winged horse Pegasus, but even insects and inanimate objects are endowed with personal characteristics. The supernatural is treated quite simply as an extension of the natural; not only does human life open supernaturally outwards to the life of gods and goddesses, but it is in its own turn a supernatural enlargement of that of insects, trees, and stones. Powys does in his own homely and familiar manner embody in a fable the evolutionary vision of a Teilhard de Chardin. What has been implicit in the earlier novels, giving them a curious intensity, is now brought forward to the centre of the action. In *A Glastonbury Romance* there is a certain straining at the seams of the fabric of the novel, but in *Atlantis* the world and the fable are at one. Acting as commentators on the unfolding drama are a moth and a fly who together inhabit a crack in the club of Herakles, now wielded by Odysseus. The moth is a

11. ibid., p. 215.

mystic by nature, the fly informed by scientific curiosity—though not a curiosity of the kind denounced by Powys elsewhere in the various embodiments of 'the Professor'. They speak what the fly calls 'the alphabet of matter' in which 'the sensations that certain words convey to us are [more important] than the precise nature of the words used or the number of the syllables they contain ... in the science of language it is a combination of assonance and allitera-tion that conveys the idea; and thus it is only in poetry that the real secret of what is happening is revealed'.[12] Powys would here seem to be relating the nature of speech to some kind of group un-consciousness. In these later novels his approach is increasingly Jungian, and in the fantasies he objectifies the unconscious in a world of sunlit myth and marvel. It is notable that both moth and fly, intellectual and dreamer, are dependent on the great phallic club of the giant Herakles; and that this club of its own accord attacks both the deadly monster Keto and the sinister ruler of Atlantis.

The latter is a magnificent creation, the most successful, because most remote, of Powys's denunciations of the false scientific spirit. Atlantis itself occupies an ambiguous position in the novel. The revolt against the gods is generally regarded with favour; but Zeus has sunk Atlantis for a refusal to believe in his existence. One may see in it an image of a technological civilization, at once a thing of marvels and beauty, but at the same time a threat to older, more established human values. Nisos feels that

to see the terrible beauty of this majestic face mauled, crushed, churned up ... would be to assist at the most savage crime that his wickedest imagination had ever pictured. But there was an 'I am I' within him that was deeper than his divided soul; and with this he felt that the only con-ceivable alternative to letting the club obliterate this Ruler of Atlantis was to let the Horror have its way, to give up himself to it with absolute submission ... He couldn't let this Being, whatever the mystery of its creative power, whatever the ineffable beauty of its face, whatever its justi-fication as the arch-enemy of Olympus, triumph over all he loved, unresisted![13]

In this scene at the bottom of the ocean, when Odysseus and Nisos confront the androgynous ruler of the drowned city sprawled on a vast heap of rotting seaweed, Powys brings together a num-ber of images from his earlier work. The ruler of Atlantis is the most sinister embodiment of the bisexual figures who have appeared else-where in the novels; and also raging in the deep are the monsters

12. *Atlantis*, p. 155.
13. ibid., pp. 449–50.

Orion and Tryphon. Professor, giant, and fairy are here seen as elements of one another; but sexual energy and mystical and poetic illumination have become subservient to an overriding curiosity divorced from any purpose but the desire to experiment. The denunciations of science which occur in *Wolf Solent* and the succeeding books are here seen as denunciations of false science, science regarded as an end in itself, science divorced from its purpose of succouring human need and enlarging human hearts. The ruler has a deadly fascination because Atlantis is so near the truth; but Odysseus has to sail over it and beyond it before he can find his new-found land. And with him go the affections of the past and the hope of the future in the persons of Arsinoë and Nisos. Powys denounces the false spirit of science in the name of the very human values it ostensibly exists to serve. The world is so full of mystery that scientific dogmatism is as unacceptable as religious: only the agnosticism of Zeuks can be a satisfactory response to life, an agnosticism which takes us back to the attitude of John and Mary Crow: Defy, Forget, Enjoy. But while Zeuks dies at the end of the book in an ecstasy of pure happiness, because there is no need to feel alone, since 'there are vibrations from one organism to another throughout the entire universe'[14] the hero is still Odysseus, the ever-questing voyager.

Atlantis abounds in haunting scenes—the whole visit to the drowned city, the attack of the furies upon Atropos, the ride across Ithaca on the winged horse; and it abounds also in the little homely details of which Powys was such a master. It is in the name of all the small entities of life, of the Worm of Arima, of the cow Babba, of the olive shoot in the floor of Odysseus' palace, of the simple farmers and herdsmen that Powys protests against a view of human power that rules out the human involvement in; and responsibility to, the life of nature. The book embodies a world which is its own message. It may lack the intellectual and imaginative control of *Porius* but it has its own vitality. Its long-windedness is less oppressive than in the other novels, and if many of the characters and incidents seem irrelevant to the plot they are consistent with the over-all design. Thus the family of Nisos, introduced so gradually, are necessary contrasts to the world of Odysseus: the murder of Eurycleia by Leipephile is the more horrible because of the laconic manner of its narration. Leipephile has been frequently mentioned; we know that she is strong, pretty, and simple; now, suddenly, that simplicity or stupidity comes to the fore and she is a killer. There are no heroics: this is what life is like.

14. ibid., p. 461.

It is the Ithacan passages which account for over two-thirds of the book and give it its particular appeal: once on board the ship the narrative slackens. Powys was more at home on land. His Ithaca is a marvellous creation, a vigorous transfiguration of all his Cimmery Lands and Mathrafals back into human terms. As in *Owen Glendower*, a slow, detailed early narrative stamps its character on the rest. That character is increasingly idiosyncratic: the dialogue is everywhere Powysian and nowhere realistic but the vocabulary notably rich; and the whole novel, for all its extravagances and vagaries and waywardness remains a major affirmation of life in its diversity, its narrative zest, and its sympathetic concern for every form of consciousness.

3

In *The Brazen Head* Powys returned to the Middle Ages and to Wessex. But the Wessex of this novel is a mythical Wessex, its landscape of heaths and swamps and woodland only broken by castles and abbeys of such unaboriginal names as the Fortress of Roque, Bumset Priory, or Lost Towers; nor is the historical background treated with the serious and meticulous scholarship of *Porius* or *Owen Glendower*. Indeed the famous historic figures who are the novel's leading characters are used simply as mouthpieces for particular Powysian themes, and the mental and spiritual world which they inhabit is that of Rabelais rather than the idealism and intensity of the thirteenth century. *The Brazen Head* is a historical fantasy, like *Atlantis* a vision of man-in-nature, and the most genial and robust of all the author's novels. The Wessex it portrays questions the Wessex of the earlier books, at the same time illuminating their particular quality.

Was it . . . that ever since Joseph of Arimathea brought the blood of Jesus to this coast, consecrating thereby the Mystery of Virginity and throwing a strange and desecrating shadow upon the greater Mystery of Procreation, there had been a craving, a longing, a hungering and thirsting, in the whole earthy substance of this portion of the West, so that the actual soil and sand and stones and rocks and gravel and pebbles of Wessex, along with the very slime of the worms beneath and the slugs above and the spawn of the frogs and the scum of the newts, and the cuckoo-spit of the smallest insect, had been roused to revolt against this preposterous edict of unnatural purity.[15]

It is precisely this sense of revolt, of strain, that is lacking in these final books. Like *Atlantis*, *The Brazen Head* is a kind of hymn of

15. *The Brazen Head* (Macdonald, 1956), p. 290.

liberation. In inventive qualities it falls short of its predecessor, nor does it possess, except momentarily, the poetic qualities of the other novels; but it is humorous and written in a far more muscular style. Its plot is virtually non-existent. The book is really a portrait of a group of eccentrics, or rather of eccentric attitudes: the characters are more vaguely defined than in the earlier books. It is possessed of mental rather than of imaginative energy, and is something of a conversation piece. It is the most Peacockian of the novels.

Its original title was 'The Three Barons', but its final one might well have been 'The Four Theologians'. Roger Bacon's brazen head plays relatively little part, save as a bone of contention between the two theologians who want to preserve it and the two who want to destroy it. Although Powys presents sympathetic pictures of Albert of Cologne and Roger Bacon, his sympathies lie outside the realm of theology proper. He sees dogmatic beliefs of whatsoever kind as a threat to human happiness. So at the very start of the book the giant Peleg prays to the moon:

Heal us ... O Goddess, of the hurts and wounds in our souls that ache and bleed today because of the false doctrines about gods and men that have been inflicted upon us, false doctrines about all things in heaven and earth!

Have they not taken on themselves, these priests of pain, these ministers of blood, to invent signs and tokens and symbols and sacraments out of privation and deprivation, out of suppression and frustration, out of denial and negation? Have they not defied the revelations made by thy blessed mystery, and turned to nothing the secret of thy holy rapture, of thy sacred madness, of thy entranced, thy transporting ecstasy? Make them give us back the pulse of our life, great Goddess, give us back the beat of our heart, give us back the dance of our blood![16]

The book ranges from moods and scenes of wild extravaganza to moments of seriousness and romantic beauty; the latter, however, are in a minority. The darkest element in the book is the character of the soldier of fortune, Peter Peregrinus, who incarnates not only the mania for destruction glimpsed in earlier figures but also the power to carry it out. His magic lodestone is operated through contact with his own genitals, and sex is shown in its negative as well as in its healing aspects. Indeed, in Peregrinus Powys portrays evil as an active force in the world. His encounter with two derelict beggars at a lonely turnpike crossing, and the curse put upon him by the woman, lead him to a memory of an act of cruelty committed by Edward, Prince of Wales, and of his vow to pay back the 'powerful, dominating, ruggedly handsome, battle-loving, strong willed Lord

16. ibid., pp. 14–15.

Edward'. Vengeance is exacted on the Prince's son, and Peter actually wills into the future the murder of Edward II in Berkeley Castle—an event which, as we have already seen, had a terrible fascination for Powys. It is his own belief that Peregrinus voices when he declares that 'there are certain turnpike valleys, in the future lives of us all ... in which things can be made to happen to us, either as a blessing or as a curse, by concentrated will supported by concentrated prayer addressed to Heaven or—mark you!—to Hell ...'[17] Half-ruefully in the *Autobiography* Powys admits to the suspicion that he may have kindred powers himself. Certainly he records his conviction there that 'the cause of every natural phenomenon is personal—the exertion of energy by a conscious, or at any rate a half-conscious *will*'.[18]

Peter's counterpart is a wickedly caricatured but extremely funny portrait of St. Bonaventura; and the self-consciously righteous man is thus set alongside the self-consciously wicked one—for Peter fancies himself as an anti-Christ. Both Roger Bacon and Albert of Cologne, on the other hand, are uninterested in their own merits or defects, and are impelled by a spirit of proper curiosity and reverence for life. Even Peregrinus is forced to admit Bacon's superiority.

'It shows that when a man is quiet and peaceful and timid and philosophical, and scared of both God and the Devil, and longs to live entirely for his own lonely sensations and for his fine points of learning and for the mystery of words, there may come a moment when he suddenly finds himself with a power of plunging into action and of abandoning himself to reckless and desperate moves, such as much stronger characters and much more formidable wills would never dare to display.'[19]

This is Powys's ideal of the good man.

The three barons are conceived in a mood of broad comedy, while the family at Lost Towers seem to have wandered straight off the drawing-board of Charles Addams. The young people, on the other hand, are most tenderly and sympathetically drawn. The book's centre of regulative normal sexual power is the couple Peleg the Giant and the Jewish girl Ghosta, who is his lover; they are rather solemn. But the misuse of sexual energy by Peter Peregrinus is contrasted with the wholeness and strength of Peleg and Ghosta, and he and Lilith of Lost Towers are specifically likened to Satan and the first wife of Adam.

17. *The Brazen Head*, p. 296.
18. *Autobiography*, p. 55.
19. *The Brazen Head*, p. 314.

The Brazen Head is stronger in its parts than as a whole. But its world is typical of Powys's last period, being earthy, speculative, and genial in tone. And the book contains at least three passages which bring us to the heart of Powys's secret, a secret which he is continually illuminating by such asides. The first of these concerns the philosophy of Sir Mort Abyssum (the name is clearly significant) which is a summary of Powys's beliefs about the nature of psychic reality expressed in most of novels from *Glastonbury* on. Sir Mort believed that

there was what he was pleased to describe as an invisible Dimension that existed over the whole surface of land and sea; and that into this Dimension rushed all the thoughts and feelings and passions and even sensations of everything that was subject to these things ... while we live we are all, including the myriads of sub-human lives in air, on land, and in water, from whales to earth-worms and the tiniest gnats, in constant contact with an invisible over-shadowing atmospheric mist, crowded with feelings and dreams and emotions and what might be called sense-emanations and thought eidola issuing from all that exists, whether super-human, human, or sub-human, whether organic or inorganic.[20]

Powys's last novel, *All or Nothing*, might have been written by Sir Mort Abyssum.

This belief in a circumambient dimension is the source of some of his most curious imaginative effects. A second passage from *The Brazen Head* reads like a piece of surrealistic metaphysics.

They were sitting side by side with their backs to a wall of wet dark stone. Down this wall dripped continually small trickles of water; while the wall itself was broken here and there by deep greenish-black clefts of incredible depth. In fact these cracks in the wall gave the impression that, were they enlarged so that a small person could worm himself into them, they might be found to lead, if the explorer had the courage to persevere and follow one of them to the bitter end, right to the very centre of the whole planet, where such an explorer would be liable to be devoured by that fabulous creature called the Horm, the legends about whom were evidently so appalling, and so likely to be disclosing a horrible reality, that, long before any written chronicle existed, they must have been deliberately suppressed by the self-preservative consciousness of the human race.[21]

This kind of epistemological sleight of hand is the equivalent in Powys's metaphysical speculations of the quality of wit. The interpenetration of physical and mental, central to his vision, is here used half-playfully in an image that is both amusing and disturbing.

20. ibid., pp. 165–6.
21. ibid., p. 149.

The very length of the sentence and the curlicue nature of its construction further the effect. Indeed, Powys went on improving as a
writer almost to the end of his life. *The Brazen Head* has a far more
flexible and lively style than the more famous novels preceding it.

The third and last of these representative passages gives us perhaps as good a description of Powys's own art as a novelist as any.
Ghosta is speaking.

Everybody's life's like a star with at least forty points branching out in
all directions, and every one of those points can turn eventually into a
life-long road of unending interest. But at the heart of that star the real
Peleg and the real Ghosta can sit at their hearth over their crock of pot-
tage, and watch the shadows on the wall, and hear the wind in the chim-
ney and the rain on the roof, and take to themselves the mystery of
everything.[22]

There is a Shakespearean ring to this: it recalls *King Lear*. It is this
apprehension of the eternal that makes Powys the satisfying writer
that he is.

4

Powys published two books between *The Brazen Head* and *All or
Nothing*. Following *Up and Out*, there is *Homer and the Aether*.
This is not a novel, but it throws light on this last stage of the
author's work. It is a free rendering and abridgement of the *Iliad*,
and as such not altogether successful, for the style is frequently
slangy, especially in the dialogues. The interest lies more in what
Powys makes of the matter of the poem rather than in its rendering
into modern English. The book is indeed less the 'walking commentary' he describes it as being, than a descant on the *Iliad*; and,
as it proceeds, Powys abandons translation and paraphrase for
commentary, interpolating glosses of his own, making Briseis, for
instance, a characteristic Powysian elementalist; and enlarging,
perhaps from schoolboy recollections, upon Thersites' ability to
tease. He attributes to the gods attitudes of his own and adds
humorous touches to heighten his interpretation of Homer's characters, as when he makes Diomed, after the wounding of Aphrodite,
walk away with the words 'If I turn round she'll know well why, and,
by Zeus, she shan't see me do it!'

In his description of the Aether Powys enunciates explicitly not
only his ideas as to the nature of the creative imagination, but also
his own purpose in these last imaginative works. The Aether has the

22. *The Brazen Head*, p. 151.

power of reading men's thoughts and is Homer's inspirer; but it is
not the Muse of poetry. Rather it is the author of what may be
called the poetic experience. In the introductory chapter called
'The Aether Speaks' it is clear that by this experience Powys means
one that he has already frequently described: '... the special kind
of ecstatic trance that I alone in the whole world have the power
of creating. I do it, of course, through the elements of air and water;
but I can only do it when these elements are transfigured by the
particular and special light with which I suffuse them'.[23] The Aether,
'the gleaming sky shining above and below Olympus' (we have
come a long way from the clogging oppression of the Somerset soil
in *Wood and Stone*), the Aether declares that the human mind has
the capacity to endue the inanimate with consciousness of a kind,
'gradually created in them by the person who habitually glances
at them'. This reciprocity between mind and matter is the natural
term of Powys's particular vision. And it springs from a romanticism
based not on aspiration but on recollection:

O my Homer, remember that the poetry of all your days and the days
upon earth of the race to which you belong comes from memory. Now
and then, perhaps, but O so rarely, come gleams to you of something,
something beyond all horizons, to which your race is slowly moving, but
the weird feelings that these gleams bring with them are ecstatic emotions
untranslatable in definite words. No, it is the memories that come to all
men, called up by particular objects in their daily life, in their dwellings,
rocks on the banks, stones on the paths, fallen trees in the copses, broken
masts by the edge of the sea, that call up the memories, sometimes
almost too wistful and poignant to be borne, by which the poetry of life
is created.[24]

This may not have much to do with the *Iliad;* but it is the very
stuff from which John Cowper Powys's imaginative world was
made.

His animism is the product of this close sense of belonging to
the physical cosmos, of being a part of its organism; and his rejection of purely rational or cerebral values is summed up in his comment upon Achilles:

What a tedious and uninteresting life the wife of Achilles would have
led! The sole purpose of his existence was to win glory for himself. He
was not interested in science like Hephaestus. He was not interested in
the government of men like his father. He was not interested in all the
magical secrets and under-sea mysteries familiar to all the Nereïds in the

23. *Homer and the Aether* (Macdonald, 1959), p. 23.
24. ibid., p. 27.

caves of the Old Man of the Sea. To be known by everybody a hundred thousand years hence as the swiftest runner and strongest spearman who ever lived, *that* was all he wanted! Glory, glory, glory! And to gain this he was ready to soak himself in blood.[25]

The pacifist, anarchist side of Powys made him reject such ideals as much as did his animism; but the rejection limits his understanding of the *Iliad*. The violence in his later writing has all the uneasy ferocity of one who dislikes a fight.

If in *Homer and the Aether* we find Powys fettered to some extent by his material, the same can certainly not be said about the final stories. Their particular type of fantasy, however, was not an entirely new development. In a long short story called *The Owl, the Duck, and—Miss Rowe! Miss Rowe!*, published in 1930 by William Targ of Chicago in a signed limited edition of 250 copies, he produced what is not only his single piece of fiction based on his life in America, but also his first experiment in animistic fantasy. The setting is the small apartment in Patchin Place, New York, of which he was to write in the *Autobiography*, where 'a group of Persons lived, two of whom were human, two Divine, one an apparition, several inanimate, and two again only half-created'. The last two are the fictional creations of a former tenant; and the whole little tale, with its poignant evocation of domesticity, is a portrait of the overlapping dimensions of material and spiritual worlds. Fanciful though it is, however, it has a strong hold on observable reality—a point demonstrable by reference to Powys's account of the relations between the old woman and her kettle, in which the play of his imagination works through a close observation, both visual and verbal, of the boiling kettle itself:

The tea-kettle on the stove began rattling its lid and letting fall small jets of boiling water which hissed down its heated metal sides and struck the hot stove with a gasp of disaster that made it seem as if a miniature cosmic cataclysm was in progress behind the screen. It was an old feud between these two feminine arbiters of the household. The very shape of the tea-kettle, whose straightness expressed the rigorous conception of feminine rectitude it held, was in part responsible for its incapacity to contain the water one second after the successful consummation of its boiling had been achieved. The old woman's former profession alone was sufficient to implant a strong suspicion and dislike in the kettle's hearth-bound domestically despotic heart, and it used these eruptions caused by the impersonal Laws of Nature as every member of the Feminine sex uses them—for her own psychological and emotional ends— which in the kettle's case were, namely, to upbraid and scold the old

25. *Homer and the Aether*, p. 246.

woman for the careless, shiftless hussy she was in not paying attention
to the primal unequivocal duties and concerns of one in possession of an
old man, a kettle and a hearth.[26]

   This and the last books present something of a problem to the
critic. It would be easy to regard the latter, and they have been so
regarded, as the self-indulgent day-dreams of extreme old age, re-
grettable eccentricities of a writer always notoriously eccentric.
But undisciplined and wayward though they are, *All or Nothing*
and the two shorter tales included in *Up and Out* are full of originality and vigour; and beneath the implausibility and farce there
lurks a serious purpose. They develop out of the author's earlier
work, and the elements of giant, fairy, and professor are as integral
to them as to the major novels.
   'Up and Out', the first story in the book of that name, is the least
satisfactory of these tales, and reads like a compendium of all
Powys's worst faults as a writer. It is the only one of his works which
genuinely deserves the charge of being childish and irresponsible:
there is a real and persistent feeling of self-indulgence about it.
The naming of his characters is now so odd and arbitrary as to be
positively repellent; and all attempts at verisimilitude are dropped.
The story, such as it is, tells of the destruction of the world by a
host of simultaneous nuclear explosions, and the subsequent adventures in outer space of the four survivors. These are the narrator,
Gor Goginog and his girl Rhitha; a monster called Org, the victim
and creation of vivisectionist experiments; and his girl, who is called
Asm. The nature of these names and the summary way in which
the catastrophe is dismissed in a single off-hand sentence introduce
quite the wrong kind of frivolous note for the allegedly serious dis-
cussions that follow on the small shred of the earth's surface on
which the party finds itself floating through space. In the course of
this journey they encounter personifications of Time, as a slug; of
Eternity, as a sickly yellow mist; of various gods and philosophers,
and finally of Jehovah and the Devil. The central theme is the
voluntary self-destruction of the created order; and at the end of the
tale the earthly quartet, together with God and the Devil, take the
leap into the ultimate dimension and are destroyed. The conclusion
is thus nihilistic. The main bias of the tale is against the idea of the
Absolute or the Eternal. The idea of eternity was anathema to
Powys who saw in it the stick used to beat poor suffering humanity
by religious dogmatists. But the relativism in religious matters
which is preached so persuasively in earlier books is here presented

   26. *The Owl, the Duck, and—Miss Rowe! Miss Rowe!* (William Targ,
Chicago, 1930), pp. 40–2.

with a testiness very rare in Powys, and the total effect of the story is to belittle rather than to honour the science of metaphysical speculation. 'Up and Out' is Powys's most cynical work, its over-all note of impatient jeering only relieved by periodic flashes of good-humoured raillery.

Its companion piece, however, is the most successful of the three fantasies. 'The Mountains of the Moon: a Lunar Love Story' has a coherence, a unity both of tone and of design expressed in the plainest of prose (plain, at any rate, by Powys's normal standards) and its themes and story express the quintessence of the author's final views on life. For all its oddness of setting and of characterization, it has something of the persuasiveness of myth.

Powys's moon is an idyllic, sparsely inhabited world, a world which can be reached by the astral bodies of dreamers upon earth. Its natives live from their spontaneous selves, know things intuitively; they live, that is to say, according to the inner world hinted at in the earlier novels. But the moon is also a type of the individual consciousness. As the moon-philosopher Om says to his young pupils,

'There is not only one creator. There are as many creators as there are living creatures. Each creature creates. That is why the only sensible meaning of the word "universe" is the particular collection of created worlds that surrounds each creature. We each have our own universe, so that in any philosophical sense the word "universe' is nonsense ... There are only universes, and all these universes interlock and intertwine and melt into one another.'[27]

For him 'the one and only category of every living creature's consciousness' is space. Time exists for reason and memory alone; it is not fundamental to our experience. Powys here is positing a timeless world.

The lovers in the story are the two motherless children of the Lord of Zed, Rorlt and Lorlt. They are descendants of a long line, and Powys reproduces his mythology of vegetable origins in the shape of an ancestor of theirs who 'preferred embracing trees to embracing women'.[28] Both boy and girl are looking for a mate, to save themselves from incestuous attraction, a theme to be taken up in *All or Nothing*. Neither of these stories has the nihilism of 'Up and Out'. Lorlt finds a lover in the son of the giant Oom; and Rorlt has to descend into the giant's underground cave before he can find Lorlt and as a result of looking for her, his own mate Helia, the

27. *Up and Out* (Macdonald, 1957), pp. 218–19.
28. ibid., p. 127.

only daughter of the moon. In Helia he finds his other self, his anima; and once again we find both giant and sylph, the sexual and mental energies of the unconscious, necessary for man's completion.

In addition to these characters we have a homely old philosopher and a lunar version of the Powysian old maid; and a second giant, a son of the moon who is firm in his belief that his father is Mars instead of the life-giving sun—a belief which is declared to be mistaken: the symbolism is obvious enough, though Powys hardly bothers to develop it. He is writing instinctively by this stage, and the various elements in his imagination fall simply into place without elaboration. More vivid is the curious collection of articulate inanimates (rather in the manner of those described in T. F. Powys's *Fables* but without any of the power of that unique book) who are emblems of certain events in world history—the heel of Achilles, for example, and a feather from the dove on Noah's ark: they form a kind of miniature satire on world history, or on the historical consciousness. But it is the undertow of human affairs that interests Powys. The giant Oom has a countenance 'that seemed to be rather the expression of elemental happenings than of supernatural intelligence'[29] and the philosopher whose name is Om (a contraction and concentration of the giant's energies?) voices another aspect of his creators gospel.

'The wiser any of us are, the more we confine our individual contribution to our race's future to a certain dull, regular, and resolute repetition of some monotonous but absolutely necessary daily labour ... I believe myself ... that this very dullness gives us sometimes a strange and mysterious feeling that, by thus sharing the submissiveness of what we call the Inanimate, we are really in touch with the deepest of all the mysteries of creative Nature.'[30]

This feeling for the inanimate is extended in the part played in the story by Rorlt's club Blob, a lunar version of the club in *Atlantis*, which leads him to his love, and which is made from the Orvod trees, fruit of Rorlt's ancestor's vegetable eroticism: again we are shown that there is no way to fulfilment that does not involve a return to roots. Coupled with this elementalism is an insistence on the permanent reality of spiritual forces, thought-projections, dreams: a vision of human life is presented that extends both inward to the forces of the unconscious and outward to the spiritual dimension. The speculation is conducted quietly, without rancour, and the whole little tale is suffused with peace. It carries

29. ibid., pp. 143–4
30. ibid., p. 194.

little emotional weight, and is uncertain in tempo and occasionally yields to one of the shortcomings of Powys's last phase, an injudicious use of outdated slang; however, it succeeds, not by virtue of its technical competence but by its consistency of vision. Powys's powers were on the decline; but they did not swerve from their self-chosen path.

5

All or Nothing is the longest and most important of the final fantasies. Though more uneven in quality than 'The Mountains of the Moon' it is more inventive and far-ranging, richer in pictorial qualities and humour; and the childlike simplicity of its narrative style conceals a certain complexity of theme. In it Powys gathers up the essence of his attitude to life as evolved through the major novels, and plays football with it in a wild phantasmagoric mixture of space-fiction, domestic comedy, metaphysics, fairy-tale, and farce. The book is both preposterous and profound, though it must be admitted that the former attribute outweighs the latter.

It is the story of four young people and of their adventures in space. John o'Dreams and Jilly Tewky are twins, with a close and, like the couple in 'The Mountains of the Moon', an almost incestuous affection for each other. Ring and Ting are the children of Urk, one of several giants who take part in the story. Again like Rorlt and Lorlt, both couples are descended from people with an especial affinity with vegetable growths—the giant's wife has been a lover of trees, while John and Jilly's irascible grandfather, old Grumble Nu, has created a vegetable called Gog-Magogs—in both pairs there is thus a union between the vegetable world and the world of sexual potency. But whereas the Nu family are full of warm human feeling (the tea-table at their house, Morty, being an obvious reminiscence of the Powys tea-table at Montacute Rectory, so vividly described in the various family memoirs), Giant Urk is a life-hater, with the spirit of resentment and defeat in his blood. The antimonies of the early novels are thus revived.

The space adventures are three in number. In the first and shortest John and Jilly visit the heart of the sun, and John kills Giant Urk when he tries to devour it, much as Moloch was seen eating the moon in 'Up and Out': in all three tales swallowing is an image of evil as the lust to devour and destroy. The killing of Urk by a series of violent blows on the head, described in rather sickening detail, echoes in an interesting manner the sadistic imaginings of Mr. Evans in *A Glastonbury Romance*; here in this final act of

violence Powys exorcizes the evil impulse by putting it to a good
end.

The second voyage is to a star in the Milky Way called Vindex,
and takes place under the aegis of the Arch-Druid, a disappoint-
ingly colourless individual. Vindex is rife with political and racial
tensions, plots, and schemings; not surprisingly the most sympathetic of its inhabitants are the most ancient ones, the Horners,
who seem to have strayed out of the pages of Swift. On Vindex the
travellers meet the Cerne Giant and bring him back to earth; and
the final voyage is undertaken in his company. It involves the
creation of a new star altogether, a star made out of the soil of
Wessex and dedicated to Boadicea, the embodiment in this book
of the wise old matriarchal rule envisaged in the Welsh novels—a
rather surprising embodiment, it must be admitted, in view of
her traditional warlike character. But she is portrayed at the end of
the book, when the two young couples and their children go with
the Cerne Giant to the Tower of London to offer her homage, as a
wise and gracious figure.

All these wild adventures are narrated in the most perfunctory
manner, and nowhere is it more evident that Powys was not interested in the practical details of his plots, but only in the private
feelings of his characters. Landscape is but lightly sketched in, and
the trips through space are barely imagined at all. What keeps the
book going is its sheer energy, evidenced in a proliferation of characters and a lively stream of philosophical discussion. The characters
include, in addition to those already mentioned, a worm and a
slug, a country rector, a cyclops, a nightmare called Lorm, two wise
old spinsters called Auntie Oh and Miss Posh, God (incarnate first
as a newt and then as a cockroach), a Space Monster, a couple of
village girls straight out of the pages of *Wolf Solent*, and a falling
star. Powys's doctrine of universal consciousness here finds its logical
embodiment.

The heart of the book lies at the strangely imagined fountain of
Bubble and Squeak. The fountain is flanked by

what looked like a fossilized skull on one side of the over-hanging rock,
and what looked like a petrified flower-bowl on the other side of the over-
hanging rock ... at regular intervals, lasting only two ticks of a clock,
there fell simultaneously little blobs of earth upon the very broad and
flat top of the fossilized skull, and drops of water into the middle of the
flower-bowl, which was already filled with water up to the brim. The top
of the fossilized skull was indeed already carrying a pillar of earth ... a
pillar of earth that had even now come to resemble a thick totem pole
balanced upside down. But as opposed to this slowly developing inverted

pole on the right, the perfectly formed bowl on the left, brimming with water, showed not the slightest change from what it must have become, and in what it must have remained, for a thousand years . . . Each drop of water as it fell made a splash, and each splash created a bubble which rose and burst in the air. But the weird thing about the whole matter was that, simultaneously with the bursting of the bubble, there came from the mouth of the skull a clear, definite and unmistakable squeak.[31]

It is characteristic of Powys to make out of a nursery phrase a metaphysical image. The bubble represents the nothingness against which all existence is defined, and to which all existence is pulled; the skull, of the First Man, embodies the urge to creation, the All which in another light includes even Nothing. The two concepts are set against each other repeatedly throughout the tale, and are related to the concept of space. Powys's particular cult of the present moment, of the transcending of bodily sensations by a deliberately diffused sensuality, led him to a reverence for space as against time —Time he saw as a false God, Space as the primal category. Various interpretations of the nature of space are voiced. The Space Monster, an amiably philosophical spherical swallower, finds the idea of infinity meaningless; but the Cerne Giant is prepared to entertain the idea of other dimensions, that 'we are living in one world, while another world parallel to it exists side by side with it—another world, or a dimension wherein we would be surrounded by a totally different aspect of the whole of life'.[32] It is God who, appropriately enough, seems to provide the real answer, not in what he says so much as in what he is. Space is all there is, but differentiation, which is necessary to consciousness, involves the idea of nothing. However impossible the idea, nothing is an aspect of existence—both the bubble and the skull comprise the fountain. Powys in this final work seems concerned to reconcile two moods, the creative and the destructive urge—we are back in the world of *Rodmoor* and *Ducdame*. The final conclusion voiced by Boadicea is that it is only in the human heart, that is to say in the consciousness, that the meaning of life is to be found: speculation cannot answer the ultimate questions as effectively as the romantic yearnings of John o'Dreams.

No, the difference between his feeling for Jilly Tewky and his feeling for Ting had nothing to do with right and wrong or good and evil, nothing to do with the dark wickedness of what people called incest. It had something about it, this difference, that resembled the difference between those far-away glimpses of a sea-horizon just visible between rocks and trees and beyond the far-flowing estuary of a mighty river, and the out-

31. *All or Nothing* (Macdonald, 1960), pp. 22–3.
32. ibid., p. 192.

lines of a forest and lakes and towering crags and a ruined castle rising up in the immediate foreground. Magnificently imposing though that castle and lake and forest might be there was something infinitely more strange and poetical in that far-away horizon beyond the mouth of the wandering river. And if Jilly Tewky was the exciting, massive castle reflected in the deep lake with its romantic lights and shadows and its overhanging battlements, Ting was that far-off glimpse of an horizon retreating into the mystery of forgotten memories, and even into a half-conscious sense of lives lived long, long ago, before our mother gave us birth into this present world.[33]

In this passage we have the essence of Powys's romanticism as freshly presented as when he first began to write. His love for painting, especially the paintings of Claude, is evident here, together with his capacity for assimilating personality to landscape, and the peculiar blend of forward-looking romantic yearning combined with a sense of primeval origins. And all this is transmitted in a prose of childlike spontaneity and grace.

But by the time he came to write *All or Nothing* Powys's powers were waning, and the book suffers from a certain impatience and from perverse changes in mood; his characters are more than usually unhappy in their way of speech, and John o'Dreams in particular is an unattractive mixture of violent language, mental sophistication, and schoolboy behaviour. There is far too abrupt a shift between the plane of the commonplace and the fantastic, and the constant implausibility becomes wearing, though as Powys himself contends, 'however gravely and logically we look at things, there remains in life an element of pure bedlam'.[34] The bedlam breaks out in this book in passages of hilarious and unexpected farce, a crazy mix-up of physical and psychic; but coupled with this is something more permanent, that sense of wonder and mystery and veneration for life which makes Powys the profound imaginative visionary that he is.

33. ibid., p. 149.
34. ibid., p. 77.

CHAPTER SIX

The Novelist and his Art

1

In coming to any assessment of Powys's achievement it is necessary to make certain preliminary reservations. It is as a novelist and autobiographer that he is likely to be remembered: the rest of his output is chiefly valuable for what it tells us about the man who wrote the prose romances. He was a lively and idiosyncratic letter writer; but, as with his poems (written for the most part in the earlier stages of his career), one is led to feel that he conveyed himself in direct personal expression less satisfactorily than in the more indirect methods of fiction. The *Autobiography* indeed draws much of its strength from the way in which Powys treats himself as if he were one of his own characters. In the criticism and philosophical writings he effaces himself rather more than in the letters and poems; but interesting though they are (in spite of frequent repetitions and *longueurs*) they are more probably enjoyed by admirers of Powys the novelist than by systematic critics or philosophers; they have all the vices as well as all the virtues of amateur work—though the word 'amateur' should perhaps be replaced by the word 'independent': Powys wrote out of a wide and pondered range of reading. All his work bore the unmistakable stamp of his personality; but the very strength of that personality lends enchantment to its distancing.

Most of the novels are flawed by tricks of style. The same could be said of writers as different as Dostoevsky and Hardy; but Powys's shortcomings are less easy to escape than theirs, being built into even his finest passages. He frequently writes slackly, with garrulity and clumsiness; his chapters are far too long, his metaphysical asides frequently intrusive and implausible. The use of capital letters and constant exclamation marks, the whimsicality, the coyness, the fustian literary echoes of Carlyle and Scott, the irrelevancies and distortions, the flagrant disregard for verisimilitude, the euphemistic circumlocutions, above all the self-indulgent airing of private fancies and peccadilloes are constant sources of alienating irritation. More seriously, such bad writing weakens confidence in what he has to say; it is fatally easy to damage his reputation by

random quoting. And he is easily parodied. Such an exercise might
run as follows:

What our inscrutable friend then proceeded to do next was nothing less
than to cast his prematurely attenuated frame at the dainty feet of this
buxom daughter of Eve whose sidelong glances, cast provocatively and
with winsome artlessness in his direction, seemed to be imploring him not
to delay any further his indulgence in the sweet dalliance of prolonged
and vicious love-making; and then to select with an exquisite and at the
same time whimsical nicety certain wafer-thin slices of brown bread and
butter cut only an hour before by the soap-scrubbed hands of none
other than that elderly damsel Totty Buttercup, and greedily to devour
these delicious morsels of wheaten sustenance with a whole series of
scooped-up, rinsed-out, downward-gurgling, upward-snorting gobbles of
incredible appreciation, gobbles which, if the truth be told, had not been
heard in that particular corner of our terraqueous planet that lies between
Bickery Heath and Plimsolbury, since the last slimy-scaled crustaceous
dragon winged its flight beyond the uttermost reach of the furthest stellar
galaxy in this problematical universe that is, if the deductions of certain
scholarly philosophers be correct, not a universe at all *but a multi-parti-
tional, inter-veritudinal superverse!*

But parody can be a mark of respect and affection as well as one
of mockery, and the major writers can survive it. (Lesser ones are
helped by it to survive.) Max Beerbohm's celebrated burlesque of
Henry James's style in *A Christmas Garland* contains appreciation
as well as merriment. Parody, and the occasion for it, are alike
penalties of being a strong personality, and only dull or faultless
writers are exempt.

More important than the easy task of noting Powys's faults is the
recognition of his merits. One of the least deliberate and most spontaneous of twentieth-century writers, probably one of the greatest
and certainly the most neglected of those with kindred gifts, his
name appears in relatively few histories of the novel or surveys of
the literary scene. That this is in part owing to historical causes
has already been indicated: romantic novelists have been out of
vogue because they work from premises which criticism, and indeed the popular urban temper of the time, refuse to take seriously.
The possibility of Powys's relevance not being admitted, the
seriousness of his achievement is ignored. His faults are of a kind
which current standards find abhorrent, and he stands so far outside the mainstream of twentieth-century literature that he is
neglected both by literary historians and by writers on the novel.
His reputation is kept alive not by academic critics or teachers or by
popular reviewers but by general readers content to accept his

novels on their own merits, innocent of the predetermined pattern of what is considered significant for English literature.

Enough has perhaps been said, in expounding the novels themselves, about the more esoteric aspects of his message and vision: what it is important to stress is that a satisfying response to his fiction does not depend on full comprehension of, or assent to, this aspect of his work. Powys's greatness as a novelist is independent of his status as a seer, although, having said that, one must add that the actual breadth and wisdom of his total outlook is part of the secret of that greatness. But his real strength lies in the creation of a solidly realized, imaginatively consistent and, for the most part, artistically persuasive fictional world—a world whose landscapes and characters and dramas have a profound bearing on the consciousness of men and women living in the age of the industrial and technological revolutions, and on the understanding of what it is to be a human being at all.

2

To start with his landscapes. That Powys is one of the great masters of landscape portrayal is generally admitted: even his adverse critics concede his effectiveness in this. We have noted in his work a gradual absorbtion of landscape into the central themes of his novels: from the relatively detached 'background' descriptions in *Wood and Stone* through the symbolic use of natural scenery in *Rodmoor* and *Ducdame* to an account of the interpenetration of landscape with character in the Wessex novels. In his later work Powys relies increasingly on the minutely accurate recording of detail to stress the integral part physical environment plays in consciousness and to expound his vision of man's involvement in the inanimate—a vision to which all his earlier work had been tending. There is thus a wide variety not only of actual scene (scenes ranging from the dense woodlands of Dorset to the wide East Anglian sea-scapes, from the Welsh mountains to the Glastonbury water-meadows, with all their different imaginative and symbolic overtones) but of presentation of scene, not only landscape faithfully observed but landscape emotionally experienced. This includes not only, as in Scott's novels, the back-cloth or underlining uses of landscape—one recalls the vast storm-tossed marshland of *Rodmoor* which heightens and emphasizes the lost bewilderment of the characters—but also the use of landscape in the manner of Lawrence, to blend in with and further his characters' self-awareness. *Rodmoor* provides an example of this method in the

'Sun and Sea' chapter, and others occur in *Wolf Solent* (Wolf's seduction of Gerda in the water-meadows, his visit with Miss Gault to King Aethelwolf's tomb in the Abbey Church) and in *Weymouth Sands* (Perdita's and the Jobber's love-making at the Clipping Stone, Magnus's visit to Curly at the Wishing Well) where the actual setting of the scene is a contributory factor in the characters' actions. More frequently, however, he uses landscape as a diffused element in his people's communal awareness, and nowhere more notably than in *Porius* where we are transported into a world in which natural forces are the predominant factor in human lives, more important even than the issues of love and war because more general and more enduring. It is in this kind of natural description that Powys excels and through which he conveys the burden of his message. Landscape is not an addition to his fictional world but a vital part of it, and the weakest novels are precisely those in which landscape plays a relatively unimportant role.

But this feeling for physical environment extends beyond the world of scenery: Powys's use of domestic interiors is no less impressive and effective. It is here that he shows the breadth of his psychological understanding, as well as his affinities with painting. Readers of the novels will have little difficulty in summoning a large number of interiors to their minds—the plainly furnished bedroom of Darnley Otter, Christie's little sitting-room, the drawing-room at Spy Croft with all its late-Victorian impedimenta, Owen Glendower's dining-hall, Gipsy May's hut, the untidy muddle in the sitting-room at Glymes, the mysterious haunted chamber in Mark's Court, the armoury in the Fortress of Roque, the little dairy shop where John Crow first meets Edgar Athling—interiors described with a faithfulness worthy of Dürer and with not a little of the imaginative force of Dickens. But whereas Dickens's art is essentially impressionistic, Powys is concerned to combine description with reflection. He can do this by a meticulous use of detail that leads up to an illuminating comparison that successfully places the room's occupant:

Funny old things they were—Mrs. Geard's possessions—the woollen antimacassars, the sickly yellow pears and blue grapes under a big glass covering, with red plush round its base, the staring picture of her father, the Plymouth Brother, with whiskers like a sailor and a mouth like a letter-box closed for Sunday; the old, worn, ash-coloured carpet, the black bear rug with broad red-flannel edgings and more mouse-grey skin than black hairs left to view, and all the ancient, stained, blotched, greasy cushions that always were to be, and never *had* been, re-covered; and the rickety little tables with glaring tablecloths, and so many brackets with green and red tassels hanging from photograph frames, containing groups of Geards and Rhyses, the former a good deal less pompous-looking but hardly less stiff and uncomfortable in their photographer's parlours—all these things made up a sort of dusty, cushiony ensemble, like the huge nest of some kind of stuffed bird, now extinct.[1]

Or he can convey the scene more indirectly through the meditations of an observer: here is Magnus Muir in Miss le Fleau's drawing-room at Kimmeridge House:

'It *is* a brown room, this room,' he thought. And he remembered how he had told its owner on one occasion that it was like a 'brown study', and with what a wry face she had received that remark. But the effect of it *was*, in some odd way, brown; though except for the round mahogany table, and that was polished till it looked like deep water, there was not an actual brown thing in it. The wallpaper was a pale 'Dutch pink', bordering on yellow. The cushions and carpet were a dull, rather muddy plum-colour. The pictures were all old, coloured prints, most of them of that smooth, mellow, *greasy* effect that is so peculiarly soothing—as if a misty, oily film, stolen from many natural twilights, had been spread over sketches in crayon; while the books in the three solid rosewood bookcases were almost all green and gold, their bindings carrying all those quaint curlecues and flourishes so popular in the middle of the nineteenth century.[2]

In both these descriptions we have the evocation of that late nineteenth-century world that Powys makes particularly his own, a world in which the crowded display of material things, a thick sense of physical actuality, is seen in a dim light as from a certain distance, a faded air imparting a sense of something insubstantial to lighten the solidity of the original impression. It was a world peculiarly suited to convey Powys's presentation of reality, a blend of homeliness with the nostalgia for the far away, of present actuality with an underlying feeling for the past.

3

This density of physical detail is an important element in those big crowd scenes in which Powys excelled, and in which his technique again resembles that of Dickens. But Powys's big scenes are more than great set pieces: they are narrative watersheds, and from them flow different currents in the novel's total theme. A good example of this is the chapter in *A Glastonbury Romance* called 'The Christening'. The christening is that of Nell Zoyland's son by Sam Dekker.

1. *A Glastonbury Romance*, pp. 675–6.
2. *Weymouth Sands*, pp. 34–5.

Will Zoyland, realizing, unknown to Nell, that the child is not his, loves it all the same; but tension exists between them on account of his intrigue with their servant Doxy Pippard. The guests at the christening are likewise in a state of sexual frustration and include Mat Dekker, himself deeply in love with Nell, and Dave and Persephone Spear, estranged husband and wife. A second party goes on in the kitchen, involving a number of the subordinate characters and described with lively humour. Attention shifts from this party to the one in the dining-room with the move from one to the other of Mrs. Legge; and with her, the local procuress, the sexual tensions work up to breaking-point. Will and Persephone wander out into the dark and make love in a boat; Mat's desire for Nell all but makes him break down; Will and Nell quarrel violently over the child; and the scene ends with Nell's resolution to leave Will and move to the protection of the Dekkers, and with the loss of the christening cup, the 'dolls house grail', in the river. The development of events is slow, full of the ebb and flow of humour, and realized down to the last detail; the various thoughts and reactions of the participants are contrasted with and comment on each other. The final breakdown of Nell comes as a relief to the reader as much as to her, so vivid has been the building up of tension. And there is a touch of brilliant comic invention when Will and Persephone return to the others, relaxed and satisfied after love-making but affected by acute post-coital hunger, only to find in their absence that the supper has been eaten by the rest of the party and that there is nothing left. The realism and ironic humour of this is very characteristic of Powys.

For all the multiplicity of its points of interest, however, the scene does not develop casually: there are a number of pointers marking the development of its inner meaning. The main theme centres round ideas of order and disorder in the sexual field. The chapter, after noting the baptism of Tossie Stickles's illegitimate twins, offspring of Tom Barter, goes on to describe that of a more significant child, the bastard born by Nell to Sam—both of them types of the natural goodness of the earth, Nell in her warm sexuality and motherhood, Sam in his saintliness and preoccupation with botany and the vegetable world—always a favourite element in Powys's scheme of values. As against this 'good' adultery, so to call it, for it is the fruit of genuine love, is set the trivial adultery of Zoyland with the servant girl—an intrigue described with the kind of circumlocutory coyness of which Powys was so disastrously a master. Doxy and her mother prove to be dissentient factors in the kitchen; when the innocent and charming Nancy Stickles rebukes

Doxy for her intrigue with Zoyland she is in turn accused of one with Red Robinson: but this confusion of values is roundly dealt with by old Abel Twig. 'Thik Red Robinson were zour, no doubt, when Mistress Nance didn't let 'un do what 'a wanted to do ... and so 'a went and cast up this tale agin' her, as thik dirty Potiphar-scrub did agin' King Joseph in History.'[3] The theme of adultery is furthered by Will's seduction of Percy in the boat, and is given its Arthurian reference afterwards when the lovers sit drinking whisky out of the same glass, 'which might have been drugged for them by that same Dame Brisen, who, in the days when love was all, brought Lancelot du Lac to the bed of young Elaine'. And that quietly placing phrase, 'when love was all', is taken up specifically by Percy's husband, the idealistic and Christ-like Dave Spear, as he watches the lovers gazing at each other.

'And this sort of thing is what they call a personal life! These people are thinking of nothing else but their own personal emotions; and they are proud of it ... I'll teach these good friends of mine how to be imper-sonal! These people think that their feelings are the only serious thing in the world. *Their feelings!* When, at this very moment in China, in India, in New York, in Berlin, in Vienna—Good God! ... *their feelings!* When, at this moment, if all the pain in the world caused by this accursed personal life, by this accursed individual life were to rise up in one terrific cry ... It would'—The little Henry's crying—as if to round off Dave's thoughts—rose to a pitch that was distressing to hear.[4]

The subsequent loss of the baby's christening cup, indirectly a re-sult of Persephone's drinking neat whisky out of it at Zoyland's drunken urging (a kind of physical and spiritual blasphemy), comes as another image of the failure to achieve the Grail. The party breaks up in disorder, and only Dave is left quietly reading a book about the lost Atlantis. 'But he read only three pages. It is hard to be impersonal in a cosmos that runs to personality.'[5] The whole scene had no central meaning, but there is a kind of spiritual logic in events. Powys records and comments, but he never directs, never points out to the reader what he considers they ought to be think-ing: his approach is dispassionate and uncritical, save for the kind of dramatized internal criticism voiced by Dave—and Dave is as much shown up by the other characters as they are by him. The over-all impression is tragic, but the tragedy is shot through with comedy, even in the seduction of Persephone by Will, where the disparity between their two attitudes to sex is almost cruelly shown

3. *A Glastonbury Romance*, p. 840.
4. ibid., p. 860.
5. ibid., p. 870.

up. And the setting encompasses the scene: all that happens takes place in a house in lonely isolation in the marshes, and the sense of that house's gradual abandonment as the guests leave it one by one is powerfully conveyed. This physical vividness, coupled with the scene's apparent indirection, goes far to explaining the particular imaginative appeal of Powys's novels: it is impossible to forget what they show, but very hard to understand at a first reading what they mean.

The vividness is often heightened, even in a brief scene, by a kind of lighting, reminiscent sometimes of a painting by Rembrandt —that in which Mr. Evans and Cordelia come across Mad Bet and Finn Toller in the sheepfold plotting the murder of John Crow comes immediately to mind, or that in which Sylvanus and Marret say goodbye beside Tup's Fold in the light of dawn. In one scene, that of the Maundy Thursday feast in Glastonbury vicarage, Powys specifically likens the spectacle to a picture by Breughel. As we have seen, dawn and twilight had an especial appeal for him, and some of his most memorable impressions are of these half-lights— perhaps because they so naturally embody his double vision of reality. All the major novels abound in scenes where the weather is a predominating element—the gusty wet night in which Perdita arrives at Weymouth, the scorching noontide when Dud is confronted with his father, the bright morning air through which Rhisiart and Tegolin journey towards Owen's house, the strange watery light in which so much of *Wolf Solent* is suffused:

It was one of those Spring evenings which are neither golden from the direct rays of the sinking sun, nor opalescent from their indirect diffused reflection. A chilly wind had arisen, covering the western sky, into which they were driving, with a thick bank of clouds. The result of this complete extinction of the sunset was that the world became a world in which every green thing upon its surface received a fivefold addition to its greenness. It was as if an enormous green tidal wave, composed of a substance more translucent than water, had flowed over the whole earth; or rather as if some diaphanous essence of all the greenness created by long days of rain had evaporated during this one noon, only to fall down, with the approach of twilight, in a cold, dark, emerald-coloured dew.[6]

This kind of observation transcends mere precision: it enlarges awareness altogether. The novels are full of this kind of transmutation, so that the physical environment not only offsets but interpenetrates the mental dramas of the characters.

6. *Wolf Solent*, pp. 23–4.

4

Coupled with this sensitivity to surface and appearance we find a
brilliant handling of physical dimension. The novels are full of a
kind of spatial distancing—a device that Powys perhaps learned
from Hardy. Figures are occasionally depicted from far off, as if
they were figures in a painting. *Rodmoor* is especially rich in such
effects, and a similar one is found in *A Glastonbury Romance*
shortly before Young Tewsy catches the great chub of Lydford,
when the converging movements of Edgar and Lady Rachel, Sam
and James Rake are plotted or mapped out from afar before they
actually encounter. Such long-distance portrayals add greatly to
the sense of significance, a mysterious significance, of the various
movements of Powys's people. We oscillate between a close, in-
tricate acquaintance with the movement of their inmost thoughts
and a remote, almost Olympian view of their physical activities.
Their world thus feels intensely real and yet at the same time is
clearly fictional.

But it is the close intimacy with their inmost selves which is
predominant. Powys's characters, strange and eccentric though they
may be, have enormous vitality as individuals. And this vitality
stems, not only from the inventive genius of the author, but also
from their own articulation of what it feels to be alive. Dave Spear's
mutterings about personal relationships are endorsed by the way in
which Powys treats the private lives of his characters. Introspective
they may be, but it is an introspection concerned with their relation to the world that surrounds them. In none of his central
characters is there a vestige of self-pity: their problem is not loneliness but relatedness.

In claiming that there is an absence of self-pity one might seem
to be ignoring the character of Wolf Solent. Wolf is certainly shown
as often being very sorry for himself but his fundamental problem is
how to contain and channel his exuberant sensationalism, his intense
inner feelings. Powys always starts from the positive affirmation of
vitality, even when many of his characters such as Perdita or Adrian
Sorio or Mr. Evans are frequent victims of depression. Underlying
his work there is an enormous, deeply pondered optimism.

This optimism is the more convincing because it involves an
examination and acceptance of tragedy. *Weymouth Sands*, for all
that it contains more purely comic writing than the other novels,
is the one in which this tragedy is most overt, but it sounds again
and again in all of them, nowhere more plangently than in *Owen*

Glendower, in Owen's final withdrawal to the ancient camp. Tragedy in Powys's world centres around the impossibility of fulfilling romantic longings and the continuing presence of physical pain. His sceptical spirit prevented him from portraying a tragic hero in the conventional sense; but the tragic flaw as it exists for example in Mr. Evans does touch the note of genuine tragedy in the extraordinary scene where he attempts—and fails—to turn his sadistic impulse back upon himself by being crucified in the Glastonbury pageant. More common is the tragedy of unrequited love, treated with a wide variety of mood but with an equal intensity and vividness in such characters as Selena Gault, Mat Dekker (an especially sympathetic portrait), and Euphemia Drew. The destructive aspect of withheld passion is powerfully suggested, as are the tense relationships in *Maiden Castle*. Coupled with this feeling for repressed energies is an awareness of cruelty that makes itself apparent not only in a repeated reference to the obvious case of vivisection, but also in such deliberate actions as Mad Bet's attempted murder of John Crow and Owen's actual treatment of Lord Grey of Ruthin or Lowri's tormenting of her besotted lover Simon. Powys's novels, for all their reticence, give a powerful sense of the possibilities of evil, most especially perhaps in the frightened whispering world of Kings Barton in *Wolf Solent*. Evil is for him always associated with fear and furtiveness—a clear example of this being the experiment on the dog carried out by the young French ambassador in *Owen Glendower*. And it is in his three greatest novels, *Wolf Solent*, *A Glastonbury Romance*, and *Owen Glendower*, that these intimations of evil are most keenly felt.

The darkness, and awareness of morbidity and cruelty, are offset, however, by the pathos of so many of the characters, especially the forlorn or downcast—people like Peg Frampton in *Weymouth Sands*, the boy Elphin in *Glastonbury*, or the dwarf Sibli. Powys is without illusions as to Peg's promiscuity or Sibli's sadistic tendencies; but their essential situation is so firmly apprehended in relation to the society in which they live that he is able to portray their derelict state without any recourse to sentimentality. Indeed Powys is among our least sentimental writers, avoiding as he does the extremes of over-optimism or extreme disillusionment. His most pathetic characters have a way of seeming funny even when they are being most sympathetically presented.

Indeed, it is the comedy in Powys's novels which in the last resort gives them their enduring appeal and power to enlighten and refresh. This comedy takes many forms. There are, for example, the numerous rustic or yokel figures, figures whose function is primarily to provide humorous relief, figures like Isaac Weatherwax and Abel Twig in *A Glastonbury Romance* or Mr. Torp in *Wolf Solent*; their speech, a decidedly mannered 'Mummerset', is excellently managed of its kind, and challenges comparison with T. F. Powys's essays in the same sort of thing. It might be argued that this is a cheap and easy way of attaining a humorous effect; but these figures are never *merely* humorous, and have other attributes as well—Abel Twig being as sympathetic and kindly as old Weatherwax is the reverse. In *Weymouth Sands* there is a splendidly managed scene in which an assemblage of old women comment on the events of the Cattistock wedding: each speaker is distinctly characterized, and their different social attitudes epitomize the life of the town. And as an example of Powys's genial, sardonic, and inventive tone when introducing one of his rustics, there is the case, also in *Weymouth Sands*, of the unfortunate Mr. Dandin:

Mr. Dandin screwed round, on the pivot of his thin neck, his scarecrow physiognomy, with its retreating chin and enormous knobbly nose and stared at each of the company in turn. But the responses he received were torpid. The old clerk was so used to having that lack-lustre, bored look fixed upon him that he had come to assume that this look was the natural look of the human race! It certainly was the look of the whole Radipole congregation when he repeated 'And with thy spirit', in the Church responses. It had been the look of Shepherd Rugg all the way to Weymouth in the 'bus this morning. Herb had only to turn his face towards any living thing and the eyes of that thing grew as glazed as the eyes of old Gideon. When he went to his privy these autumn mornings and just glanced through the wet mist over the nettles and burdocks of Mr. Cole's hedge to catch the yellow eye of Mr. Cole's great sow, the creature, in plain pig-language, told him he was a nuisance.[7]

Often the humour is slipped in in parenthesis: ' "What was that?" cried Mrs. Gadget in alarm at the terrible strength of the wind for she had always said to her husband even in the by-gone days when she resisted his passion, "Our place be too near the edge of the cliff, John." '[8] But more generally there is a play of humour over the entire action of each book, nowhere more evident than in the mixture of the grotesque with the serious, as in the character of Sylvanus Cobbold and John Geard, and of which the love-making of Cordelia and Mr. Evans is the most poignant example:

Their wet cold faces, her shapeless nose and his grotesque hooked nose like the caricature-mask of a Roman soldier, their large, contorted, abnormal mouths, made, it might seem, more for anguished curses against God

7. *Weymouth Sands*, p. 463.
8. ibid., p. 262.

than for the sweet usage of lovers, were now pressed savagely against each other and, as they kissed, queer sounds came from both their throats, that were answered by the groanings of the tree and by the raindrops as the wind shook it.[9]

In emphasizing the grotesque element in Powys's humour there may be a danger of forgetting how subtle he can be. We have already noted the masterly portrayal, in *Wolf Solent* and *Maiden Castle*, of domestic quarrels; and what is especially remarkable about those portrayals is the fact that they are as funny as they are touching and observant. Few authors can excel Powys when it comes to depicting the discomfiture of the male before the female. In *Weymouth Sands* there is, in the description of the relationship between Magnus Muir, Richard Gaul, and Sippy Ballard, a delicately humorous and exactly caught rendering of masculine psychology in its bachelor aspect; while *Wolf Solent* shows the matter in its more sinister light in the threefold relationship between Parson Valley, Jason, and the Squire. Powys was acutely sensitive not only to sex differentiation but also to the exchange of masculine and feminine qualities between the sexes, and this is matter for some of his finest comedy.

5

Indeed in his treatment of sex Powys is very far from being the old-fashioned novelist that he at first appears to be. His treatment of passion and its side-issues is extremely subtle and sophisticated, not least because he is prepared to allow for the element of humour. That he fully understood the nature of straightforward passion his account of Nell's and Sam's night together in Whitelake Cottage is ample proof; but his especial concern seems to have lain more in the less common kinds of sexual attraction and repulsion. In the *Autobiography* he gives a frank account of his own sexual peculiarities, especially his attraction to those sylphlike girls who figure so frequently in the novels, and his obsessed voyeurism on Brighton beach. It is rather typical of Powys that, whereas most autobiographers when they refer to their sexual lives do so in boastful terms, he should relate his failures and inadequacies. Indeed it is his concentration on sexual inadequacy that makes him a distasteful writer to some people, for in doing so he is not, except in the remarkable scene where Wolf Solent finds himself unable to make love to Christie, describing a failure. Dud's and John Crow's sterile love-making is deliberate. Powys's reticence is a little frustrating in

9. *A Glastonbury Romance*, p. 785.

the latter case—John and Mary's sexual encounters are described as
'vicious', but it is never made quite explicit why this word is justified,
although enough is given for the reader to make his own guesses.
But this is characteristic of Powys: it is not the physical activity
of sex which interests him, but its mental and psychic aspects; and
it is this concentration on the imaginative force of sexual fantasy
that enables him to declare at one point that of all the people in
Glastonbury 'John Crow, contemplating the real figure of Mary
toying with the little wild pansies, and Angela Beere contemplating
the imaginary figure of Persephone, first in one aspect and then in
another, as she sketched the famous ruin usually known as St
Joseph's chapel, were the two ... whose amorous excitement was
most intense.'[10] Typical of him too is the note on the activities from
which both lovers are at the same time detached.

The power of sexual fantasy is one of the leading motives in
Maiden Castle, where, as in *Weymouth Sands*, Powys makes play
with the traditional notions, found in magic, of the spiritual powers
inherent in the unravished love of virgins. This magical aspect of
sex is, however, secondary to the extremely convincing way in which
the particular energy of repressed sex is palpable in characters like
Thuella or Angela Beere; and to Powys's disturbing power of describing and evoking the sensation of sexual titillation. Indeed this
aspect of his writing is one where his very stylistic faults serve him
well, since the tendency to arch circumlocution that mars much of
his work is itself an embodiment of the particular aberration he is
describing. But there is a wide range of treatment here: the episode
in *Weymouth Sands* when Larry Zed gets Perdita to lie down on
his bed is a far cry from the mutual teasing of Dud and Thuella
by the scummy pond in *Maiden Castle*, just as the curiously sibling-
like relationship between Rhisiart and Tegolin in *Owen Glendower*
is unlike the fierce sensuality of John and Mary Crow. But underlying all these different manifestations of cerebralized sexuality we
find an insistence on the diffused nature of sex, its intricacy and
power for both good and evil.

The lack of solemnity in his handling of sex is a welcome corrective to the more exalted or embittered treatments of the matter
to which one has become accustomed. And this note of humour is
entirely lacking in any sense of mockery or abuse. The description
of Larry Zed's adolescent yearnings is a remarkable example of
Powys's honesty and tenderness, as is the account of Peg Frampton
and of the lady-in-waiting Luned in *Owen Glendower*; while his
sympathy extends over the entire age-range of sexual yearning—he

10. ibid., p. 623.

portrays the elderly John and Megan Geard, for example, as still being lovers. Above all it is sex as an element in life rather than sex as a passion which interests him—and this gives to his writing a curious detachment, a detachment which, however, enables him to extend the field of his erotic awareness into that of fetishism. People's relationships with objects are a recurring phenomenon in his world—Daisy May and her doll Quinquetta in *Weymouth Sands*, and Mrs. Wohntcher and the mahogany table in *The Inmates* come immediately to mind—and no hard-and-fast line is drawn between what is sexually motivated and what is not. Where he does excel, however, is in the delineation of different sex-responses in the act of love itself: Will's curiously detached relations with Persephone in *A Glastonbury Romance* have already been alluded to, and there is a memorable instance of this also in *Porius* in the fine scene between Rhun and Morfydd on the latter's wedding morning, as well as in the whole account of Wolf's relationship with Gerda, and of Dud's with Wizzie. A word that frequently recurs in Powys's writings about sex is the word 'nerves'; and it is the tension suggested by his use of this which is predominant in his treatment of the matter. He is the novelist of the unfulfilled, and in a time when sexual performance seems to be the mark of orthodox maturity his observations on the subject are as valuable as they are unusual.

They are, too, bound up with his particular view of life. Sex in most novels is described as an end in itself, but with Powys, as with Lawrence, it is a mark of a man's inmost being. However, whereas Lawrence at times sees in sexual intercourse a kind of parable of healing both of body and soul (most notably in *Lady Chatterley's Lover*), for Powys it is the spring-board for an extended awareness, both sensuous and spiritual, of a man's entire material and spiritual ambience. Another word he uses in this connection is the word 'drugged', and again and again he portrays sex-fulfilment as a condition which opens on to other worlds of deeper and more mysterious experience. His mystics, Sylvanus and Uryen, and to a lesser extent Owen himself, all seek to make use of the withheld sexual energy of virgin girls for spiritual purposes; and in his scenes of happy love, such as those between John and Mary Crow or Porius and Morfydd, it is the extra-sensual perceptions upon which he concentrates. Because of this diffused sex-awareness, this freedom from preoccupation with the genitalia, he is able to describe calmly and with naturalness homosexual attractions and bisexual natures, and treat with quiet ease matters which in other novelists would be sources of sensationalism or selective concern. As an example of

his insight into the relationship between the sexes, and his command of both comedy and pathos in dealing with it, his account of
Mary Crow listening to John and Barter through John's door is out-
standing in its sureness of touch; while the death of Princess Erdudd
in *Porius* is a vivid instance of his ability to make the implausible,
in this case death through an excess of sexual joy, both touching
and convincing.

One can illustrate the particular Powysian approach and achieve
ment by specific comparison with the work of Lawrence. Here is the
latter describing the love-making of Gerald and Gudrun in *Women
in Love*:

He had come for vindication. She let him hold her in his arms, clasp her
close against him. He found in her an infinite relief. Into her he poured
all his pent-up darkness and corrosive death, and he was whole again.
It was wonderful, marvellous, it was a miracle. This was the ever recurrent miracle of his life, at the knowledge of which he was lost in an
ecstasy of relief and wonder. And she, subject, received him as a vessel
filled with his bitter potion of death. She had no power at this crisis to
resist. The terrible frictional violence of death filled her, and she received
it in an ecstasy of subjection, in throes of acute, violent sensation.

As he drew nearer to her, he plunged deeper into her enveloping soft
warmth, a wonderful creative heat that penetrated his veins and gave
him life again. He felt himself dissolving and sinking to rest in the bath
of her living strength. It seemed as if her heart in her breast were a second
unconquerable sun, into the glow and creative strength of which he
plunged further and further. All his veins that were murdered and lacerated, healed softly as life came pulsing in, stealing invisibly into him as
if it were the all-powerful effluence of the sun. His blood, which seemed
to have been drawn back into death, came ebbing on the return, surely,
beautifully, powerfully.

He felt his limbs growing fuller and flexible with life, his body gained
an unknown strength. He was a man again, strong and rounded. And he
was a child, so soothed and restored and full of gratitude.[11]

The passage needs to be quoted at this length to be understood. In
its intense urgency, its instinctive understanding of a living process,
it is an example of something that Lawrence does particularly well
—a dramatic description that is also a more generalized analysis. His
language, simple, reiterative, mimetic, is designed to convey the
immediacy of the event, as well as to place Gerald's experience in
relation to his total stage of growth. The passage is essentially
dramatic, it describes a process accomplished, in terms of the primeval forces of light and heat and magnetic attraction; and yet the
actual personalities of the lovers have disappeared for the moment

11. *Women in Love*, Chapter 24.

within the experience they are undergoing. The novelist, for all his engaged quality of writing, is speaking to the reader away from their experience.

Powys's approach is interestingly different. Here are Nell and Sam, in *A Glastonbury Romance*:

His authentic love for her, his pity, his tenderness, his feeling for her beauty, had simply opened wide the gates of ecstasy. Through these gates there rushed now a rapture of bodiless, mindless, delirious sensation. This sensation, dominating now the whole field of his conscious and unconscious being, was much blinder, simpler, less complicated than anything which she felt. Both their sensations centred in *her* body, not in his. His body was merely the engine of the well-known personality that was now enjoying her. His body might have been ugly, coarse, deformed, grotesque. It might have been made of clay. It was her man's dear body; and that was enough! If it had been the body of a leper, it would have been the same. But with him, once again, it was otherwise. His consciousness, even at the beginning of his delight, could only have expressed its rapture by the concept—'She is too sweet.' Then there came a further point in his ecstasy when he could not even have articulated as much as that; when he could perhaps have said no more to describe what he felt than some perfectly incoherent gibberish, some subhuman gibberish that would be identical with what a bird, a beast, a reptile, would utter, or try to utter, as it plunged into that sweet oblivion.[12]

What is at once apparent here is a far less urgent tone, reflected in the leisurely prose that takes its time, that makes its points by weighted phrases, judicious repetition, copious illustration. It is a talkers' prose. And coupled with this slowness of tempo is a greater detachment than we find in Lawrence, a pondered consideration of this act of love rather than a dramatic representation of it. It is related to the whole of man's evolution and to the very nature of physical life. But at the same time the feelings of the actual couple, Sam and Nell, are fused with this more generalized portrayal: the passage is in this sense more intimate and immediate than the one by Lawrence.

One further comparison between Powys and Lawrence may further clarify their difference. Here is the account of an embrace between Ursula and Skrebensky in *The Rainbow*.

Then he turned and kissed her, and she waited for him. The pain to her was the pain she wanted, the agony was the agony she wanted. She was caught up, entangled in the powerful vibration of the night. The man, what was he?—a dark powerful vibration that encompassed her. She passed away as on dark wind, far, far away, into the pristine darkness of

12. *A Glastonbury Romance*, pp. 310–11.

paradise, into the original immortality. She entered the dark fields of immortality.[13]

Here are Perdita and the Jobber in *Weymouth Sands*:

... as they pressed their bodies and their faces together they were beyond any definite kisses, just as they were beyond astonishment, surprise, thankfulness, happiness even. He could taste the salt of her tears, pouring, pouring, from what seemed like the whole surface of her face, and she could feel herself rising and falling, up and down, on the crests and troughs of his immense, slow, shaking sobs. It was as if they were not just human lovers, not just sweethearts finding each other again. It was as if they were animals, old, weak, long-hunted animals, whose love was literally the love of bone for bone, skeleton for skeleton, not any mere spiritual affinity, not any mere sexual passion.[14]

The far greater actuality of this is at once apparent. Admittedly in context the two passages will be seen to be performing different functions, the passage from *The Rainbow* forwarding the movement of the novel's theme, that from *Weymouth Sands* describing the final reunion of the lovers as it feels to them and might look to an observer. But even allowing for this difference one may claim a greater humanity in the Powys passage because of its complexity of mood and immediacy of sensual impact. By standing further back from his characters Powys enables us to draw closer to them. His very identification with them means that his own personality does not compete with theirs.

6

When his characters lie outside his own immediate concerns and problems (as do Red Robinson or Dunbar Wye, both of them politicians of a sort) they are unconvincing. This is admittedly a limitation in his inventive power; but if it is complained that all his principal characters are embodiments of aspects of his own character, then one answer lies in the reminder that objectivity is in fact impossible, and in John Bailey's contention, in connection with Tolstoy, that such solipsism 'is, ironically enough, the answer to the novelist's problem of abstraction and alienation. He identifies in his own body all the other bodies of the world.'[15] Those words might equally well have been written about John Cowper Powys. And what is so remarkable about him is the range of this inner world of his: his capacity for self-identification transcends boundaries of age

13. *The Rainbow*, Chapter 15.
14. *Weymouth Sands*, p. 565.
15. *Tolstoy and the Novel* (Chatto & Windus, 1966), p. 60.

and sex. (Like Lawrence he had an uncanny knack of portraying a woman's point of view: indeed he declares in the *Autobiography* that he was attracted to women 'much more as a Lesbian is attracted to them than as a man is attracted to them'.)[16] Only in *Wolf Solent* does he filter his story through the consciousness of a single character; and while this gives the novel an intensity unequalled by the rest, it also deprives it of the characteristic Powysian spaciousness of atmosphere. The most unified of the books, it is also the most claustrophobic.

This spaciousness is the product of the peculiar blend of reality and unreality within each novel. Reference has already been made to Powys's use of the world of his boyhood to provide the external frame of reference for his romances; and the story-book character of his settings and backgrounds, and the anachronisms of dress and habit, the oddities of speech and irrationality of behaviour, are all elements that go to make a world of curious unreality: one cannot see Powys's people as existing in the world of any other novelist, any more than one can see most of Dickens's. But out of this external implausibility Powys creates a world of hypnotic credibility, a world totally self-consistent, a world which enables him to select those aspects of life which seem to him to be significant and to relate them to each other with liberating effect. Physically and psychically his world is totally convincing: what is lacking is the everyday stuff of social commerce and, in the broadest sense, of politics. It is this search for an abstracted world that led Powys's imagination from Wessex through Wales to the Ithaca of *Atlantis* and, finally, beyond the Milky Way. The surprising thing is that whereas the minor novelist tends to describe the real world and to make it unreal in so doing, Powys begins with an obviously unreal world and makes it credible, and not only credible but relevant as well. It is not an abstraction merely, but rather a visionary extension of the world we ordinarily know.

Within that world his characters have their rich and varied being. They do not exist to point their creator's moral or to adorn his tale: rather, they *are* his moral and his tale. His fictional world is realized not only through their physical and psychic impact, but also through the movements of their minds and hearts. And although the same types recur from novel to novel, the same individuals do not. The magician figures—John Geard, Sylvanus Cobbold, Uryen Quirm, Myrrdin Wyllt—are as sharply differentiated as his old maids— Selena Gault, Euphemia Drew, Miss Le Fleau, or the three old princesses in *Porius*. Each one is an entirely new creation, with his

16. *Autobiography*, p. 594.

or her own particular characteristics, physical and spiritual. John
Crow and Wolf Solent may be half-brothers of Rhisiart and Dud
No-Man, but there is no confusing one of them with any of the
others. The young women are, it is true, less individuated—there
is much in common between Mary Crow and Perdita Wane, between Nell Hastings and Nell Zoyland, while the various girls in
the final novels are virtually indistinguishable; and it is interesting
to note that the novels with the most effective female characters—
Wolf Solent, Ducdame, and *Maiden Castle*—are the ones in which
there is the most tightly organized plot, and those in which the
central character himself comes under threat of domination by the
female. The urgency in the man–woman confrontations is the dramatic hub of Powys's work, and his exploration of such relationships
as those between Dud and Wizzie in *Maiden Castle*, Nell and Sam,
John Crow and Mary in *Glastonbury*, and the fascinating triangle
in *Porius* between Porius, Rhun, and Morfydd, go to the very heart
of sex differentiation, just as the studies of friendships, like those
between John Crow and Tom Barter or between Wizzie and
Thuella, put a good deal of emotive writing about homosexuality in
perspective. And in all these cases the characters are memorable
because presented from within, and not only from within but also
with their external projections in the way of dress, habits, movements, and emotional force. They are not only seen and felt, but also
felt *with*. How effective Powys's method can be is evidenced by
the success of his portrayal of Miss Le Fleau in *Weymouth Sands*.
She plays a relatively small part in the action of the novel, but by
dint of recording her lodger's impressions of her house, of letting
us see, for example, her cake of lavender soap in the bathroom
while he is washing his hands, and giving us indirect glimpses of
her habits and of her effect upon him, she becomes a potent presence in the novel, and stays in the mind for far longer than her
actual appearance within its pages would seem to warrant.

7

Keen and imaginative sense-perceptions, a highly developed sense
of comedy, compassion and insight into human fears and failings,
a strong controlling imaginative vision to order all his enormously
vital responses—all these are elements in Powys's equipment as a
novelist. As a creator of character, of individuals who are not merely
types, he has few equals in our time, and none in his courtesy and
deep understanding of the people whom he has created. There is a
Dickensian richness about his world: this enormous gallery of

figures—old men and children, lovers, magicians, maiden ladies and tramps, clergymen and gypsies, timid bachelors and boastful workmen, house-proud wives and slovenly housekeepers, publicans, lonely eccentrics, gardeners, businessmen, monks, servant girls, poets, perverts—not to mention the long list of animals and inanimates—are the fruit of a marvellously apprehended experience of life that derives its force and particular appeal from its abstraction from day-to-day reality as much as from its approximation to it at a deeper level. The novels, the major ones at any rate, bear the test of a repeated re-reading. There is always something new and enlightening to find.

For underneath the frequent extravagance and foolishness there is wisdom: the more one reads John Cowper Powys the more one is made aware of his fundamental and possibly prophetic sanity. Comprehensiveness is perhaps the secret of his world, his capacity to combine deep spiritual and psychic insights with an unassuming homeliness, his feeling for that quality which Gertrude Stein called 'stupid being'. Certainly he frequently quoted the term, and while few of our novelists have so closely rivalled Dostoevsky in the depiction of nervous tension, few of them have had a stronger command of the calm undercurrent of everyday existence. The secret of the latter lies in his feeling for nature: as he himself wrote, and it is true of himself, 'the real Nature-lover does not think primarily about the beauty of Nature; he thinks about her life'.[17] Sensitiveness to the life of the earth, he declares, 'is the beginning and the end of a person's true education'.[18] Powys's feeling for nature was a feeling for the recurrent rhythms of the world, and for man's part in them: robust and yet delicate in his apprehensions, he always interprets nature in terms of the great mother just as the old matriarchal societies were to remain his ideal. In his extreme old age he had a great devotion to the nymph Egeria, who was the counsellor of King Numa of Rome, and the long procession of wise old unmarried ladies is one of the most attractive features of his novels. His reverence and liking for women does not, however, preclude a very masculine consciousness of their power to disturb. Nature for him is never a placid back-cloth but always the place of making.

The childlike quality of his vision has already been remarked upon; and in the last section of his book on Rabelais, the most attractive of all his critical writings, he in effect describes his own aims in defining the achievement of his master:

17. *The Meaning of Culture*, p. 180.
18. ibid., p. 175.

In the genius of Rabelais, Erasmus-worshipper though he was, the Privileged and the Academic received a jolt from which they still stagger. In him, by him, and through him the common herd became audible; the people of France expressed themselves; and as happened in the Revolution by expressing themselves they expressed the whims, the humours, the desires, the hopes, the fears, the secret longings, the long-suppressed blasphemies, of all the under-dogs of Western humanity.

And this was done in the healthiest and most natural way of all, through the people's childishness![19]

This indicates Powys's own achievement in regard to the traditions of his day. One may criticize his detachment from current concerns, and his political non-involvement, whatever the left-wing nature of his sympathies in private correspondence; but he had the courage and the honesty to make a positive out of his limitations. He simply was not attuned to a machine age, but he used his pen constantly to champion those in similar case, and to wrestle with the problems of living in one. Hence the many philosophical books: informal though they are in presentation, they are an honest attempt to share his own solution to his problems (a solution that certainly worked for *him*) with that common reader for whom he felt such concern and from whom he was by his very genius so far removed. Removed, that is to say, by power of vision and imagination, and by the intense diversity of his intellectual interests. He was never remote in bearing, being a man of great and tender courtesy to all who came his way.

The final section of *Rabelais* also contains the best account of his fundamental attitude to men and women and thus to the point of view from which he came to write the novels. Speaking of the 'magical feeling of immensity, which Rabelais' genius can throw around or discover within' the most ordinary things, he goes on to say that

It comes from the inexhaustible energy and fecundity of a little child's awareness of life, an awareness which is totally unchristian ... But it happens that this unchristian human nature is, as Pelagius hinted and as Erasmus argued, and as innumerable millions of uncircumcized, unbaptized, unregenerate men and women have proved in their brief and forgotten lives, not under any diabolical or any divine or any self-guilty curse of 'original sin' but simply adapted by Nature, physically, mentally and emotionally, to fighting for dear life and to keeping some sort of common-sense balance between self-interest and the interest of others.[20]

19. *Rabelais* (John Lane, The Bodley Head, 1948), pp. 295–6.
20. ibid., p. 348.

CHAPTER SEVEN

The Novelist and his Time

ENOUGH has already been said about the fortuitous reasons for the neglect and lack of recognition afforded to Powys both in his lifetime and afterwards: enough too, it is hoped, about his actual gifts and aims. What still needs to be attempted is to assess his position in the general traditions of the English novel, and to justify the claim that he still deserves to be read today. Is he really as eccentric as he seems?

Eccentricity is, of course, a relative term: perhaps it would be better to describe him as 'individual'. Powys's whole output, novels, criticism, philosophy, is a vast essay in self-exploration and analysis —so much can easily be established. What is more unusual and more remarkable is the fact that his work, far from being narrowly egoistic and inward-turning, is a projection of the self into an autonomous world of the imagination which is accessible to everyone. In this respect the novels are the natural centre and consummation of his achievement. This externalization of his own life-struggle and his own introspection makes of him a peculiarly liberating kind of confessional novelist. (One might compare his novels in this respect with the self-enclosed work of Malcolm Lowry.)

We have already noted the dual nature of his response to life: his withdrawal on the one hand into an emphasis upon and acceptance of solitariness, and his intense feeling for and contemplation of the inanimate. His two sources of strength are thus the cultivation of self-acceptance, and the cultivation of the widest possible physical sensitivity. Both movements are means of combating fear, fear of the self and fear of the external world; and the two movements may best be seen personified in his stoical egoists, such as Wolf Solent and Dud No-Man, and in his magician figures; but variations and combinations of both these attitudes are to be found in innumerable lesser characters.

What gives his work its particular energy and toughness is his complete self-sufficiency as an artist; his resolute adherence to his own inner light and vision; and his complete freedom from passing fashion. This singleness of mind, and this innocence of literary ambition in any worldly sense, while they have served to deny him the acclaim that is his due, are what is likely to ensure his acceptance in the future. In the vast output of contemporary novels his stand out for their sympathy with what it is to be alone. The word 'sympathy' is exactly meant: loneliness as a condition has been dealt with exhaustively and usually with bitterness by contemporary novelists; but it is the condition of *being*, as distinct from feeling, alone that is John Cowper Powys's overriding concern. And far from protesting against the state he glories in it.

This is not to say that he rejects the concept of society, only that he will have no substitute for *true* personal communication. What emerges from his novels, from *Weymouth Sands* especially, is that there are levels of subconscious communication that make it all the more important that the individual should adhere to his own integrity, since that integrity also operates at the subconscious level, and is thus a force for both good and evil. For evil, not because the collected self is a force for evil, but because the rejection of life, that comes from a failure to relate to life at all levels of one's being, is a force of death. And it is a measure of his breadth and charity of vision that he compassionates all those who, like Mr. Hastings or Adrian Sorio or, in a different way, Red Robinson or Lowri ferch Ffraid, have this hatred of themselves and of their life. Dangerous they may be, but they are not to be rejected. Their aloneness, their separate identities, are sacred.

As a champion of the individual Powys then is both outspoken and unsentimental; and in his insistence on the shared unconscious of his characters (which comes from his identification of them with himself) he interprets society as a fundamental element in man's being. But society for him cannot be divorced from nature. Men can only effectively relate to one another if they are at one with their environment and at one with their inner selves. The interaction of the two relationships is elaborately explored in *Wolf Solent*: the novel goes far beyond a celebration of the awareness of solitude into a complex study of the self-defeating efforts to combat solitude and of the threat to fellowship when the terms of solitude are not adhered to. In Powys's world people need to be self-sufficient at the conscious level, in the assurance that by virtue of their common human nature they can communicate at the unconscious level, through their shared perceptions of, and self-identification with, the external world of nature.

It is in his treatment of nature that Powys takes his place as one of our great romantic novelists. As much as Lawrence or Forster he laments the ravages of the machine age upon the English landscape; but he is far less concerned than either of them with what may be termed the changing face of England. He does not, as

Forster does, turn to some unseen world as a guarantor of values which are being steadily threatened by the money-making way of life, although the presence of that world is felt throughout his novels. But whereas Forster, a characteristic Edwardian in this, uses fantasy with a tinge of whimsical playfulness, Powys, far more a genuine countryman, portrays the unseen as an organic extension of the seen, and finds in the very structure of nature itself the guarantee of values which protect the individual from the threat to his identity: the end of *Porius* is his classic statement of this belief. He posits for human beings values which are harder and more akin to natural processes than are the ideals of liberal humanism—though he nowhere denies the validity of those ideals as such. But he is calmly aware of man's essential egoism, and accepts it as part of his natural endowment in the life-struggle. His faith in nature, and his consciousness of human beings as participants in nature in the fullest sense, allow him to accept this without bitterness or misogyny.

Rather, his hostility is reserved for the pseudo-scientific spirit which sees men as manipulators of a world from which they deny their derivation and in which they ignore their own participation. Powys as much as Blake is a contender that 'everything that lives is holy'. The animism of the final fantasies is governed by this conviction: it is what protects them from being merely whimsical. That he was not a mere anti-scientific obscurantist is attested by a passage from *The Meaning of Culture* which indicates where his true sympathies lay:

What . . . used to be derided fifty years ago as the pathetic fallacy, namely that Nature feels, in some intimate way, even as we ourselves feel, must now be regarded as something approximately true. Fast and faster every year is the purely mechanistic conception of life receding and being discarded; and thus the instinctive old-world response to Nature, as something living . . . returns upon us today as the most comprehensive as well as the most simple reaction which our mind, under its present mortal limitations, is able to experience. It is indeed only when we are, for a little while, quite alone with Nature, that our basic philosophy falls into focus and we are able to see things in a true perspective.[1]

Powys is being optimistic when he suggests that the Cartesian presuppositions as to the distinction between mind and matter are being generally abandoned in popular attitudes; but it is significant that he does not, in his assertions about the livingness of Nature, suggest the existence of any World Soul existing over and above our human consciousness. Always it is the interaction of interior vision and outward tangibility which is at the heart of his view of nature;

1. *The Meaning of Culture*, p. 196.

and throughout his work he insists upon the importance of the *will* in creating the kind of worlds which we inhabit.

His novels are themselves examples of this process. They are not objective records of the already known, either by way of social realism, psychological observation, or poetic mimesis. They do not analyse society or seek to capture the relationship of the individual to society in society's terms. They do not attempt any surrealistic vision, nor do they promulgate problems and resolutions. They are very patently fictions, but fictions which take the known facts of sensual experience and make of them a world which is both in its subject-matter and obviously in its construction an example of that creative vision of external nature which is Powys's interpretation of reality. And this private world it is the individual's responsibility to create, and for whose creation he is responsible when it is accomplished. In Powys's world character is fate.

This emphasis on individual creativity makes his fiction of great significance. It exemplifies the message he states explicitly in the philosophical books. That message concerns the primary right to happiness of every individual, and sees that happiness as bound up with the proper cultivation of the individual's sensibility. That sensibility is seen in terms of a psycho-sensuous response both to its physical environment and to the reanimating powers of memory—and both these things as being also part of a corporate consciousness that goes deeper than any shared social awareness. The more the individual can live in and respond to his own inner needs and responses, the more will he be a source of life and comfort to his fellow humans. Powys is concerned with the bed-rock essentials of personality: as much as his father he was an evangelist; but his evangel, instead of coming down from heaven, is drawn out of his vigilant sensuous responses. His metaphysic is only one way of coming to terms with his psychological needs: the real source of his message is his trust in the bond between man and matter.

His affinities with Hardy and with Lawrence have already been noted; he belongs in the same tradition, but expands it. Whereas Hardy colours his portrayal of the decay of rural England and the loss of man's roots in Nature with a bitter fatalism, Powys, unconcerned with the social aspect, is less inclined to lament the severance from Nature than to expose its folly by demonstrating how vital to human happiness communion with one's natural environment is. His work partakes more of comedy than of tragedy. And whereas Lawrence sees man's return to wholeness and wisdom through an obedience to his instinctual life, Powys, more detached, explores that instinctual life in terms not only of sexuality but also of fantasy, social habit, and contemplation. His work partakes more of anthropology than prophecy. Above all, where Hardy and Lawrence use the world of their boyhood as evidence of social change and as a text for their view of life, Powys uses his as a means of imaginative creation of a fictional world which exemplifies what for him stands over and above all social change. He is concerned with the constant adjective that qualifies each changing noun.

It is his insistence on the autonomy of the creative imagination, and on its participation in the given physical and psychic facts of human life, which gives to his work both its fundamental optimism and its sense of permanence. In this he differs from the other novelists of his generation. A certain ungainliness, and a certain fustian quality in much of his work, have been used by critics as alibis for a neglect that is really based on an unwillingness to reckon with the kind of subject-matter that he deals in. Thus, for example, his use of fantasy, not as an exclusive category but as an element within a broadly realistic whole, is an offence in an age of scepticism which likes its fantasy prepackaged and used for parabolic or symbolic purposes in children's books: the work of David Garnett and C. S. Lewis comes to mind here. And so because his own outlook transcends the outlook of the majority of his contemporaries, Powys's work is ruled out of court. Religious novelists like Graham Greene can be more readily accepted, for their premisses are expressed in psychological terms—Greene's natural world is achingly devoid of God—and can equally well be dismissed on those grounds; while the novels themselves can be read in the same terms, because they are of the same kind, as those of social observers like Anthony Powell or Evelyn Waugh. To mention these three supremely dexterous and technically elegant writers is to place John Cowper Powys in an odd perspective: it is rather like encountering a Druid at a literary luncheon. But the druidic element in Powys, that primitivism which is one of his popular attributes in current literary chat, is only temporarily a disadvantage. His work is not likely to be dated: it is available to each reader to make of it what he will.

For this is one of the most unusual aspects of Powys's art as a novelist. His work is peculiarly open to the reader. Although he planned and revised his novels more thoroughly than is generally imagined (there are manuscripts of *Porius* and *A Glastonbury Romance* extant to prove it) his essentially instinctive method of composition kept him from that over-careful disposition of material which is a characteristic of so much post-Jamesian fiction. He wrote out of an inner necessity to write, and once a book was finished he never re-read it, but moved on to the next one. Each book was a work of exploration, rather than a statement: his novels are not therefore susceptible to the kind of evaluative criticism that is currently the norm. In terms of writers like Jane Austen, George Eliot, or Henry James, Powys's romances seem muddled and messy. (Henry James would have deplored them, just as he deplored the novels of Dostoevsky.) But the best of them belong to the number of those which, to quote Q. D. Leavis's properly exacting definition, 'an adult can read at his utmost stretch—as attentively that is, as good poetry demands to be read—instead of having to make allowances for its being only a novel or written for a certain public or a certain purpose'.[2]

The word 'adult' is of course critical here, especially in view of the emphasis Powys places in his fiction on the continuing existence of the child within the man. The singular width of his imaginative vision allows not only for a continuing awareness of the past of places and peoples but also for the continuing presence within individuals of the infancy from which they have sprung. Many novelists (Dickens, George Eliot, and Proust come immediately to mind) have written memorably about the childhood of their characters; but it is always a childhood that is left behind. Even Proust, vivid as are his recollections of Combray, carries a fully adult intelligence and sensibility into the drawing-rooms of Parisian society. But in John Cowper Powys's novels a continuing childishness of behaviour is presented in almost all the leading characters, not only in their fantasy lives but in their small everyday actions and secret thoughts. It is this childish element in the novels which disconcerts many readers coming to them for the first time, though to others it is a means of illumination and refreshment. In the final novels it does tend to get out of control; but in his best work it is the quality which most distinguishes that work and relates it too to elements in the work of Dickens. Above all it allows for a measure of collusion between author and reader; there is no sense in a novel by Powys that the author is writing down to us.

Most definitions of what constitutes an 'adult' novel are essentially critical definitions; by which is meant, not that they are definitions made *by* literary critics but definitions made *for* them. The standards invoked and the methods applauded are standards and methods which readily lend themselves to criticism for they are themselves a work of criticism: author and critic can thus work comfortably hand in hand (as one currently sees them doing in study after study of George Eliot, Henry James, and Joseph Conrad). But this, perhaps inevitably, tends to lead to a judgement of a

2. 'Gissing and the English Novel', *Scrutiny*, vii (1938).

novel as if it were in effect a work of criticism only, however dramatically embodied; and such a critical approach leads to a greater
and greater severance between the ideas of the critic and the reasons
why people actually read novels.

In terms of this kind of critical approach John Cowper Powys
emerges very badly. His novels provide no clearly marked critical
pointers, no obviously key paragraphs for quotation and commentary. (One has only to compare a number of studies of, say, E. M.
Forster, to note how often the same passages recur for purposes of
exposition.) Powys's novels have no very obvious design, they seem
to invite the Jamesian description of 'fluid puddings'. That this impression is deceptive should be apparent by now, but in any case
the books work less by plot or development of theme or character
than by the invocation of a complex experience of outward and inward vision. And the particular way in which Powys identifies with
his characters, in which he *becomes* them, merges with them, is
more enlightening and more memorable than any amount of detached analysis could be: his characters are conveyed to us primarily through their responses to their environment—and that environment includes the men and women with whom they come in contact. All those men and women are seen as centres of energy, rather
than as static and fully moulded entities. Their very vivid external
traits and appearance are secondary to their vividness as mediums
for psychic and sensuous experience. Thus Powys's fictional world
is really more consonant with contemporary attitudes than was the
work of those novelists who were his contemporaries in age —Wells,
Bennett, Maugham, and, in America, Dreiser and Upton Sinclair.
Older than Lawrence, Joyce, and Virginia Woolf, Powys belongs
with them in that essentially 'modern' tradition of the novel that
thinks in terms of symbol, and of fluidity in personal awareness and
relationships. And if in style he belongs to an earlier generation than
theirs, in his imaginative scope and extended range of speculation
he goes beyond them, though it needs to be added at once that
for intensity and skill in the handling of words he is notably
their inferior. But he belongs in their tradition, rather than in
that other tradition which continues the nineteenth-century solid
world of character analysis into the twentieth—one thinks of Elizabeth Bowen and Angus Wilson as distinguished exponents of this,
exponents who have also learned from the other tradition, as Elizabeth Bowen has learned from Virginia Woolf, and Angus Wilson
from John Cowper Powys himself.[3]

Powys's work is being read with increasing interest in France, in

3. See *New Chapter*, i, No. 3 (Sept. 1958).

Germany, and in the United States; and he has a wide readership in his own country, unassisted by any place on academic syllabuses. This is not surprising. To read his novels is to enlarge one's mental horizons and to extend one's sensibilities. His work demands the kind of reading and attention that current religious and philosophical outlooks make it hard to come by—and, as has been seen, it does itself grave damage when it seeks to embody directly its extra-temporal apprehensions; but for those ready to respond to his view of human life in all its diverse aspects, the satisfaction that his novels generate is of a rare and continually rewarding kind. His defects do not distort or undermine his purpose, and they pale before the imaginative richness of his work, its finely wrought texture of imagery, its ripe humour, its broad unsentimental tolerance, and abounding vitality and wisdom. In his ability to quicken the senses and to reorder the emotions and to enlarge the capacity for self-acceptance and responsiveness to life, Powys deserves to be ranked among those major novelists who, in the words of F. R. Leavis, 'count in the same way as the major poets, in the sense that they not only change the possibilities of the art for practitioners and readers, but that they are significant in terms of that human awareness they promote; awareness of the possibilities of life'.[4]

And though in relation to the art of the novel Powys is not an innovator (not an innovator, that is to say, in terms of presentation), in terms of sensibility he is. In his hands the novel, while losing none of its hold over what may be called the prose of life, takes on some of the characteristics of poetry—it becomes the vehicle of the inner self; and that not simply in confessional terms but as the vehicle of a self bent on relating all levels of its experience to the world around it. In that sense Powys's own extraordinary character and Merlin-esque appearance are a key to the peculiar magic of his work. He was no mere man of letters in his own life, and his novels no more than himself fit easily into the world of current literature. But as long as people are responsive to novels that are written out of a deeply cherished feeling for the past and a seriously considered and uniquely personal experience of the present moment, then it is likely that his books will continue to be read. They, like all major work, are the measure of their readers.

4. *The Great Tradition*, p. 8.

APPENDIX

IN addition to his published books a large amount of Powys's work exists in manuscript, much of it in the collection of Mr. E. E. Bissell. (See Derek Langridge: *John Cowper Powys, a Record of Achievement,* The Library Association, 1966.)

Besides a 70,000 word book on Keats, Powys wrote a three-act play, *Paddock Calls* (1920), and even a number of short stories, three at least of which survive—*The Spot on the Wall, The Incubus* (which contains the character of Romer Mowl, mentioned in Malcolm Elwin's *Life of Llewelyn Powys* (John Lane, the Bodley Head, 1946), pp. 67, 69) and *The Harvest Thanksgiving.* Three chapters of a modern novel laid in Corwen were written in 1940 and then laid aside. At least three short novels subsequent to *All or Nothing* remain unpublished.

But the most important manuscript, a copy of which is now in the Powys collection at Churchill College, Cambridge, is the missing portion of *Porius.* Powys abridged and extensively rewrote the book for publication, not altogether successfully as certain mystifications and abrupt shifts in the narrative bear witness. The surviving fragment, while impossible to reincorporate into the book as it stands, does however shed a good deal of light on the author's intentions, as well as containing a number of fine scenes entire in their own right. Selections from it should certainly be printed in any republication of *Porius* itself.

Powys was forced to change his intentions with regard to the novel quite early on. In a letter to Clifford Tolchard dated 2 March 1943 (printed in *World Review,* July 1950) he writes of the book, 'I start here in the *prehistoric* encampment on our actual Corwen hills above the little town with a Welsh hero & shall take him to Italy & to Athens by sea as described by St Luke in the "ACTS".' But by October 1946 his plans have changed.

I see I shall have to end without even leaving home, far less getting a ship for Piraeus, tho' I've got a Greek captain on a ship ready to sail & I've got an elderly much travelled scholar and collecter of Mss & of whatever monastery-bound & copied classics were to be found there, who receives letters from France & Italy & Athens from Sidonius and Cassiodorus and Damascus of those three centres of civilization and from the young Boethius in Rome.

The planned sea-trip was to be postponed till *Atlantis* (and even then Powys only just leaves Ithaca in time). *Porius* was to have an altogether different theme.

For what the cancelled fragment makes clear is that the novel was to centre even more surely than it does upon the significance of the primeval forest and the forest people. This theme links Merlin, who is identified specifically with Saturn or Cronos (pp. 506-7) with Taliessin, who was to have played a more central part in the novel than he finally does, and who is described as

a Being set apart from others to reveal to the world what only poetry *could* reveal, that is to say a certain secret life of planetary sensation, totally independent of love and religion and nationality and power and fame and glory and learning, a life of sensation that lifted the elements to the level of vegetation, vegetation to the level of animals, animals to the level of men, and men not only to the level of one another but to the level of the immortal gods (p. 750).

The old gods of Wales, championed by Brother John, are set against the new, Pwll and Pryderi against Math and Gwydion. The whole tendency is against dogmatism, authoritarian religions, and the separation of mind from matter. The Arthurian theme becomes an example of how truth can be subordinated to the needs of dogma. One of the book's deleted characters is a chronicler called Cretinloy (the name is deliberately appropriate), described by the Henog, the mouthpiece of the 'magical and magnanimous' older gods, as one 'who ... will be fully able to transform the most cowardly retreats into heroic deeds and the most lecherous obsessions into emotions of piety and purity' (p. 1385). Powys portrays the subsequent Arthurian cultus as a Christian perversion of the truth—hence his demotion of Arthur from his traditional character. Similarly Galahalt is shown as a peeping Tom and a forlorn boaster, and the freeing of Blodeuwedd is set firmly in the same anti-Christian context, when acid reference is made to the young priest's extravagant praise of 'the noble morality of Gwydion the son of Don in punishing the unfortunate Blodeuwedd for her murderous infidelity to the man whose desires she had been created to satisfy' (p. 1426). Pelagius too is seen as a champion of a way of life that allows the supremacy of the creative imagination and the freedom of the individual to follow his own desires. *Porius* is in many ways an antisocial novel: Porius himself feels 'how remote, how absolutely alien to his whole world of sensation was the *family*—the holy, sacred, must-be-preserved, must-be-obeyed family!' (p. 1271). Matriarchy is to be preferred to patriarchy: the three Aunties conspire with Medrawd

because they think that the sister's son should have right of primo-
geniture.

Among the most extraordinary scenes in the fragment is Porius's
discovery, in the Druid's cave after the battle, of a strange red-
haired child belonging to an aboriginal race older than all in the
forest; among the most complex is the account of the death of
Prince Einion, who in this original version perishes at the same cross
roads as the Princess Erddudd, the imprint of whose body is still
to be seen upon the grasses. The role of the girl Sibilla is clarified,
and that of Teleri, curiously undeveloped in the version as we have
it, can be seen as crucial to Powys's over-all design for the novel.
Much else has been sacrificed in these unavailing cuts—detailed
accounts of the love-making of Porius and Morfydd, of Porius and
Nineue, the encounter between Porius and Medrawd on Eyri. It
is the closing chapters of the book which have suffered most. What
is above all apparent is the fact that the book should have been its
author's crowning statement, both in its formal themes and in its
prodigality of invention. The version that we now have is less the
product of a private world than would appear; and what would
seem to be taken for granted instead of explained or realized
dramatically can now be seen as the result of compression and not
of imaginative irresponsibility. Powys was more of a formal artist
than the published version of *Porius* would suggest.

SELECT BIBLIOGRAPHY

PRINCIPAL WRITINGS OF JOHN COWPER POWYS

Fiction

Wood and Stone: A Romance (G. Arnold Shaw, New York, 1915; William Heinemann, London, 1917).

Rodmoor: A Romance (G. Arnold Shaw, New York, 1916).

Ducdame (Doubleday, Page & Co., New York, 1925; Grant Richards, London, 1925).

Wolf Solent (Simon & Schuster, New York, 1929; Jonathan Cape, London, 1929; Macdonald, London, 1961).

A Glastonbury Romance (Simon & Schuster, New York, 1932; John Lane, The Bodley Head, London, 1933; Macdonald, London, 1955).

Weymouth Sands (Simon & Schuster, New York, 1934);
  as *Jobber Skald* (John Lane, The Bodley Head, London, 1935);
  as *Weymouth Sands* (Macdonald, London, 1963).

Maiden Castle (Simon & Schuster, New York, 1936; Cassell & Co., London, 1937; Macdonald, London, 1966).

Morwyn: or The Vengeance of God (Cassell & Co., London, 1937).

Owen Glendower: An Historical Novel (Simon & Schuster, New York, 1940; John Lane, The Bodley Head, London, 1942).

Porius: A Romance of the Dark Ages (Macdonald & Co., London, 1951).

The Inmates (Macdonald & Co., London, 1952).

Atlantis (Macdonald & Co., London, 1954).

The Brazen Head (Macdonald & Co., London, 1956).

Up and Out (Macdonald & Co., London, 1957).

All or Nothing (Macdonald & Co., London, 1960).

Autobiographical

Confessions of Two Brothers (with Llewelyn Powys) (The Manas Press, Rochester, New York, 1916).

Autobiography (Simon & Schuster, New York, 1934; John Lane, The Bodley Head, London, 1934; Macdonald & Co., London, 1967).

Obstinate Cymric: Essays 1935–1947 (The Druid Press, Carmarthen, 1947).

Letters of John Cowper Powys to Louis Wilkinson 1935–1956 (Macdonald & Co., London, 1958).

Letters to Nicholas Ross (Bertram Rota, London, 1971).

Critical

Visions and Revisions: A Book of Literary Devotions (G. Arnold Shaw, New York, 1915; William Rider & Son, London, 1915; Macdonald & Co., London, 1955).
One Hundred Best Books (G. Arnold Shaw, New York, 1916).
Suspended Judgments: Essays on Books and Sensations (G. Arnold Shaw, New York, 1916).
Dorothy M. Richardson (Joiner & Steele, London, 1931).
The Enjoyment of Literature (Simon & Schuster, New York, 1938); as *The Pleasures of Literature* (Cassell & Co., London, 1938).
Dostoievsky (John Lane, The Bodley Head, London, 1946).
Rabelais (John Lane, The Bodley Head, London, 1948).
Homer and the Aether (Macdonald & Co., London, 1959).

Philosophical

The Complex Vision (Dodd, Mead & Co., New York, 1920).
The Meaning of Culture (W. N. Norton & Sons, New York, 1929; Jonathan Cape, London, 1930).
In Defence of Sensuality (Simon & Schuster, New York, 1930; Victor Gollancz, London, 1930).
A Philosophy of Solitude (Simon & Schuster, New York, 1933; Jonathan Cape, London, 1933).
The Art of Happiness (Simon & Schuster, New York, 1935; John Lane, The Bodley Head, London, 1935).
Mortal Strife (Jonathan Cape, London, 1942).
The Art of Growing Old (Jonathan Cape, London, 1944).
In Spite Of (Macdonald & Co., London, 1953).

Poetry

Odes and Other Poems (William Rider & Sons, London, 1896).
Poems (William Rider & Sons, London, 1899).
Wolf's-Bane: Rhymes (G. Arnold Shaw, New York, 1916).
Mandragora (G. Arnold Shaw, New York, 1917).
Samphire (Thomas Seltzer, New York, 1922).
Lucifer (Macdonald & Co., London, 1956).
Selected Poems, edited by Kenneth Hopkins (Macdonald & Co., London, 1964).

PRINCIPAL WRITINGS ABOUT JOHN COWPER POWYS

Richard Heron Ward: *The Powys Brothers* (John Lane, The Bodley Head, London, 1935).
Louis Marlow: *Welsh Ambassadors* (Chapman & Hall, London, 1936; Bertram Rota, London, 1971).

Malcolm Elwin: *The Life of Llewelyn Powys* (John Lane, the Bodley Head, London, 1946).

Louis Marlow: *Seven Friends* (Richards Press, London, 1935).

Bernard Jones: *John Cowper Powys* (Dorset Natural History and Archaeological Society, 1962).

G. Wilson Knight: *The Saturnian Quest* (Methuen & Co., London, 1964).

H. P. Collins: *John Cowper Powys: Old Earth-Man* (Barrie & Rockliff, London, 1966).

Derek Langridge: *John Cowper Powys. A Record of Achievement* (Bibliography. The Library Association, 1966).

Kenneth Hopkins: *The Powys Brothers* (Phoenix House, London, 1967; Warren House Press, Southrepps, Norfolk, 1972).

G. Wilson Knight: *Neglected Powers* (Routledge and Kegan Paul, London, 1971).

Belinda Humfrey (ed.): *Essays on John Cowper Powys* (University of Wales Press, Cardiff, 1972).

INDEX